The essential guide to
paying for
university

THE ⬤ TIMES

The essential guide to
paying for
university

Effective funding strategies for
parents and students

Catherine Dawson

**KOGAN
PAGE**

Publisher's note

Every possible effort has been made to ensure that the information contained in this book is accurate at the time of going to press, and the publishers and author cannot accept responsibility for any errors or omissions, however caused. No responsibility for loss or damage occasioned to any person acting, or refraining from action, as a result of the material in this publication can be accepted by the editor, the publisher or the author.

First published in Great Britain in 2009 by Kogan Page Limited

Kogan Page Limited
120 Pentonville Road
London N1 9JN
United Kingdom
www.koganpage.com

British Library Cataloguing in Publication Data

A CIP record for this book is available from the British Library.

ISBN 978 0 7494 5635 1

Typeset by Saxon Graphics Ltd, Derby
Printed and bound in Great Britain by Thanet Press Ltd, Margate

Contents

List of tables   x

Introduction   1

Part One: How much does it cost?   5

1. Paying tuition fees   7
    *Understanding the background 7; Knowing about fee
    levels 8; Making payments 10; Financial help with
    paying fees 12; Part-time tuition fees 14; Tuition fees
    for EU students 15; Summary 15; Further information 15;
    Useful organisations 16; Further reading 16*
2. Paying for accommodation   17
    *Knowing about costs 17; Questions to ask when choosing
    accommodation 24; Living at home 28; Paying for
    food 29; Paying for utilities 30; Paying council tax 33;
    Summary 35; Useful organisations 35*
3. Paying for books, stationery and course materials   36
    *Knowing what to buy 36; Making the most of library
    resources 37; Knowing about costs 38; Using reading
    lists 39; Finding bargains 41; Summary 41; Useful
    organisations 42; Useful websites 42*
4. Paying for sports, leisure and entertainment   43
    *Knowing about entertainment costs 43; Knowing about
    sports and leisure costs 46; Knowing about costs for clubs
    and societies 47; Knowing about costs off campus 48;
    Paying for a TV licence 49; Summary 51; Useful
    organisations 51; Useful websites 52*

5.   Paying for field trips and study abroad   53
     *Knowing about the cost of field trips 53; Knowing about
     the cost of study abroad 55; Paying for passports and
     visas 56; Buying an international student identity card 57;
     Summary 58; Useful websites 58; Further reading 59*
6.   Paying for IT and communications equipment   60
     *Using university equipment 60; Buying your own IT
     equipment 61; Paying for internet access 63; Using
     mobile phones 66; Knowing about photocopying and
     printing costs 66; IT costs for a full degree course 68;
     Summary 69; Useful websites 69*
7.   Paying for a full degree course   71
     *Weekly budget 71; Monthly budget 73; Annual
     budget 73; Payment calendar 75; Summary 76;
     Useful websites 77*

Part Two: What funds are available?   79

8.   Government funding (England)   81
     *Knowing about the types of funding 81; Knowing about
     eligible courses 84; Applying for government support 85;
     Summary 86; Further information 86; Useful websites 87*
9.   Government funding (Wales)   89
     *Knowing about the types of funding 89; Knowing about
     eligible courses 93; Applying for government support 94;
     Summary 96; Further information 96; Useful websites 96*
10. Government funding (Scotland)   97
     *Knowing about the types of funding 97; Knowing about
     eligible courses 101; Applying for government support 102;
     The Graduate Endowment 103; Summary 103; Useful
     organisations 104*
11. Government funding (Northern Ireland)   105
     *Knowing about the types of funding 105; Knowing about
     eligible courses 110; Applying for government support 111;
     Summary 111; Further information 111; Useful
     organisations 112; Useful websites 113*

12. University bursary scheme funding   114
    Knowing about bursaries and scholarships 114; Knowing
    about bursary levels 115; Bursary administration 128;
    Bursary take-up rates 129; Summary 130; Useful
    organisations 130; Useful websites 131; Further reading 131
13. Funding for students with disabilities   132
    Knowing about the type and amount of funds 132;
    Eligibility criteria 133; Making an application 134;
    Obtaining help after enrolment 136; Summary 137;
    Useful organisations 137; Further information 138
14. Funding for specialist courses   139
    Funding for teacher training 139; Funding for healthcare
    courses 146; Funding for dance and drama courses 148;
    Funding for social work courses 149; Funding for fine and
    performing arts 150; Obtaining financial help for study
    abroad 151; Summary 152; Further information 153;
    Useful organisations 155; Useful websites 158
15. Funding for adult students   160
    Government funding for adult students 160; Adult
    education bursaries 164; Adult Education Allowance
    Scheme 167; Trade union funding 167; Receiving tax
    credits 169; Receiving benefits 170; Summary 172;
    Further information 172; Useful organisations 173;
    Useful websites 175
16. Taking advantage of government and university funding   176
    Knowing what is available 176; Knowing when and how
    to apply 180; Raising levels of success 181; Overview of
    funding in the United Kingdom 182; Summary 185

Part Three: How can I pay, as a parent?   **187**

17. Providing financial support for your child   189
    Understanding the parental contribution 189; Making
    financial gifts to your child 191; Loaning money to your
    child 193; Ensuring take-up of statutory support 193;
    Helping with costs 194; Tips from parents 196;
    Summary 197; Further information 197; Useful websites 197

18. Making use of children's savings plans 199
When to start investing 199; Investing in Child Trust Fund accounts 200; Investing in children's savings accounts 201; Investing in children's bonds 202; Maximising your investment 203; Protecting your investment 204; Understanding tax issues 206; Summary 206; Useful organisations 207; Useful websites 207

19. Making use of general investment opportunities 208
When to start investing 208; Investing in National Savings and Investments 209; Investing in unit trusts, open-ended investment companies or investment trust savings plans 211; Investing in individual savings accounts 211; Maximising your investment 213; Protecting your investment 213; Understanding tax issues 214; Summary 215

20. Investing in property to pay for university 216
Buying a second property 216; Buying a property for your student child 218; Investing in buy to let 219; Choosing the right property 222; Maximising returns 223; Knowing about tax implications 224; Avoiding pitfalls 226; Summary 227; Further information 228

21. Raising cash from your property 229
Downsizing 229; Releasing equity in your home 231; Remortgaging your home 233; Understanding tax implications 234; Avoiding pitfalls 235; Summary 235; Useful organisations 236; Useful websites 238

Part Four: How can I pay, as a student? **239**

22. Earning during a gap year 241
Knowing about types of work 241; Knowing about salary levels 243; Paying tax 244; Paying National Insurance 245; Saving your wages 246; Summary 247; Useful websites 247

23. Undertaking part-time and vacation work 249
Knowing about student employment services 249; Knowing about types of work 250; Knowing about salary levels 252; Knowing about working conditions 253; Paying income tax 253; Paying National Insurance 256; Summary 256; Further information 257; Useful websites 257

24. Obtaining sponsorship   258
     Sponsorship for sports 258; Company sponsorship 261;
     Armed Services sponsorship 263; Summary 267; Further
     information 267; Useful websites 267
25. Obtaining trust or charity funding   269
     Obtaining money from trusts and charities 269; The
     Helena Kennedy Foundation 270; The Leverhulme Trade
     Charities Trust 271; The Gilchrist Education Trust 272;
     Summary 273; Further information 273; Useful
     organisations 274; Useful websites 275
26. Becoming a student entrepreneur   276
     Assessing the feasibility 276; Developing your idea 278;
     Deciding how to trade 279; Sorting out your finances 280;
     Understanding tax implications 282; Building your
     business 283; Managing work and study 285; Summary 286;
     Further information 286; Useful organisations 286;
     Useful websites 287
27. Reducing the cost of university   288
     Reducing expenditure on accommodation 288; Reducing
     expenditure on utilities 290; Reducing the cost of IT
     equipment 291; Reducing the cost of travel 291; Reducing
     the cost of course materials, books and stationery 292;
     Reducing your spending on entertainment and social
     activities 293; Reducing the cost of sports and leisure 294;
     Knowing how to budget 294; Managing your money 296;
     Summary 299; Further information 299; Useful websites 300

     Appendix 1: Case studies   *301*
     Appendix 2: Budget planner   *305*
     Appendix 3: Graduate employment opportunities and wages   *307*
     Useful websites   *312*
     Useful organisations   *317*
     Index   *327*
     Index of advertisers   *333*

Tables

2.1	Weekly accommodation costs (2008/09)	18
3.1	The cost of books, course materials and stationery	38
6.1	University photocopying costs (2009/10)	67
6.2	University laser printing costs (2009/10)	67
6.3	IT costs for a three-year degree course	68
7.1	Weekly university budget	72
7.2	Monthly university costs	73
7.3	Annual university budget	74
7.4	University payment calendar (instalments)	76
7.5	University payment calendar (lump-sum payments)	76
12.1	University bursaries in England, Wales and Northern Ireland (2008/09)	120
16.1	Easy reference to government and university funding	185
22.1	Employment opportunities for gap-year students	244
23.1	Student employment and salary levels	252
26.1	Conducting a risk assessment	277

Introduction

Over the past decade the cost of university education has soared. This is due, in part, to the introduction of variable tuition fees, which means that students in England, Wales and Northern Ireland have to pay up to £3,225 per year in tuition fees for a full-time undergraduate course (2009/10 figures). Many student and parents are now finding that the cost of university is a huge financial burden. For some, the costs are so great that they decide to delay or cancel their plans to go to university.

However, there are grants, loans, bursaries, scholarships and other sources of finances available for students to help them pay for university, especially if they are from low-income households. Yet some of these schemes are not widely advertised and some students, for whatever reason, do not take up the money that is available to them. Others believe that a university education is far too expensive and decide not to go to university in the first place because they perceive that they cannot afford to do so.

This book seeks to address these issues. It begins by discussing the various costs associated with a university education, including tuition fees, accommodation, books and course materials, leisure and entertainment, sports, field trips and information technology. It goes on to look at the sources of statutory funding: that is, public funds that are distributed to students by the government. The second part also discusses university funding, which includes bursaries that are made available for students from low-income families and scholarships that are available for high-achieving students.

Parents are increasingly involved in raising finances for their child's university education, and the third part of the book goes on to consider ways that parents can help to pay. This includes information about the parental contribution, which has to be paid by parents who have dependent children, if they have a household income over a specified amount. It

discusses the topic of making gifts and loans to children, and how these might be affected by inheritance tax issues. This section of the book also looks at short and long-term savings plans that can be utilised to build up a sum of cash that can help to pay for a child's university education.

Another way that parents can help to pay for their child's university education is to raise money through property. This could be through buying a second property that can be sold once the child reaches university age, or through buying a property in which children can live while they are studying. Other parents choose to raise the money by downsizing or releasing equity in their homes. This course of action is not without its risks, especially within a volatile property market, so information and advice about all types of property investment for parents and students is offered in Part Three of this book.

The final part of the book goes on to look at ways that students can raise finances themselves, in particular if they are mature students or have parents who are unwilling or unable to help out financially, but also if they need extra cash to see them through their studies. This section includes information about employment during vacations, gap years and part time work, sponsorship, charitable funding and money raised through self-employment or entrepreneurship. It concludes by illustrating how students can reduce the costs of university.

The appendices provide some case studies, a sample budget planner, and examples of student employment opportunities and wages. The book concludes with useful addresses and websites for students and parents.

I have worked within higher and adult education for 25 years, and most of this time was spent conducting research with students who were seen to be 'non-traditional': that is, students from poor backgrounds, mature students and those from a variety of minority ethnic backgrounds. Part of my research included an analysis of the financial barriers to participation and an assessment of what was required to overcome them. I found that one of the main issues was lack of advice and information about financial matters for both students and parents. This book has been written as a result of this research: I believe that students and parents should be able to make informed decisions about university armed with the most up-to-date and complete facts. Financial pressures should not be a barrier to participation.

In addition to my work in higher and adult education I am a shareholder of a family property business, for which I conduct the research and

development. We let our properties to students and have wide experience of dealing with colleges, universities, students and parents. As a family, we have found that property is a useful and viable source of income for the education of our children. The information and advice provided in Part Three of this book is based on our family experiences with property.

I firmly believe that financial barriers and fear of debt should not be a barrier to participation in higher education for young people or adults who wish to return to education. I hope that this book helps you to overcome these barriers and that you feel able to make informed decisions about beginning university. I wish you every success in obtaining the appropriate finances and good luck with your studies.

Part One

How much does it cost?

1 Paying tuition fees

At universities in the United Kingdom 'tuition fees' are the fees that students have to pay for their course. This does not include the cost of accommodation. Universities in England, Wales and Northern Ireland are now able to charge 'variable' tuition fees for full-time undergraduate courses. These fees are variable because universities are able to decide how much they wish to charge, up to an amount that is specified by the government. Although universities can set their own fees, in practice most choose to charge the full amount (see below).

Scottish students do not pay tuition fees if they study in Scotland. However, if they wish to study in England, Wales or Northern Ireland they will have to pay the variable fee. More information about the background to variable fees and fee levels in each part of the United Kingdom is discussed in this chapter.

Understanding the background

Legislation to introduce variable fees was passed through Parliament in 2004, with the fees introduced in 2006. At the time there were two main reasons for this legislation: universities said that they needed more money, and the government said that students benefited from a university education through receiving higher wages and, therefore, should contribute towards the costs. There was huge opposition to the introduction of variable fees, so two amendments were included to appease the opposition. The first imposed a duty on the education secretary (rather than just a power) to decree a £3,000 cap on fees so that no university could charge above this amount. (There is an index-linked rise on this figure each year.) The second ensured that any attempt to raise this figure above £3,000 in 2010 would require a vote of both Houses of Parliament.

Variable fees were initially referred to as 'top-up' fees because they provided additional money to universities that was nearer to the actual

cost of a course. Previously, fees had been 'capped' by the government and only covered a small proportion of these costs. However, costs vary considerably, with some courses costing much more than the £3,000 that students pay in fees. This has led many universities to push for higher fees, and in some cases they believe that students should pay around £8,000. A review of the system of university funding and student support, which includes a decision about the amount of tuition fees that can be charged, is now taking place. Opponents fear that if fees are increased many students, in particular those from poorer backgrounds, will be put off university.

Interestingly, however, the initial rise in fees to £3,000 does not seem to have had a significant impact on applications to university. In 2006/07 there was a slight drop in applications, but these have risen each year since. One reason for this is highlighted in the quotation below.

Michelle, third-year mature student, Sheffield Hallam University

I had been thinking about going to university for a few years, then I heard all this stuff about top-up fees or whatever you want to call them. I must admit it really made me think whether it was a good idea, you know, to go to university, what with me being a mum and all... but I needed to do it, for my children and for me... Then I found that I didn't have to pay straight away, you know, I didn't have to pay my fees at the beginning of the course. So that made me think that's great, you know, it was better for me, 'cos I didn't have the money at the start... I should have it at the end when I've got a job.

Knowing about fee levels

In 2009/10 the index-linked maximum tuition fee level was set at £3,225. Universities in England, Wales and Northern Ireland are able to charge up to this amount. These fees are also paid by Scottish students who decide to study in other parts of the UK. This figure will not rise by more than the rate of inflation before 2010 at the earliest, after the result of the planned review is known.

Fees are variable, and in practice universities can charge anywhere between nothing and £3,225 for their courses. Although most colleges and universities have chosen to charge the maximum amount for a full-time undergraduate degree course, there are some that have decided to charge a smaller amount. In 2008/09 the colleges and universities that did not charge the full fee were:

- Leeds Metropolitan University (£2,000);
- the University of Greenwich (£2,835 for undergraduate honours degree programmes, except the Medway School of Pharmacy, and £2,270 for honours degree programmes at partner colleges);
- University College Plymouth St Mark and St John (£2,825 and £2,300, depending on the course/combinations studied);
- Trinity and All Saints, Leeds (£2,390 on all undergraduate programmes);
- Writtle College (£2,835 for full-time undergraduate programmes).

Fees are not fixed for the duration of a course of study but are subject to annual increases. However, if fees were to rise considerably from 2010, existing students would not be affected by the rise, but would continue to pay an index-linked fee based on the £3,000 maximum.

Equivalent and lower qualifications (ELQs)

In September 2007, it was announced that from 2008/09 funding would no longer be provided to students who study for a qualification that is equivalent to, or lower than, a qualification they already hold. This means that universities will have to decide whether to raise their tuition fees for this type of student because they will receive no extra funding from the government. However, certain courses will be exempt from this policy, such as teacher training, nursing and social work (see Chapter 14).

There was much opposition to this new ruling, particularly because it affects mature students and people wishing to update their qualifications to improve their employment prospects (see quotation below). It also seriously affects the funding for universities that specialise in providing courses for this type of student.

Bridget, 43, Southampton

I took my first degree straight after school. It was a BA combined humanities at what was then West Midlands College of Higher Education. It has long since been incorporated into another institution, first Wolverhampton Poly and then Wolverhampton University, I think. Anyway, I worked for a while after I got my degree and then I left to have my three girls. Now they are grown up I thought it would be nice to do another degree. But I found out that they won't fund me. What this means is that the university will have to put up the tuition fees by at least 50 per cent, they've said. This means that my course would cost over £6,000 per year. There's absolutely no way that I can afford to do that, so I can't fulfil my dream and go back to study geology. It's such a shame.

In Scotland the Student Awards Agency for Scotland (SAAS) will not usually pay your tuition fees if you have previously been on a full-time higher education course at HNC, HND, degree or equivalent level, and had help from public funds for this study. However, there are exceptions to this rule so if you are in any doubt about your entitlement, you should contact the SAAS to confirm whether they can pay your tuition fees for your new course (see Chapter 10).

Making payments

One of the main changes to be introduced in the 2004 legislation was that students would no longer be required to pay their university tuition fees at the start of their course. This was seen to be a fairer system because it enables students to pay for their university education once they begin to reap the financial benefits. Instead of paying up-front (and perhaps relying on their parents for financial support) they are able to take out a loan to pay for their fees and then begin to pay back the loan once they have finished their course and are earning over £15,000 a year. Welsh students who study in Wales and Scottish students who study in Scotland may not be eligible for a full tuition fee loan, although they are eligible for a loan for maintenance/living costs (see Chapters 9 and 10).

Some students, however, decide to pay the fees at the start of their course, usually because they can afford to do so and they do not wish to be saddled with debt once they have left university. If you decide to follow this route, some universities will offer a discount, which can be as much as 5–8 per cent.

If you choose to take out a loan to cover fees the Student Loans Company (SLC) will send payment direct to your university at the start of your course, and each year thereafter (details below). If you intend to pay your fees yourself, payment methods will vary. However, most universities will offer the following ways to pay tuition fees:

- In full, by cheque, credit/debit card or sterling traveller's cheques before the start of term. The discount (if offered) will be included in the bill.
- By instalment over the academic year. This is usually in two, three or monthly instalments. Most universities will require that you set up a direct debit agreement at the start of each year of study and will require the first instalment and bank registration details at the time of registration. Also, most universities will impose a financial penalty for late payment of fee instalments. For example, the University of Manchester charges £25.00 for a late payment and this rises to £50.00 if the instalment remains outstanding for 28 days (see quotation below).
- In full by bank transfer. This option may be suitable for overseas students who have to pay full course fees and are not subject to current variable fee legislation. Bank transfers from outside the United Kingdom may be subject to bank charges that have to be borne by the payee.

Non-payment penalties

Penalties for non-payment vary. As we have seen above, some universities will charge a late payment fee that can increase as the length of non-payment increases. Others have more severe penalties that can include the following:

- The university will not let you register for the next year of your course.
- If you have tuition fee debts (or other university debts, such as outstanding library fines or accommodation debts) some universities will not let you attend your degree ceremony.

- Some universities will not provide you with a degree certificate if you have outstanding university debts. This could make it difficult for you to apply for a job or for further study when you need to provide evidence that you have passed your degree.

All universities have a student financial adviser who will be able to offer advice if you find that you are unable to pay your fees. Contact this person immediately, and also speak to the finance officer, who may be able to arrange an easier payment plan for you. Alternatively, you could seek help from your parents (see quotation below).

Charlie, second-year student, University of Manchester

I was a bit of a twit really. I went overdrawn without knowing it. What a wally! So the bank bounced my direct debit and they charged me for it and then the university charged me for it as well. The bank charged me £20 and £5 for a letter to tell me they'd charged me £20. Then the university charged me £25 and said they would charge me even more if I didn't get it sorted in the next 28 days. I had to go and beg to mum to help. What a wally! When you're living on not much, having £50 in charges whacked on you is no joke. Do you know what my mum's done? She's a gem. She's made me open another account this year and set up a direct debit from that account and she's put some money in to help. It's great. Mum's great.

Financial help with paying fees

There are various funds available to help you to pay your fees. The money that you can access depends on what and where you decide to study and on the level of your household (or family) income. The type of financial help that may be available to you is summarised below and discussed in more detail later in the book.

Student loans

As we have seen above, students are able to defer payment of tuition fees until they have finished their course. Students from England and Northern Ireland can take out a loan for their fees, while Welsh students who study in Wales can receive a Tuition Fee Grant to help with the cost of tuition (see below). Scottish students who study in Scotland are not eligible for a student loan for fees because, in most cases, they do not need to pay tuition fees (see below). More information about student loans is provided in Part Two of this book.

The Tuition Fee Grant (Wales)

The Tuition Fee Grant is available for students who normally live in Wales who choose to study at a university there. In 2009/10 the grant is worth £1,940 and is paid irrespective of family income, direct to the university at the start of the course and each year thereafter. Welsh students who choose to study in other parts of the UK are not entitled to this grant but may be eligible to apply for a student loan to cover tuition fees. This grant is also available for non-UK EU/EEA students who choose to study in Wales. Currently, a review is taking place and it is possible that this fee grant could be scrapped in the future, with the finances refocused elsewhere (see Chapter 9).

University bursaries

If universities wish to charge maximum tuition fees they must provide additional financial support for people from low-income families. In 2009/10 these bursaries must be at least £319, but many universities are offering larger sums. If you are from a low-income family, or from a group that is under-represented in UK higher education, you may be entitled to receive a bursary to help with your tuition fees. Some universities also offer bursaries to students who are entering the university from local schools or from local areas. Maximum levels of university bursary are shown in Table 12.1, along with the amount of tuition fee charged (see Chapter 12).

Financial help (Scotland)

If you are a Scottish student and you intend to study at a Scottish institution, the SAAS will pay your tuition fees. If you are Scottish and you intend to study elsewhere in the United Kingdom, the SAAS will assess your entitlement to help with tuition fees. This will depend on your family income. If you are eligible for help with your tuition fees, the SAAS will pay your tuition fees straight to your university. Student loans will be available for students who wish to study outside Scotland who are not entitled to help with tuition fees (see Chapter 10).

Part-time tuition fees

In most cases the financial help described above relates to full-time undergraduate courses. Also, variable fees and associated rules only apply to full-time degree courses. If you are thinking about studying part time, fees vary considerably, so you will need to contact the university in which you are interested to find out more about their part-time course fees. As a general guide fees tend to range from £300 to £600 for a 15 or 20-credit unit. As a part-time student you can choose how many units you wish to take a year and there is some government funding available to help you to pay for the course, depending on the intensity of your study.

In England and Northern Ireland there is a fee grant of up to £1,210 from the government for part-time students who are studying at a rate of 50 per cent or more of a full-time equivalent course (2009/10 figures). The amount you will receive is based on family income and is linked to the intensity of study at the following levels:

- 50–59 per cent of an equivalent full-time course: maximum fee grant £805;
- 60–74 per cent of an equivalent full-time course: maximum fee grant £970;
- 75 per cent+ of an equivalent full-time course: maximum fee grant £1,210.

Part-time students in England and Northern Ireland can also receive a grant of up to £260, depending on household income, to help with course-related costs. Schemes for part-time students in Wales and Scotland differ slightly (see Chapters 9 and 10).

Tuition fees for EU students

EU students studying at English, Welsh or Northern Irish universities pay the same fee as UK/home students. However, in Wales non-UK EU/EEA students are eligible to apply for the fee grant of £1,940 from the Welsh Assembly Government (2009/10 figures). Although EU students are able to take advantage of the deferred fees scheme, which means they only pay after graduation, they are not entitled to maintenance support in the same way as home students. However, if EU students have been settled in the UK for more than three years they will be classed as home students and may apply for financial support in the same way as home students.

Summary

Tuition fees are the fees that you have to pay for a university course. Universities use tuition fees to pay for the cost of running the course and the university, and to fund bursaries that help students from low-income families. Students studying full time in England, Wales and Northern Ireland, and Scottish students who choose to study outside Scotland, must pay variable fees. The amount of fee charged is decided upon by the university, up to a limit set by the government.

The cost of university accommodation is not included in the tuition fee figure; students must pay for accommodation separately. The cost of university accommodation and private rented housing is discussed in the following chapter.

Further information

More information about tuition fees can be obtained from www.direct. gov.uk. Further details are provided in *A Guide to Financial Support for Higher Education Students in 2009/10*. The guide can be obtained from the website above, by telephoning 0800 731 9133 or by contacting your local authority (England and Wales) or Education and Library Board (Northern Ireland).

Useful organisations

Student Loans Company Limited

The Student Loans Company (SLC) administers government-funded loans and grants to students throughout the United Kingdom. You can find out more information about the company and obtain contact telephone numbers from the website.

Student Loans Company Limited
100 Bothwell Street
Glasgow G2 7JD
Tel: (0141) 306 2000
Fax: (0141) 306 2005
www.slc.co.uk

Further reading

Dawson, C (2009) *University Tuition Fees and Bursary Schemes, 2009/10*, available from www.studentcash.org.uk. This book contains comparative tables of all universities in England, Wales and Northern Ireland, listing the tuition fee charged, bursary available, eligibility criteria, application procedure, contact details and other sources of funding that are available from each university.

2 *Paying for accommodation*

As we have seen in the previous chapter, the cost of accommodation is not included in the tuition fee for your course. Therefore, when working out how much you need to pay for university, you will need to consider your accommodation costs for each year of study. Today there is a wide variety of university and private rented accommodation available, to suit all tastes and budgets. Costs vary a great deal, depending on where you decide to study and the type of accommodation in which you wish to stay.

When choosing accommodation you need to know about the costs involved and be clear about what the price includes, such as meals and utilities. Some students also find it useful to weigh up the pros and cons of living at home while they study, as this tends to be the cheapest option. Advice and guidance about all these issues is offered in this chapter.

Knowing about costs

Accommodation costs vary enormously throughout the United Kingdom and, as you can see in Table 2.1, some universities provide the option of both cheap and expensive residences on their campus. The cheaper accommodation tends to be self-catered, basic rooms with washbasin and no internet access, shared bathrooms and communal kitchens, with the cheapest accommodation in double or triple sharing rooms. The more expensive accommodation tends to be for single occupancy, en-suite rooms, catered, with internet access. For private rental, the cheaper end tends to be for shared terrace housing, excluding bills, while the more expensive tends to be flats or lodgings (often including breakfast) that are inclusive of all bills.

Table 2.1 provides a general guide to what you can expect to pay for accommodation throughout the United Kingdom. Prices quoted are per

week for university (catered and self-catered) and private rental. Many universities had not set their 2009/10 accommodation costs at time of writing so 2008/09 prices have been quoted, unless otherwise indicated. To gain a better picture for 2009/10 you should note that universities add another 3–7 per cent to rental costs each year. In most cases prices have been supplied by university accommodation officers/housing staff. Where no response was received from a university, prices have been obtained from university websites and/or prospectuses.

Table 2.1 Weekly accommodation costs (2008/09)

	University accommodation	Private rented accommodation
A		
Aberdeen, University of	£72–£137	£80–£120
Abertay Dundee, University of	£52 £100.66	£40–£90
Aberystwyth University	£61.75–£96	£55–£90
Anglia Ruskin University (2009/10 figures)	£63.65 £120	£86.37–£92.70
Arts Institute at Bournemouth, The	£85 £100	£45–£85
Arts, University of the	£123.20–£166.60	£70–£120
Aston University	£65–£101.11	£50–£88
B		
Bangor University	£63.21–£98	£55–£80
Bath Spa University (2009/10 figures)	£75–£135	£64–£80
Bath, University of	£74.50–£115.50	£65–£80
Bedfordshire, University of	£68.50–£81	£50–£80
Belfast Metropolitan College	NA	£37.50–£75
Birkbeck College	NA	£70–£120
Birmingham, City University	£64–£94.52	£45–£75
Birmingham, University College	£67–£85	£50–£80
Birmingham, University of (2009/10 figures)	£78.45–£130.98	£45–£80
Bishop Grosseteste University College	£63–£87	£45–£65
Bolton, University of	£60	£45–£60
Bournemouth University	£74.50–£101.56	£70–£90
Bradford, University of	£64.90–£82.40	£40–£70
Brighton, University of	£66–£127.40	£70–£155

	University accommodation	Private rented accommodation
Bristol, University of	£76–£152	£60–£90
Brunel University	£81.41–£99.96	£65–£90
Buckinghamshire New University	£68.60–£87.85	£65–£80
C		
Cambridge, University of	£70–£100	£60–£100
Canterbury Christ Church University	£65–£123.40	£67–£80
Cardiff University	£56–£84	£50–£80
Cardiff, University of Wales Institute	£72.50–£114.00	£60–£70
Central Lancashire, University of	£69.93–£81	£65–£85
Central School of Speech and Drama	NA	£90–£140
Chester, University of	£45.50–£125.65	£55–£85
Chichester, University of	£73.50–£126.30	£65–£90
City University, London	£97.37–£169.12	£80–£140
Conservatoire for Dance and Drama	NA	£90–£140
Courtauld Institute of Art	£110–£153	£90–£140
Coventry University	£60–£94.50	£49–£75
Cranfield University	£68–£120	£60–£90
Creative Arts, University for the	£63.20–£105.30	£55–£120
Cumbria, University of	£48–£78	£45–£70
D		
De Montfort University	£77–£90	£52–£75
Derby, University of	£65.03–£87.01	£35–£60
Dundee, University of	£67–£105	£65–£140
Durham University	depends on college	£50–£87
E		
East Anglia, University of	£57.75–£92.96	£48–£70
East London, University of	£95–£128	£70–£120
Edge Hill University	£51–£82	£60–£70
Edinburgh College of Art	NA	£60–£120
Edinburgh, University of	£67.34–£165.34	£60–£120
Education, Institute of	£88–£170	£70–£120
Essex, University of	£61–£96	£65–£75
Exeter, University of	£64.40–£156.03	£68–£85

	University accommodation	Private rented accommodation
F		
Falmouth, University College	£89.55–£98.49	£60–£85
G		
Glamorgan, University of	£78	£47–£55
Glasgow Caledonian University	£70.40–£81.20	£60–£90
Glasgow School of Art	£69–£89	£60–£90
Glasgow, University of	£81–£118	£60–£90
Gloucestershire, University of	£69 to £102	£55–£80
Glyndwr University	£50–£77	£49–£58
Goldsmiths, University of London	£88–£114	£70–£140
Greenwich, University of	£77.35–£170	£70–£90
Guildhall School of Music and Drama (2009/10 figures)	£112	£70–£140
H		
Harper Adams University College	£57–£125	£45–£55
Heriot Watt University	£57–£103.50	£55–£85
Hertfordshire, University of	£61.53–£96.67	£65–£85
Heythrop College	NA	£70–£140
Huddersfield, University of	£65.95–£99.95	£35–£55
Hull, University of	£55–£123	£40–£80
I		
Imperial College London	£54.46–£168.77	£70–£140
K		
Keele University	£61–£95	£45–£55
Kent, University of	£83–£122	£67–£80
King's College London	£70.49–£128.52	£70–£140
Kingston University	£87.50–£109.75	£70–£140
L		
Lampeter, University of Wales	£58.50–£75	£35–£80
Lancaster University	£75–£98	£55–£75
Leeds College of Music	NA	£55–£85
Leeds Metropolitan University	£63.70–£120	£55–£85
Leeds, University of	£63–£140	£55–£85
Leicester, University of	£65.38–£141.96	£52–£75

	University accommodation	Private rented accommodation
Lincoln, University of	£86–£95	£45–£65
Liverpool Hope University	£66.66–£88.75	£45–£140
Liverpool Institute for Performing Arts	£64–£97	£45–£70
Liverpool John Moores University (2009/10 figures)	£65–£98	£45–£70
Liverpool, University of	£72.80–£106.40	£45–£70
London Metropolitan University	£101	£70–£120
London School of Economics and Political Science	£126.98–£195.93	£70–£120
London South Bank University	£86.50–£106.00	£70–£140
London, University College	£86.03–£145.18	£70–£120
Loughborough University	£67.80–£147.33	£37.50–£95
M		
Manchester Metropolitan University	£63.00–£100	£32–£75
Manchester, University of	£70.73–£103.35	£32–£75
Middlesex University	£81.41–£97.09	£70–£90
N		
Napier University	£80.36–£81.41	£60–£120
Newcastle upon Tyne, University of	£65.45–£107.80	£35–£70
Newman University College	£73–£97	£35–£93
Newport, University of Wales	£62–£75	£50–£70
Northampton, University of	£37.50–£79.75	£40–£75
Northumbria University (2009/10 figures)	£58–£126	£35–£75
Norwich University College of the Arts	£74–£98	£50–£60
Nottingham Trent University	£65–£105	£45–£80
Nottingham, University of (2009/10 figures)	£65–£172.98	£47–£82
O		
Oriental and African Studies, School of	£109.90–£181.30	£70–£120
Oxford Brookes University	£83–£120	£65–£120
Oxford, University of	depends on college	£65–£120
P		
Plymouth, University of	£74–£134	£55–£125
Portsmouth, University of	£73–£113	£50–£80

	University accommodation	Private rented accommodation
Q		
Queen Margaret University, Edinburgh	£91–£96.25	£70–£80
Queen Mary, University of London	£64.82–£115.64	£70–£120
Queen's University Belfast	£60.51–£86.32	£35–£55
R		
Ravensbourne College of Design and Communication	£66–£82	£75–£125
Reading, University of	£75–£125	£65–£75
Robert Gordon University, The	£65–£86	£60–£90
Roehampton University	£87.99–£119.58	£70–£140
Rose Bruford College	£85	£70–£90
Royal Academy of Music	£88–£114	£70–£140
Royal Agricultural College	£137–£183	£60–£100
Royal College of Music	£69–£122	£70–£140
Royal Holloway, University of London	£96.07–£127.88	£69–£100
Royal Northern College of Music (2009/10 figures)	£97.75	£55–£75
Royal Scottish Academy of Music and Drama	£80–£90	£50–£90
Royal Veterinary College	£108–£180.60	£70–£140
Royal Welsh College of Music and Drama	£79.95	£50–£80
S		
Salford, University of	£56–£90	£45–£60
Sheffield Hallam University	£45–£135	£45–£85
Sheffield, University of	£76.16–£129.64	£45–£85
Southampton Solent University	£46.55–£96.95	£50–£70
Southampton, University of	£65.45–£145.60	£50–£70
St. Andrews, University of (2009/10 figures)	£57.75–£165.62	£52–£90
St. George's, University of London	£90–£100	£70–£95
St. Mark and St. John, University College Plymouth	£63–£67	£38–£120
St. Mary's University College, Belfast	NA	£37.50–£50

	University accommodation	Private rented accommodation
St. Mary's University College, Twickenham	£80.85–£136.85	£75–£100
Staffordshire University	£40–£85	£40–£60
Stirling, University of	£60–£88	£46–£71
Stranmillis University College	£80–£90	£37.50–£75
Strathclyde, University of	£66–£94	£60–£90
Sunderland, University of	£54.19–£99.02	£32–£77
Surrey, University of	£57–£121	£63–£119
Sussex, University of	£68–£102	£69–£100
Swansea Metropolitan University	£50.25–£66.25	£50–£65
Swansea University	£62–£109.50	£55–£65
T		
Teesside, University of (2009/10 figures)	£44–£71	£35–£41
Thames Valley University	£89–£159	£60–£120
Trinity and All Saints	£69.92–£109.69	£55–£85
Trinity Laban Conservatoire of Music & Dance	£113–£144	£85–£130
Trinity College, Carmarthen	£72–£90	£45–£80
U		
UHI Millennium Institute	£60–£90	£40–£80
Ulster, University of	£40–£95	£35–£70
W		
Warwick, University of	£60–£100	£40–£75
West of England, University of the	£86–£123	£60–£90
West of Scotland, University of the	£55–£66	£40–£80
Westminster, University of	£67.35–£153.02	£80–£140
Winchester, University of	£69.09–£117.53	£60–£78
Wolverhampton, University of	£58–£86	£35–£60
Worcester, University of	£69–£100	£55–£90
Writtle College	£89–£111	£55–£75
Y		
York St. John University	£72.33–£125.08	£60–£80
York, University of	£68.39–£107.31	£60–£80

Length of stay

When working out accommodation costs you need to work out your length of stay because prices vary accordingly. For example, some halls of residence may require you to pay for 44 weeks of residence, while others charge for only 38 weeks. It may be cheaper for you to choose a shorter contract and live with your parents for a longer time during the vacations, although you will need to check that this fits in with the length of your course. Also, if you are choosing to live in private rented accommodation, some landlords will offer discounts, or half rent through the summer, so again, check this information when working out costs.

If you are entering university from care, some universities will offer you a 52-week contract on their accommodation, so check with individual universities if this applies to you. You will not have to vacate your room or move out your possessions with this type of contract.

Payment methods

Universities offer a variety of methods to pay for university accommodation. These include the following:

- Instalment plans (for example, nine monthly instalments or three term instalments).
- Payment up-front, sometimes with a discount that could be up to 8 per cent.
- Payment can usually be made by direct debit, cheque or credit/debit card. Bank transfers are available for overseas students, although there may be additional bank charges to pay.

Questions to ask when choosing accommodation

It is important that you do not accept any offer of accommodation, or sign a contract, until you are completely sure of the terms and conditions. The following questions will help you to clarify the pertinent issues. These depend on whether you are choosing to live in university-owned accommodation or private rented accommodation.

University accommodation

- For how long does the contract run? (Some universities refer to this contract as a 'licence'.) Contract periods vary considerably, so check carefully as this could have an effect on how much you pay and how long you can stay in your accommodation.
- What are the payment methods? If you are relying on loans and grants to help you to pay for accommodation, will the money be in your bank account so that you can pay in a way and at a time that is suitable for you and the university? Recently, there has been a problem with late payment of grants and bursaries; would the university penalize you for late payment if you were unable to pay through no fault of your own?
- Are there any discounts for early payment (in part or in full)?
- Is any interest charged on instalment plans?
- How much is the late payment charge, or default payment charge? Some universities may charge up to £30 for late payment on each instalment.
- How much is the booking/reservation fee? Is this a one-off payment or will you have to pay it each term? Is the fee refundable if you are unable to take up the offer of accommodation?
- How much is the deposit? Universities tend to ask for a deposit once you have accepted a firm offer of accommodation (usually in the region of £150–£500), although some universities combine their deposit and reservation/booking fee. If this is not paid within a specified time, your offer will be withdrawn and your room will be allocated to another student. Also, some universities will not refund the deposit if you cancel your room less than a month before your contract begins, or if you leave your accommodation before the end of your contract. Your deposit will be returned at the end of the contract period once deductions have been made for arrears, specified administration fees and damage (if relevant).
- Do you need to pay an extra vacation retainer? In the past universities have not charged to keep a room, but recently some have started to ask for an extra payment to guarantee that the room will be available.
- Do you need to move out during the vacations? Some university halls of residence are used for conferences during the vacations, so you may be required to move all your belongings from your room. Will you have somewhere to live during the vacations, and will you have to pay extra for vacation accommodation?

- Are there any discounts over the vacations, especially if you have to remove your belongings from your room?
- What utilities, if any, are included in the rent? Most university accommodation includes utilities, but you should check that this is the case as some have started to request an additional weekly payment.
- Is internet access included in the rent? Some universities will provide this service free of charge (in more expensive rooms), whereas others will ask for an additional payment to cover costs, usually between £100 and £200 per annum.
- Are any meals included in the rent? If they are, find out how many and whether cooking facilities are available for times when meals are not provided (see below).
- What cooking facilities and utensils are available for self-catered accommodation?
- Is any equipment included in the rent? For example, some universities now offer a complimentary bedding pack (duvet and cover, pillow and cover and fitted sheet), although they will not launder bedding. Some provide a variety of kitchen equipment and utensils, whereas others will only provide the basics. Other universities will provide a 'utensils pack' for an additional fee.
- Is insurance covered in the rent? Some universities will not insure your personal belongings, so this is something you will have to arrange yourself. However, over recent years more universities have decided to arrange block insurance for their accommodation, so check whether this is the case. This insurance will cover your personal possessions up to a certain amount, usually around £3,000. When you move into your accommodation you will be offered advice on registering and downloading your insurance documents. In certain circumstances your belongings may be covered on your parents' household insurance, but you will need to check whether this is the case.
- Is car-parking/bike storage available? Is there an extra cost? Some universities will charge up to £150 for an annual parking permit and up to £20 for annual storage in the hall bike shed.
- Are there any compulsory charges you will have to pay? For example, Imperial College London asks you to pay 'a small compulsory contribution to the social amenities of the hall' and 'a small compulsory contribution to the shuttle bus service (where applicable)'. Are you happy to use the services and pay this extra cost?

Private rented accommodation

- How much is the rent? Does the contract state start and finish dates, and clearly state how much rent is to be paid for this time? Check that the contract runs for the length of time you require and that you are able to pay your rent on time. This is of particular importance if you are relying on grants and loans to make rent payments.

- Check the contract very carefully. Is it an individual or joint agreement? If it is an individual agreement you are responsible only for your share of rent and bills. If it is a joint agreement you will be liable for everybody's rent and bills. Some landlords prefer to issue joint agreements because it covers them financially if someone in the house refuses to pay. However, as a student it is not in your interests to be liable for everyone else's debt. Also, you should note that individual agreements will require you all to purchase separate TV licences, whereas one licence will suffice for properties on which there is a joint agreement (see Chapter 4).

- Do you need to pay a retainer for the landlord to keep the accommodation for you over the summer vacation? This is a practice that is discouraged by some universities and the National Union of Students (NUS) but it is not illegal for a landlord to do this. If you do pay a retainer ask for proof in writing, along with a written guarantee that the landlord will keep the accommodation for you.

- How much is the deposit? Most private landlords will require a deposit, usually equivalent to one month's rent, and they will need to provide information about the tenancy deposit scheme that they intend to use (see Chapter 20). They will also need to provide you with a receipt for the money you have paid.

- Are bills included in the rent? If not, ask for a copy of previous bills so that you can work out how much you will have to pay for utilities (see below).

- What is to be provided in the property? Your landlord should provide you with an up-to-date inventory of all items in the property and their condition. Ask to see the inventory and check that everything is available as described. This will help you to work out what else you will need to buy. University-approved landlords who provide student accommodation should provide everything you need in a fully furnished property.

Living at home

Many students are now finding that it is cheaper to live at home while they are studying, especially in cases where parents are willing to pay for their board and lodging. This is a decision that will have to be made carefully. Are you happy to live in the parental home while you are studying? If you are a parent, are you happy to support your child and enable him or her to live in your home, perhaps rent free, for another three years?

One of the important points about studying at university is the opportunity to move away from the parental home and learn the life skills that are associated with independent living, such as financial management, cooking, organising a household and so on. If you live in your parental home while you are studying, you will miss out on some of these opportunities, although you may not have to worry about bills and your personal finances so much. If you are a parent, would you prefer your children to learn these life skills while they are studying, before they enter the world of employment, or would it give you peace of mind to know that they are financially secure and safe in your family home? Frank and honest discussions will be required to make sure that everyone in the household is happy with the decisions that are made.

Juliet, final-year student, Bournemouth University

I did live at home while I was at university. Funnily enough the main reason wasn't lack of money… it was more to do with the fact that lots of my mates were going to our home university and they did exactly the course I was interested in. But I soon found out that money was one of the main advantages because mum and dad really helped me out and I didn't have to buy food or anything like that… No, I don't think I missed out too much really on a social life… The only problem was that I had to get a bus to university and that was a pain for nine o'clock lectures. I had to get up really early. But other than that, no, I can't think of any problems really. I still went to parties and all that sort of thing.

Paying for food

There are different ways of paying for food, depending on the type of accommodation you choose and the university at which you wish to study. These are described below.

Full board residences

With this type of arrangement three meals a day, usually seven days a week, are provided along with your accommodation. The fee that you pay will cover all meals for the period of your contract, with specified breaks during vacations. Since residential halls can be used for conferences you may be required to leave your room and clear it of possessions during vacations.

Although your rent will be a lot higher with this type of arrangement, an advantage is that all your meals are paid for and you do not have to buy food or cook for yourself. It is for these reasons that full board residences tend to be available mainly for first-year students who have less experience of self-catering. This type of arrangement is also popular with people who don't like cooking or who know that they would spend too much on food if they prepared it themselves.

Semi-catered residences

Many universities provide this type of arrangement, whereby two meals are provided, five or seven days a week, because it offers students a little more flexibility but still provides enough meals for students not to have to cook themselves.

If you are interested in semi-catered halls you should find out exactly what meals are offered and at what time, to make sure that they fit in with your preferences and with your course. For example, if you never eat breakfast, you would be better choosing a hall that offers lunch and an evening meal, and perhaps brunch at the weekend. Some halls will only offer meals during the week, so you will need to make your own arrangements at the weekend.

This type of hall will usually provide kitchens and equipment for you to cook light meals and snacks. Again, although this type of accommodation will be more expensive, an advantage is that you pay for many of your

meals with your rent, so you don't have to budget for extra food costs, and you will still be able to eat if you run out of money at the end of the term.

Self-catered residences

Self-catered university accommodation offers a room without meals and rent, and therefore tends to be cheaper, although luxury self-catered accommodation with en-suite facilities will still be expensive. Fully equipped kitchens are provided for you to prepare all your own meals, if you wish. However, most universities will enable you to join their meal scheme, which will allow you to take a certain number of meals at university catering outlets for an additional cost. Although schemes vary, they tend to offer a choice, such as buying a card that enables you to take lunch and dinner five days a week (costing approximately £400–£500 a term) or one that enables you to take just lunch five days a week (costing approximately £200–£300 a term). In most cases you are not tied in for the whole year, but can choose which scheme, if any, to join each term.

Self-catered halls are popular with older students and those who are happy to cater for themselves, as they can be much more flexible and don't tie you to specific meal times. Also, with careful planning and budgeting, and by cooking meals together, this option can work out cheaper.

Private rented accommodation

Most students who live in private rented accommodation will have to buy and prepare their own meals, although it is usually possible to take part in the types of meal scheme described above if you prefer. In some cases, lodgings may be available where students live with families and take some meals with them. This type of accommodation is more expensive because food is provided. However, some international students prefer this type of arrangement because it enables them to live with a family and learn more about the British way of life while they are studying.

Paying for utilities

If you choose to live in a hall of residence, the cost of gas, electricity and water is usually included in your rent, although, as we have seen above,

this may not always be the case. If you choose to live in private rented accommodation, some rents will be inclusive of water, gas and electricity, whereas others will not. You should check with your landlord what bills you are expected to pay before moving into the accommodation. If you are offered a property in which rents are inclusive of water bills, you could be expected to pay an extra £2.00–£3.00 per week on top of your basic rent. If the rent is inclusive of all bills, you could be expected to pay an extra £6.50–£8.00.

If you have to pay all bills you will need to budget carefully and make sure that you have the money available when bills are due. Late payment can result in penalties, the most serious of which can be disconnection and possible eviction if your landlord is successful in taking you to court for non-payment. The following examples give you an idea of how much you could expect to pay for utilities, but since all accommodation has different usage, equipment and levels of insulation, you should ask for previous bills from your landlord so that you can budget carefully.

Gas

The cost of your gas will depend on the number, type and age of gas appliances in the accommodation, the amount of gas you use, the amount of insulation in the property and the price charged by the gas supplier. To give you an example, a four-bedroom, terraced house in the south of England, occupied by four students with a new gas boiler and central heating system, gas cooker and good level of insulation, was billed the following:

29 October, 2007	£45.36
30 January, 2008	£127.20
25 April, 2008	£118.42
23 July, 2008	£40.79
Total	£331.77

The students in this house made sure that they did not use too much gas and took advantage of the prompt-payment reduction. This meant that each student paid a total of £82.94 for gas in one year.

Electricity

The cost of your electricity will depend on the number, type and age of electrical appliances, the amount of electricity you use, the energy-saving devices and equipment installed in the property and the price charged by your electricity supplier. In the same house in the south of England the students had two computers, one television, a microwave, a kettle, a fridge, a freezer and lighting in all the rooms. The landlord had taken care to source the property with the most energy-saving equipment he could afford. The students were billed the following for their electricity:

21 October, 2007	£58.45
21 January, 2008	£99.41
22 April, 2008	£89.82
18 July, 2008	£83.38
Total	£331.06

The students made sure that they saved as much electricity as possible and again took advantage of the prompt-payment discount. This meant that each student spent £82.76 on electricity for one year.

Water

Some water bills are based on the rateable (chargeable) value of a property. From this rateable value the water company works out how much you have to pay for your water supply and how much you have to pay for your sewerage services. The bills also include a standing charge for both water supply and sewerage services.

However, some properties receive a metered supply of water, which means that the people living in the house only pay for the water they use. When you choose a property check with your landlord whether the property has a water meter. If it does you can control the amount of water you use and cut costs. However, you would have to make sure that all your housemates had the same attitude towards saving water so as not to cause conflict.

Using the example above, the house in the south of England did not have a water meter and students had to pay the water bill based on the rateable value of the property. They were billed the following in 2008/09:

Water supply charge	£158.67
Water standing charge	£7.00
Sewerage service charge	£151.98
Sewerage standing charge	£7.00
Total	£324.65

The students were in the property all year, including the long summer vacation, so they had to pay the whole bill. This meant that, for the year, each student paid a total of £81.16 on water and sewerage services.

Difficulty paying bills

If you find that you have any difficulty paying bills, or that you are being billed for a previous tenant's usage, contact your students' union for advice. Deal with any problems quickly so that they do not escalate. Utility companies can be flexible with methods of payment, but you must inform them as soon as you get into trouble. You will find information about what to do if you have problems paying on the back of your bill. Don't be tempted to leave bills unpaid when you move: most landlords will ask for the address of your parents when you move into their property and will pass this on to utility companies if you have left without paying. This could have serious consequences for your creditworthiness at a later stage in life, perhaps when you apply for a mortgage or loan.

Paying council tax

Generally, anyone who is at least 18 years old and lives as a resident in a property in England, Scotland or Wales that is their main or sole dwelling is liable to pay council tax. However, full-time undergraduate students should not have to pay council tax in the following circumstances:

- If you live in halls of residence or other types of accommodation owned by the university. There is no need to apply for exemption as this will be sorted out by the university.
- If you live in a house occupied solely by full-time students. You will need to apply for exemption by contacting the local council of the area in which your property is situated and asking for the appropriate

form. (Some universities will be able to supply you with this form.) Your application will be processed faster if you return all housemates' forms together.

- If you live with other people who are working. Although you can apply for exemption, it is the property as well as the individual that is taxed, so, in certain circumstances you may need to negotiate who pays what towards the bill. For example, your working parents may require you to make a small contribution to help them to meet the bill.
- If you live with one other person who is working. Again, you should be exempt and the other person should be able to receive a single person discount of 25 per cent. However, if you are living with a spouse, for example, you may need to negotiate who pays what amount towards the bill.
- If you are an exchange student who is studying in the United Kingdom for one term only, although this will be judged on a case-by-case basis.

Some students may have to pay council tax. In general, this will be in the following circumstances:

- If you complete your course and intend to start another course a few months later; for example, you complete an undergraduate course in June and intend to start a postgraduate course the following October.
- If you are studying on a course of less than 24 weeks in length.
- If you are studying for less than 21 hours a week.
- If you leave your course.
- If you are a student owner-occupier who lets rooms in your property to people who are in paid employment. You can apply for exemption but you will also need to ensure that the council tax for the property is paid (see Chapter 20).

The Valuation Office Agency (VOA) is responsible for allocating the correct council tax band to all homes in England and Wales. If you think you may be liable to pay the tax you should visit their website to find out the band of a property in which you are interested as this will help you to budget effectively (www.voa.gov.uk/council_tax).

Summary

Accommodation costs can be significant while you are studying, unless you decide to study in you home town/city and stay in your parental home. While this course of action will be cheaper, you need to make sure that it is the right decision for you, as you could miss out on some of the life opportunities that studying away from home provides. When working out accommodation costs you need to think about length of contract, booking fees, deposits, retainers and late payment penalties. You also need to budget for food and utilities and find out whether you are liable to pay council tax.

Other important costs for which you need to budget are books, stationery and course materials. These issues are discussed in the following chapter.

Useful organisations

UNIAID

UNIAID is a charity that offers advice and support for students who may experience financial difficulty at university. On their website you can find useful interactive tools to help you to work out your finances, along with a useful student calculator. A small number of accommodation bursaries are available through UNIAID.

UNIAID Foundation
CAN Mezzanine
Downstream Building
1 London Bridge
London SE1 9BG
Tel: (020) 7785 3885
e-mail: info@uniaid.org.uk
www.uniaid.org.uk

3 Paying for books, stationery and course materials

Depending on your course and the university at which you intend to study, books, stationery and course materials can take up a significant amount of your student budget. However, there are ways to reduce your spending and cut costs without compromising your studies.

This chapter helps you to understand how much books, course materials and stationery will cost, by discussing what you will need to buy and describing the facilities that will be available at university, free of charge. It goes on to look at the costs involved, showing how you can reduce them through careful use of reading lists, understanding where bargains can be found and using suppliers that have been established specifically for university students.

Knowing what to buy

Most university students will need to buy some books. However, if you are on a tight budget you should find out how many books you have to buy as the university library may contain all you need for some courses. Also, all university libraries run an inter-library loan service that means that you can obtain books from other libraries free of charge or for a small fee (usually between £4 and £12, depending on the item, whether you have requested a printed or electronic copy, and whether you are an undergraduate or postgraduate student). Consult your university library website to find out how many books are held and the ratio of books to students, especially for key texts, which should be highlighted on your reading list (see below).

Some universities try to provide some or all of the materials required for a course, whereas others expect students to supply equipment themselves. However, all students will need to supply basic stationery. Your course literature should give you an indication of what is required, but if in doubt speak to your tutor before the course starts. If you are on a strict budget it is important that you don't spend more than you need to on books, stationery and materials.

Making the most of library resources

Most universities will provide all the books and reference material that you need, so through using the library/learning centre on a regular basis you will be able to keep your costs down. All university libraries are fully stocked with the following resources:

● books (available on long loan, short loan or for reference);
● periodicals (newspapers, magazines and journals);
● audiovisual collections (films on DVD/video and slides for teaching and presentation purposes);
● reference books (encyclopaedias, dictionaries, directories, atlases and bibliographies);
● course reference materials (photocopied material collected by tutors);
● pamphlets (usually relevant to the local area or to the university);
● electronic resources (periodicals, reference works, biographical resources, digital facsimiles of historic books, image collections, parliamentary papers, newspapers and databases).

When you begin your course your tutor will arrange for you to attend a library tour. During this tour library staff will point out what is available for your use and enable you to register and receive your library card. They will also let you know how many books you can borrow and over what period. You can renew books up to a specified number of times, if they have not been requested by another student, and this can be done electronically once you have been provided with registration details. You can also reserve books electronically, to be collected from the library when they become available. Books that are heavily in demand are usually provided on a short-term loan, which is usually for one week.

Photocopying

If you decide to photocopy any material you must do so within copyright law. This states that you cannot photocopy more than one chapter of a book or one article of a journal, and that what you photocopy cannot be more than 5 per cent of the work. More information about copyright can be obtained from the Copyright Licensing Agency (details below). For information about the costs of photocopying, consult Chapter 6.

Knowing about costs

A recent survey by the Royal Bank of Scotland calculated that students spent £330 million on books and course materials. How much you spend will depend on the requirements of your course, the number of books held in your library, the materials provided by your university and your careful planning. Table 3.1 lists the initial costs of a first-year sociology student studying at Sheffield Hallam University, to provide an example of the costs involved.

Table 3.1 The cost of books, course materials and stationery

Items	Item price
3 key textbooks (bought new)	£45.97
4 useful textbooks (bought second-hand)	£22.96
5 reams of A4 paper (draft quality)	£9.99
1 ream of A4 paper (good quality)	£4.99
Pack of 10 blue ball point pens	£0.89
5 pencils	£0.59
1 toner cartridge	£42.99
2 narrow-lined, A4 notebooks	£3.98
4 shorthand notepads	£1.96
4 A4 ring binders	£3.96
100 economy document pockets	£2.99
4 sets of file dividers	£2.36
Stapler and refills	£4.99
Hole punch	£5.99
Total	**£154.61**

The student from Table 3.1 found that she had two reams of paper left over at the end of her first year and had enough space in her notepads for another semester of study. However, she had to buy two more textbooks and two more ring binders. These extra items added a further £39.96 to her bill. Therefore, over the year, this student spent a total of £194.57 on course materials, stationery and books.

University art shops

If you are studying on an art or design course, your university will probably have an art shop (often operated by the art faculty/school) where you can buy all the materials you need at discounted prices. These shops will be run by specialist members of staff who can provide advice and guidance on materials, and provide swatches and samples for colour and materials matching. As these shops order in bulk, and work closely with course tutors, they can ensure that all the required equipment is available at discounted prices. Also, because they are often located within the faculty or school, they are very convenient for students who need equipment at short notice.

Using reading lists

You don't need to buy all the books on your reading list. Ask your tutor which are the key texts, then find out how many copies are available in the university library. If you feel you cannot do without a key text, consider buying a second-hand copy. These will be advertised on student websites, your university intranet or student noticeboards. Some students' union shops or university bookshops buy and sell second-hand books so check whether this is the case before you purchase new ones. A useful website is uni-trader, which enables you to search for textbooks and other second-hand items that are for sale at various universities in the United Kingdom (details below).

Alex, from the USA, via e-mail

I studied a Master's degree in English literature at Kent University several years ago. When I registered on the course I was given an enormous reading list; after all, that is the nature of the course. We were expected to read as much as possible before we even began our studies. I went to Cambridge, which, at the time, was near where I lived and I thought the bookshops there would have all the books I needed. I could get hold of most of them but some were so obscure that I had to order them in. In that first trip I spent £470 on books! On the second trip I spent a further £150! I had never realised that books for the course would have been so expensive. As it turns out, I didn't need some of the books because, although we had to read them as background, they weren't central to the course. I could have obtained copies from the library and returned them when read. My advice to prospective students would be to buy only what you really need. I like to write notes in my books, so I need to have my own copies. However, some didn't require any notes, so library copies would have sufficed.

University bookshops

All universities have a bookshop on, or close to, the campus. Most of these have a 'course book form' or a reading list submission policy that enables tutors and lecturers to submit their reading lists for all their courses in advance of the start of term. The tutor also gives an indication of the number of students enrolled on the course. The bookshop then orders a sufficient number of copies of each book so that there are plenty available for students who arrive at the start of term.

These bookshops can be useful if you find that you have to buy new copies of books because there are no second-hand copies available, perhaps if it is a new course or if some of the reading is quite obscure. At the beginning of term many bookshops will keep reserve stocks of books, so if you cannot find what are looking for on the shelves, ask a member of staff whether it is available in stock. Discounts will be available if you can prove your student status.

Finding bargains

Students' union shops are members of NUS Services, which is an organisation that specialises in collective purchasing and direct marketing to reach students (contact details are provided in Chapter 4). Through NUS Services special deals are made between students' unions and suppliers on all items sold in union shops. This includes stationery and course materials, and you will find that most items are offered more cheaply than they are on the high street.

On the occasions when you need to shop in high-street shops, check to find out whether they offer a student discount. Always take your library card or NUS card with you so that you can prove that you are a student. (Your library card will be issued free of charge upon registration, whereas you will need to apply at your students' union, and pay a small fee, for your NUS card.) Some bookshops, especially those situated near to a university, offer student discounts of up to 10 per cent. Although this type of discount may not be advertised, some shops will provide it when asked.

Summary

The cost of course materials, books and stationery depends on your course, what is provided by the university and the availability of second-hand resources. You do not have to buy all the books on your reading list and can reduce costs by buying only what is absolutely necessary. Your university library website should contain information about the ratio of key texts to students on your course, and your tutor will be able to offer advice about using your reading list effectively.

Another significant cost for students studying at university involves sports, leisure and entertainment. These issues are discussed in the following chapter.

Useful organisations

The Booksellers Association of the United Kingdom & Ireland Limited

The Booksellers Association of the United Kingdom & Ireland Limited represents the interests of booksellers across the United Kingdom. On its website you can use the directory to access details of independent book-shops in the United Kingdom. There is also a search facility for Open University students to find local stockists of course materials.

The Booksellers Association of the United Kingdom & Ireland Limited
Minster House
272 Vauxhall Bridge Road
London SW1V 1BA
Tel: (020) 7802 0802
Fax: (020) 7802 0803
e-mail: mail@booksellers.org.uk
www.booksellers.org.uk

Useful websites

www.cla.co.uk

This is the website of the Copyright Licensing Agency (CLA). On this site you can find useful information about copyright issues and CLA licences.

www.uni-trader.co.uk

You can buy a wide variety of items and textbooks from this site. It is a useful site to access because you can search for items at specific universities and arrange to meet the person selling the item to cut down on postage costs.

4 Paying for sports, leisure and entertainment

Paying for sports, leisure and entertainment can add a significant amount to your costs, especially if you enjoy this type of activity and want to make the most of social activities and sports opportunities while you are studying at university.

However, universities have various discount schemes available and some provide free sports and other free activities for their students. Information about these activities and the costs involved, and advice about discount schemes is provided in this chapter.

Knowing about entertainment costs

The amount of entertainment provided at your university depends, in part, on the successful activity of your students' union and the entertainment committee. When you enrol at your university you can register to become a member of the students' union, although you don't have to be a member to use their services. You can usually do this at the Freshers' Fair in the first week of term or by visiting the students' union offices. Registration is free, although there is a small fee to pay if you choose to buy an NUS card. This is a useful card to have because it enables you to access other students' unions around the country.

Prices at students' union events

Prices at all students' union events are kept as low as possible because the students' union will be a member of NUS Services (details below). This is the commercial arm of the students' union movement in the United

Kingdom. It specialises in collective purchasing arrangements and direct marketing to students, which means that students can benefit by receiving cheaper products and entertainment. NUS Services enables companies to target the student market directly by providing a sampling pack distributed to 350,000 first-year students each year. When you join your students' union you will receive a welcome pack containing a variety of free samples, vouchers, free gifts and information about local facilities.

Examples of events arranged, and prices charged, by students' unions include:

- alcoholic drink promotions and two-for-one discount (prices vary around the country, with the cost of a pint of beer ranging from £1.90 to £2.70);
- happy hours (half-price drinks);
- karaoke nights (free to £3);
- fancy dress competitions (free to £5);
- seventies/eighties discos (free to £8);
- dance nights (£5–£15);
- clubs on campus and transport to clubs off campus (£5–£20);
- pub quizzes/trivial pursuit evenings (entry fee of £2–£5);
- formal dinners/balls (£15–£30);
- bands/live music (free–£30);
- comedy acts (free–£20);
- poetry readings (free);
- film nights (free–£3);
- cultural and religious events such as Eid, Diwali, Hanukkah, Chinese New Year and Christmas (free to various prices, depending on event).

Some universities request that you buy a special entertainment card that enables you to receive cheaper drinks and/or entertainment. For example, the University of Sunderland has a scheme whereby you can buy a Students' Union Gold Card for £5 that enables you to receive discounts in the union shop and in the union bar (a pint of beer will cost £1.45 with your Gold Card at 2009 prices).

Once at university it is possible to join the entertainment committee of the students' union. In exchange for your work (such as setting up equipment or looking after entertainers/artists) you can obtain free entry to most entertainment events. Visit your students' union for more information.

Entertainment off campus

Some individual students' unions organise special offers with local companies and provide a card or booklet containing vouchers and information about discount schemes. Through these arrangements it is possible to receive discounts of up to 10 per cent on high-street entertainment such as pubs, clubs and restaurants. These vouchers might be provided in your welcome pack (provided at the Freshers' Fair) or you can find further details on your university or students' union website.

NUS Extra

This is a student discount card that can be purchased from the NUS for £10 (2009 prices). It enables you to obtain further discounts on books, entertainment, food, drinks and clothes. Examples of current deals (February 2009) include the following:

- 10 per cent discount in Superdrug when you spend £10 or more;
- 10 per cent discount in Matalan;
- 5 per cent discount at Amazon on orders of more than £15;
- free medium fries with the purchase of a Big Mac or McChicken Sandwich at McDonalds;
- 10 per cent discount at JJB Sports in store or online;
- free comprehensive annual travel insurance with any car insurance purchased from Endsleigh;
- £3 off lesson prices on a 12-week course purchased through AA Driving School;
- buy one game of bowling, get another free at Bowlplex sites across the UK;
- 15 per cent off everything at BBs cafés.

For more information, to enter competitions, to search the database for discounts and to buy a card, visit www.nus.org.uk.

Knowing about sports and leisure costs

Prices for sports and leisure vary enormously between universities. As a general guide you might expect to pay within the following ranges:

- hire of badminton court, £3.50–£8.00;
- swimming sessions, £2.00–£4.50;
- five-a-side football pitch, £6.00–£20.00;
- tennis court, £3.00–£8.00;
- aerobics session, £2.20–£3.70;
- yoga, £2.50–£4.50;
- gym session, £2.00–£8.00.

Some universities will offer discounts to students who book sports facilities on a regular basis. Also, many universities operate a sports card system. For an annual payment you are able to purchase a card that entitles you to use the sporting facilities for a reduced payment or free of charge. The price of this card varies between universities but is usually in the region of £35–£55 a year for reduced-rate cards and £70–£150 a year for cards that also provide free use of equipment.

Once you have bought a sports card you will have unlimited access to sports facilities at a reduced rate or for no payment at all. This is useful if you find that you are running out of money as the term progresses: you can still keep active and enjoy the sports facilities because you have paid up-front. It is cheaper to pay this way as long as you use the facilities on a regular basis. Also, you may find that because you have paid a fee up-front you are more motivated to use the facilities. Some universities will allow you to pay the fee by direct debit in easy instalments, and some cards will provide insurance cover once you have purchased them. You will be able to make telephone bookings using your card number, and some universities provide additional special offers to cardholders.

Although there are several advantages to purchasing a sports card, you need to think about whether you will use the facilities enough to recover the cost. If you are an occasional sports person you might be better paying only for individual sessions.

Joining a sports club

If you decide to join a sports club you will have to pay a membership fee but could receive discounts on sporting facilities. Fees vary enormously, ranging from £2 to £40, depending on the type of sport and the benefits to be gained as a member. You will have the opportunity to find out what sports clubs are available at the Freshers' Fair in the first week of term. However, think carefully about which clubs you would like to join before you pay your membership fee as this money could be wasted if you do not take up the sport.

Making use of free facilities

Although most universities will make a charge for sports and leisure facilities, you may find that some enable you to make use of certain facilities, such as football pitches and running tracks, free of charge. If you are interested in any type of sporting activity, find out whether your university has the facilities available by consulting its prospectus or website.

If you excel at a particular sport and wish to compete against other students, find out which university has a reputation for excelling at that sport. These universities may have more and better facilities available for your use, and they will be free of charge if you are committed to your training. Also, find out whether the university offers sports scholarships as these will help you to meet additional costs associated with your training and competition entry. More information about funding for sports is provided in Chapter 24.

Knowing about costs for clubs and societies

In addition to the sporting clubs discussed above, there are many different non-sporting clubs and societies available at universities in the United Kingdom. These include:

- Amnesty;
- Christian Union;
- debating;

- photography;
- drama;
- film-making;
- industrial society;
- student entrepreneurs;
- conservation;
- hill-walking;
- all political parties;
- various minority ethic groups;
- lesbian, gay, bisexual and transsexual groups (LGBT);
- gaming;
- various dance clubs;
- various music clubs.

For an up-to-date table of the clubs and societies that you can find at each university in the United Kingdom, visit the Push website (details below).

Prices for clubs and societies vary: some groups are free, whereas others request a membership fee that can be paid at the Freshers' Fair, or when you decide to join the club or society. Fees vary enormously, but tend to range up to £15, depending on the type of club and the activities undertaken. Some clubs and societies that arrange trips out will request a higher fee to cover costs, so discuss these charges with committee members before you join. If you decide to take an active role in the club, such as chairperson or treasurer, you might not have to pay a membership fee and you may be able to receive expenses associated with the work that you undertake for your club.

Knowing about costs off campus

If you choose to study in your home town you will have a good idea of the cost of leisure, entertainment and sporting activities there. However, if you decide to move away from home for your studies, you may find that prices are very different from those that you are used to, especially if you decide to study in a larger, more expensive city.

Most university websites and prospectuses will contain some information about costs, but will not be very detailed. Also, you need to remember that the main aim of websites and prospectuses is to sell their university to

you, as a potential student, so positive aspects of study in the vicinity will be highlighted and negative ones neglected. If social and sporting costs are important to you, it is up to you to obtain a detailed and up-to-date picture of these costs in the area in which you are interested. You can do this by following the example highlighted in the case study below.

Nigel, 19, Northampton

I was thinking about studying in Manchester... mainly because of the great nightlife. But I needed to know whether I could afford it... So I googled 'entertainment in Manchester'. This took me to information from their local newspapers and the local council, especially free entertainment from the council. It also got me to a website called manchesteronline that was really useful. I also rang the tourist information office and got them to send me some stuff and I looked at their website, which was www.visitmanchester.com... My brother has some friends who went to uni in Manchester so I went and talked to them. In fact I'd say that was the best information 'cos they like similar things to me and could give me the low-down, the best clubs and prices of drinks and stuff. So that's where I'm going now. I think!

Paying for a TV licence

As television is one of the most popular forms of entertainment, most students will have a set in their room/house. When you go away to university you will need to purchase a TV licence in the following circumstance:

- If you choose to live in a hall of residence and you have your own TV in your room.
- If you live in a privately rented house with other students, your need for a TV licence will depend on the type of contract you have signed. If you have signed a joint tenancy agreement, you will need to purchase a licence for a TV that is used in a communal area and this should be enough for the whole property. However, if you have signed a separate

tenancy agreement, you and your housemates will each have to buy a licence for any TV that you have in your individual room (if it is a separately occupied space).

- If you use a PC to watch live television on any device at your address, whether it is on a television set or a PC (the same rules about type of contract apply).

It is possible to get a refund on your TV licence if you leave your accommodation before the licence expires, for example if you leave before the summer vacation. A licence for a colour TV costs £139.50 (2009 price). You can face prosecution and a fine of up to £1,000 if you don't have one, so it is important to make sure that you purchase the appropriate licence as soon as you move into the property (see quotation below).

Lucy, 22, Whitstable

I couldn't believe it, we'd moved into that place the week before. Then there was a knock at the door. I was the only one in at the time so I answered it and he said he was from the TV licensing people... He said our property hadn't got a licence. I said there was a telly in the house, but we'd only moved in the week before. He said even so, we would be fined because we had been watching it without a licence... Then one of my flat mates came home and said we hadn't watched the telly because it didn't work... The man asked her to prove it and she switched it on and it didn't work. I couldn't believe it because I'd only been watching it earlier that day. So anyway he said that he wouldn't fine us but that we had to get a licence or get rid of the telly. Actually two of us also had tellies in our rooms but luckily he didn't look in those rooms. It was a real shock... Needless to say we went out and got a licence that day... We spoke to the landlord and he said some other students had been caught last year, so maybe they were watching that place.

Summary

Universities and students' unions work hard to provide a wide variety of interesting and affordable sports, entertainment and leisure facilities for their students, although the number, type and standard of facilities vary considerably between institutions. If sporting and social activities are important to you, consult individual websites and prospectuses before you make your UCAS choices. Taking part in social and sporting activities does not have to cost a lot as some facilities are provided free of charge and many universities and students' unions offer discounts for their members. A visit to the Freshers' Fair at the beginning of your course will enable you to find out what is available.

Another significant cost for some students on particular courses can be field trips and study abroad. These issues are discussed in the following chapter.

Useful organisations

NUS Services

NUS Services is owned by students' unions and the NUS. Its mission is to 'create, develop and sustain competitive advantages for member Students' Unions – reducing costs and maximising commercial revenues'. Through NUS Services students' unions can obtain goods and marketing services at reduced prices and savings can be passed onto students.

NUS Services
Snape Road
Macclesfield
Cheshire SK10 2NZ
Tel: (01625) 413200
Fax: (01625) 413400
e-mail: enquiries@nussl.co.uk
www.nussl.co.uk

Useful websites

www.hotcourses.com

This website provides comprehensive and up-to-date information about all universities in the United Kingdom. Each university has a separate entry, and this includes information about sports and entertainment. The website also contains useful reviews to help you with your course and university choice.

www.push.co.uk

You can look at each university profile on this website. Universities are rated in the following categories: academic, booze index, sports, activities, housing, welfare, reputation and living costs. You can also find out more about leisure and entertainment, along with up-to-date prices of alcoholic drinks, at each university.

5 Paying for field trips and study abroad

Field trips involve a period of study away from the classroom, led by a tutor, for the purpose of enhancing your learning through providing practical examples. This might be a morning trip to a factory or a week-long visit to a place of scientific interest, for example. Field trips can involve travel to all parts of the United Kingdom and overseas. Virtual field trips are offered by some universities if budgets and/or time are restricted. Study abroad can be a compulsory or voluntary component of your course; it can be short term, perhaps over one semester, or you can choose to study your whole degree abroad.

Field trips and study abroad can cost a significant amount of money, which has to be paid if they are compulsory components of the course. Some universities and courses use field trips and study abroad as a learning resource much more than others, so you should obtain further information from the university or course tutor before you apply. The costs involved in this type of study are discussed in this chapter. More information about funding opportunities for study abroad is provided in Chapter 14.

Knowing about the cost of field trips

The cost of a field trip depends on your university and the type/duration of the field trip. As an example, a one-week university field trip in geography or geology may cost in the region of £200–£350, depending on the location and the type of accommodation. This cost is to cover your accommodation and meals, as the cost of tuition is already included in your tuition fees in most cases. Some universities, however, may not require any extra payment for field trips as all the cost is covered by tuition fees. Consult with your tutor to find out which procedure is adopted by your university.

Buying equipment

You will need to budget for equipment when you go on a field trip. Also, if any part of your field work will be hazardous you will need to budget for the following items of protective clothing:

- safety helmets (£5–£15);
- eye/face protection (£3–£8);
- ear plugs/defenders (plugs £2–£6, defenders £6–£20);
- respiratory protection (masks £2–£10);
- high-visibility clothing (trousers £15–£22, jackets £15–£40, vests £3–£10);
- coveralls (£35–£80);
- wetsuits (full £50 £120, short £15–£30, gloves £6–£15);
- life jackets (£10–£100);
- knee pads (£3 £15);
- protective gloves (£5–£15);
- foot protection (£18–£80).

Some of this equipment may be provided for you by the university or field centre, so you need to consult with your tutor about what items to buy prior to the trip. If everyone on your course has to purchase similar safety equipment, it is often cheaper to buy in bulk and your tutor may be able to arrange this for you.

Even if you do not require any of the above safety equipment you will need to budget for the following when undertaking field work:

- warm clothing (trousers £20–£40, jumper/fleece £10–£40);
- waterproof jacket/coat (£20–£80);
- walking boots or other suitable footwear (£30–£120);
- a suitable rucksack (£7–£50).

If you buy good-quality footwear and clothing they will last a lot longer, be more comfortable and should perform better, although they will be a little more expensive, as illustrated in the quotation below.

I've never bought walking boots before, so I was a bit surprised at how much they were... my mum also told me to buy them early and walk them in. Some of my mates didn't do this and they had terrible blisters... Mine was a geography field trip and we went to Swanage and we had to walk all in all about 28 miles of the coastal path, up cliffs and down cliffs, so if I hadn't walked my boots in I would have been in no end of trouble... A good waterproof coat as well 'cos it rained and rained. Mine didn't leak, but other people's did, they were so wet and really annoyed... About £69.99 on boots and £57.99 on a good coat but they should both last for all my field trips and lots of festivals.

Knowing about the cost of study abroad

The cost of study abroad will depend on where you study and the length of time abroad. In some countries it is still possible to obtain free higher education and in other countries fees are much lower than they are in the United Kingdom. This means that studying abroad for your entire degree can cost less than it might do at home, even when extra living and travel costs are taken into account.

On the ERASMUS programme and some other study-abroad schemes you will not need to pay tuition fees in your host university. (ERASMUS stands for European Region Action Scheme for the Mobility of University Students. It is a European student-exchange programme that was established in 1987 to increase student and teaching mobility throughout Europe.) Also, you will not be required to pay other fees such as examination and registration charges. However, if you study abroad for less than a year through ERASMUS you will have to pay tuition fees in your home country, although some will offer a reduced fee if you choose to study abroad for part of the year.

When you study abroad you will be expected to meet all your living costs and pay for insurance. Some countries, such as the United States, will not grant a student visa unless you are able to show that you have

adequate money and suitable insurance. In general, it is recommended that you have at least £2,000 more than your usual annual living costs at university for study abroad. This figure will be higher for countries in which the cost of living is high and lower in countries where the cost of living is low. Insurance could range from £140 to £300, depending on where you intend to study and the insurance company that you use. Some universities have a business-travel insurance policy that covers staff and students travelling on university business, so check whether you are covered by this policy before you arrange your own insurance. All insurance forms must be completed and accepted before you travel.

Student loans and study abroad

You may be entitled to continue receiving your student loan and any other benefits that you have been granted. This is usually the case if the study abroad is a compulsory component of your course or if it is voluntary through ERASMUS. Loans will be available for no more than a year abroad and are income-assessed. More information about student loans is provided in Part Two of this book.

Student loans will not be available if you choose to study your whole degree abroad, but you may be able to obtain funding from your host country. Contact your host university for more information about funding opportunities.

Paying for passports and visas

You will need to have a current passport if you intend to study abroad. The Home Office Identity and Passport Service issues passports for UK citizens and you can find all the information you require at www.ips.gov.uk/passport. In 2009 an adult passport costs £72.

Depending on where you intend to study, you may require a student visa. Contact the international officer at your university, or contact the embassy or consulate of the relevant country directly for more information about whether a visa is required and the costs involved. As a general guide, the cost of student visas can range from £50 to £300, depending on where you intend to study and for how long. Some visas will require an administration fee that is non-refundable, even if your visa application is turned down.

When applying for a student visa you will also need to check about part-time work: some countries will make it a condition that you cannot work with a student visa, and they will need to see proof that you have enough money to see you through your studies without the need to work.

Buying an international student identity card

You can receive discounts on entertainment, books, food and drink, cultural events and travel worldwide (including the United Kingdom) if you have proof of your student status. The best way to do this is through buying an International Student Identity Card (ISIC) before you leave. This is an identity card that is recognised in over 100 countries worldwide. In 2009 an ISIC costs £9 and many students, especially those who travel frequently, find that they are able to recoup this cost easily within the first month of purchase. Current discounts and offers include:

- 25 per cent off Stansted Express tickets.
- 25 per cent off Gatwick Express tickets.
- 15 per cent discount on all sea travel with Condor Ferries.
- 10 per cent off travel packs for students from www.studentjetpacks.co.uk.
- 10 per cent off photography supplies at Jessops.
- 10 per cent off art supplies at Jackson's Art Supplies.
- Discounts in specific countries: visit the website and enter the country you intend to visit to find out what discounts and special offers are available.
- Discounts in specific cities in the United Kingdom: visit the website and enter the city that you are studying in or intend to visit to find out what discounts and special offers are available.

To be eligible and to apply for a card, you will need to supply proof of your full-time student status and proof of your date of birth. If you are not studying full time and you are under the age of 25, you can apply for an International Youth Travel Card instead. Details of both cards are available on the website www.isiccard.com. Application forms can be obtained from this website or from students' unions and university travel offices.

Summary

As an undergraduate student you may find that you have to attend field trips as a compulsory component of your course. If this is the case you need to think about budgeting for accommodation, meals and equipment. Study abroad can be a voluntary or compulsory component of your course, and if you choose this type of study you need to budget for living expenses, insurance, passports and visas. Some countries will need proof that you have enough money to see you through your studies before they will grant a visa.

Another area for which you will have to budget when you go away to university, whether you study in the United Kingdom or abroad, is for information technology and communication equipment. These issues are discussed in the following chapter.

Useful websites

www.tso.co.uk/bookshop

You can buy a number of specialist books (in printed and electronic format) about study abroad from this website. You can also obtain publications about further and higher education and books about graduate careers.

www.intstudy.com

Comprehensive information about study abroad can be obtained from this website, including information about choosing a location, applying for courses, obtaining visas, knowing what to take with you and understanding how to budget for your trip. Although the website is mainly aimed at students who wish to study in the USA, it has some useful information on all aspects of study abroad.

www.esn.org

This is the website of the ERASMUS Student Network. On this site you can find information about studying abroad, including comments and case studies from students who have been through the ERASMUS experience.

www.britishcouncil.org/erasmus

More information about all aspects of study through the ERASMUS programme can be obtained from this site, including information about the different courses, programmes and institutions, and interesting case studies from students who have taken part in the scheme.

Further reading

Barron, T (2006) *Get Set for Study Abroad*, Edinburgh University Press: Edinburgh.

6 Paying for IT and communications equipment

For some students the cost of information technology (IT) and communications equipment can be significant. This could include the costs of buying a personal computer (PC), laptop or mobile phone, and charges for services such as photocopying, printing and internet access once at university.

However, it is possible to keep costs down because much of the equipment is provided by your university, and some is free of charge. If you understand what is available you can save money by not purchasing unnecessary equipment. However, if you do decide that you need your own equipment, there are ways to reduce your costs. These issues are discussed in this chapter, with further information about reducing the costs of IT equipment provided in Chapter 27.

Using university equipment

If you are on a very strict budget you do not need to buy any IT equipment while you are at university, as all your IT requirements can be met by your university. The equipment is free to use and is up to date, enabling you to use the latest technology without any cost to yourself. You will be given an account on the central system that enables you to access the internet, store files, prepare assignments, use the latest software and send and receive e-mail.

Although the supply of equipment and services may vary between universities, in general you should be able to access the following:

- a campus network of PCs, some with 24 hour access;

- workstations and laboratories;
- advice and help desk services;
- printing and binding services;
- e-mail;
- network connection services;
- audiovisual equipment;
- remote access services;
- file recovery services;
- assistance and training in most/all aspects of IT use;
- a computer shop selling hardware and software at 'educational prices' (see below);
- sanitised equipment (see below) for re-sale to students.

Finding out what IT equipment is available

When you make your choice of university, consult its prospectus and website to find out what equipment will be available for your use. IT services departments will have their own website that lists the equipment available. If you attend an open day you will be shown the IT services and equipment that you can use as a student.

Once you enrol on your course, visit the IT services department help desk or reception, where you will be able to ask questions and pick up leaflets about the equipment, services and training courses. The staff will set you up with an account for the central system and an e-mail account. Always attend library tours at the start of your course, as these will help you to become familiar with the services and equipment. All libraries will have a help desk or reception service available where you can seek advice.

Buying your own IT equipment

If you decide to buy your own IT equipment you need to think about exactly what you need from your PC; if you are on a tight budget there is no point spending money on facilities you will never use. Choose software that you need. In general, this will be because it is required for your course, will help with your coursework, and will save you time, money and brainwork. Also, you don't always require the latest version of soft-

ware: if you have an older machine, running such versions can be slow
and cumbersome or they may not run at all.

Cheaper and discounted equipment can be obtained from various
sources:

- Each year a large amount of university IT equipment is taken out of
  service. Some universities have a disposal procedure under which
  equipment is sanitised to make it available for re-sale to students.
  Supplies may be limited so you will need to contact computer services
  as soon as possible. If you decide to buy your equipment in this way,
  think about budgeting for hardware (such as a modem) and for software. You will need to check that the specification meets your needs.
- Many universities have a computer shop where you can purchase your
  computing equipment at educational prices. These are special
  discounts worked out between hardware and software manufacturers
  and educational establishments. To purchase this equipment at
  discounted prices you will need evidence of your student status
  (usually your students' union card or your library card). If you buy
  from a university shop, find out what help you can receive with
  delivery, installation and on-site maintenance. Some universities will
  provide these services at an additional cost, so find out how much this
  will be and how it compares with services supplied elsewhere.
- Discounted software can be obtained from Microsoft if you are able to
  e-mail them from an '.ac' e-mail address, which will be your university e-mail address. Visit www.microsoft.com to find out how much
  you can save.
- Other suppliers are able to offer equipment at educational prices if
  you can prove that you are a student, so shop around for the best deal.
  Be wary of extended warranties on IT products; if you decide to
  purchase one of these, check the small print carefully to see what is
  included and make sure that the cover meets your needs. An alternative service is now offered by some suppliers whereby expert help is
  provided for specific PC projects, such as boosting memory or
  removing spyware or viruses from a computer. Again, check the small
  print and make sure that the service will meet your needs before
  paying.
- Second-hand computing equipment can be bought very cheaply, and
  many students find that it is adequate for their three years of study.

Check the university network and departmental noticeboards for items selling cheaply, or look on eBay.

Arranging insurance

If you intend to use your own computing equipment while you are at university you should obtain insurance to cover any loss or damage. As we saw in Chapter 2, some universities arrange block insurance for their halls of residence, so you should check that your IT equipment is covered on this, especially when used away from your room.

If you need to arrange your own insurance, make sure that your IT equipment is covered within the maximum cover limit on contents, or you will need to add the equipment as additional items, which will raise your premium. It is possible to use specialist insurers who will cover your laptop, PC, software and music downloads against loss or damage anywhere in the United Kingdom or overseas. However, you should note that, although insurance covers your equipment on a new-for-old basis, the replacement will be equivalent to that which is lost and damaged: it will be new but may not be state-of-the art equipment.

Paying for internet access

All students can access the internet at their university free of charge. However, some universities may limit the amount of time you can spend online and others will limit the amount of space you are given to store the information you have downloaded. All universities will have strict rules about obscene material, software theft, breach of copyright and plagiarism. You can obtain a list of rules and regulations from your university IT services department or its website. More information about e-learning, e-resources and plagiarism can be obtained from www.jisc.ac.uk.

Internet access in halls of residence

If you are intending to live in halls of residence, find out whether your room is wired for direct connection to the university network and the internet, or has wireless connection. Some halls will provide this service in all rooms, whereas others may have communal, open access computing

rooms with internet connection. Student halls might charge for the use of the network point in your room, or charge a higher rent to cover the cost. Contact the university accommodation office for more information.

Before you can connect to the campus network, universities will insist that your computer is secure, which means that you will need the following:

- the latest operating system updates;
- up-to-date virus protection;
- a firewall enabled;
- a system password set;
- safe computing configuration (this includes issues such as breach of copyright, securing against identity theft and spyware, and problems with information disclosure on social networks).

Some universities run a clean-access service that uses a technology called Network Admission Control. It checks that your computer has valid and up-to-date anti-virus software and that, if you run Windows, it is up to date with security patches. When you move into your room your connection will be immediate if your computer is up to date. If not, you will be given a series of information leaflets on how you can make your computer secure and connect to the system. If your chosen university runs this type of system, you will be given relevant information when you receive your accommodation pack, so you should be able to make sure that your PC can be connected quickly upon arrival. You may have to sign an acceptable-use policy before you can connect your PC.

TV and video

If you are intending to use your PC to watch TV and video, you must do so within the rules and regulations of the university. In particular, you need to be aware that using applications to distribute material protected by international copyright law is illegal. Your university will have a strict policy on students who use peer-to-peer software to share material protected by international copyright, with continued use leading to disconnection.

In general, video content accessed straight through a web page like YouTube or Google video is permissible. This is because you don't have to

install an application in order to view the content. However, some on-demand TV desktop applications (that have to be installed) will not be allowed because they have a detrimental impact on the delivery of the basic university online services. If you are in any doubt about what you can and cannot download, consult your IT service desk for more information. If you intend to watch TV through your PC you will need to buy a TV licence (see Chapter 4).

Internet access in private rented accommodation

If you are intending to live in private rented accommodation, find out whether internet access is provided by your landlord. More and more landlords are deciding to do this because students are beginning to demand the service. Indeed, to meet this demand, some universities are now offering a service that provides high-speed, fixed-cost internet access to student accommodation within the town/city in which the university is located. (At the moment this service is only provided to private accommodation providers offering more than 50 rooms in one development, but this could change as costs fall.)

If your accommodation has internet access you will find that, at most universities, some electronic resources can be accessed directly by visiting the website address and using a username and password to prove that you are a student from that university. You will also be able to access your university library. However, some electronic resources will not be available off campus due to licensing restrictions. Usernames and passwords are available from the IT services department, and instructions about what you can and cannot access off campus will be given when you enrol.

If internet access is not provided in your accommodation, you will need to discuss the issue with your housemates to avoid arguments about bills and access. As internet access is freely available at university, some students decide that they do not need this facility in their private rented accommodation.

Sending and receiving e-mail

Many universities automatically register new undergraduates for their central e-mail system. If this is not the case, when you enrol on your course contact staff at the IT services department who will issue you with

an e-mail address for their system. You will be given a username and password that you will need to remember in addition to your e-mail address. (Interestingly, some universities in the United States are not issuing students with e-mail addresses but ask instead for an existing one from the students. This saves the university money because they don't have to host their students' e-mail. It will be interesting to see whether this happens in the United Kingdom.)

Different e-mail systems are structured in different ways: when you register, ask staff how you get started on the system. Also, your university will have strict rules about using e-mail: make sure that you read these before you start. In most places sending offensive messages or material that belongs to other people is considered a serious offence. Some universities will restrict the amount of storage you have for messages and attachments, so you will need to organise your account regularly. Also, official university communications and important information from lecturers and tutors is sent by e-mail, so you will need to check your account on a regular basis.

Using mobile phones

Universities estimate that 99 per cent of undergraduates have mobile phones, and more and more lecturers are utilising them as a teaching and learning device. For example, they can be used on field trips to record data (text and pictures) that can be referred back to in the classroom; they can be used for audio, video or text tours of galleries and museums; or used for campus-based services such as scheduling, networking and emergency updates. All mobile phones taken to university should be insured against loss, theft, damage and airtime abuse. Premiums can be hefty, but worth the additional expense.

Knowing about photocopying and printing costs

Universities provide ample black and white and colour photocopying and laser printing services for all their students. However, there is a cost for these services (see Tables 6.1 and 6.2 below).

Table 6.1 University photocopying costs (2009/10)

Copy	Scottish university	Welsh university	Midlands university	Southern university
A4 black and white	6p	6p	7p	5p
A3 black and white	12p	15p	12p	10p
A4 colour	60p	50p	50p	50p
A3 colour	90p	70p	£1	£1
Method	Cards cost £5 or £2 from machines	Cards cost £1 and are pre-charged with 50p credit for first purchase	Cards cost £5 or £10	Cards cost £1 with 35p credit pre-loaded

Table 6.2 University laser printing costs (2009/10)

Printout	Scottish university	Welsh university	Midlands university	Southern university
A4 black-and-white draft	free	2p	free	free
A4 black-and-white, good	7p	8p	8p	7p
A4 colour	50p	50p	80p	50p
Method and offers	Free account worth £12.50 at start of year to all students	Purchase a reusable card and charge with credits	Pre-payment system from self-service kiosks	Purchase a reusable card and charge with credits

Using laser printing services

Tutors and lecturers request that all coursework is word-processed and presented neatly on one side of A4 paper. If you do not own a PC and printer you will need to use university equipment and pay each time you use their printers. However, some universities provide a cheaper or free service for printing draft copies of documents. Find out if this is the case and, if so, make sure you use the service. You need good copies only for work you are handing in to your tutor for assessment. Hunt around through

departments; sometimes this service will be offered by one department but not by another.

Many universities offer a number of printer credits to all undergraduates at the start of their course or at the beginning of each year. Find out whether your university offers this and make sure that you use your credit before paying for printing. Reduce costs by printing only what is absolutely necessary. Look after your card as you may be charged for a replacement if it is lost.

If you have a PC and printer it may be cheaper to use your own equipment. Cheap paper can be obtained from your students' union shop or from office discount stores in your local area or online. Often it is cheaper to buy in bulk, so savings can be made if you buy paper with your friends (see Chapter 3 for more information on cheap stationery).

IT costs for a full degree course

Table 6.3 below provides an example of the costs you can expect to pay on IT equipment for a three-year degree course. They are based on the

Table 6.3 IT costs for a three-year degree course

Items	1st year	2nd year	3rd year	Sub-total
PC	£499	0	0	£499
Printer	£59.99	0	0	£59.99
Software	£99.99	0	£54.99	£154.98
CDs	£19.99	£10.99	0	£30.98
Internet access	free	£191.88	£155.88	£347.76
A4 paper	£3.99	£3.99	£7.98	£15.96
Ink cartridge	£9.97	0	0	£9.97
Photocopying	0	£2.50	£7.40	£9.90
University printing	£3.60	£5.70	£8.20	£17.50
Binding (3rd-year thesis)	0	0	£16.00	£16.00
Mobile phone	£130	£110	£99.70	£339.70
Total	£826.53	£325.06	£350.15	£1501.74

reported costs of a graduate who finished his studies in 2008. This graduate chose to buy a PC instead of a laptop, although he pointed out that many of his fellow students used a laptop instead. In the first year he lived in halls so his internet access was free. In the second and third years he paid for his own broadband at a monthly rate of £15.99 (second year) and £12.99 (third year). He also tried to keep his mobile phone bill as low as possible through purchasing a pay-as-you-go SIM card.

From Table 6.3 it is clear to see that the most money for IT is spent in the first year of university study. These costs will be reduced considerably if you already have your own PC/laptop and printer.

Summary

It is not necessary to buy IT equipment for university study if you are on a tight budget, as all your IT needs can be met by the university. However, many students find it preferable to have their own equipment so that they can work in a place and at a time that suits them. Costs can be kept down by making sure that you only buy what is really needed, and through obtaining second-hand equipment where possible. Many students find that they spend the most on IT equipment in the first year, but that considerable savings can be made with careful choices and through moderate use.

Where IT and other university costs are concerned, all students have different wants and needs, which translate into different spending habits. The next chapter presents a number of budgets from different students, so that you can get a better idea of what your university education will cost.

Useful websites

www.endsleigh.co.uk

Endsleigh insurance is one of the largest insurers of student possessions and is approved by the NUS. You can obtain a personal quotation from this site and review the cover that is provided by some university halls of residence. This will enable you to check which of your personal

possessions, including IT equipment, will be covered and in what circumstances.

www.jsinsurance.co.uk/computer_insurance

This company provides specialist computer insurance for desktops, laptops, PDAs and servers. You can obtain a quotation online for easy comparison of prices.

7 Paying for a full degree course

The various costs of university study have been discussed in the previous chapters. To conclude this part of the book, you, as a student or parent, may find it useful to have a summary of these costs, broken down into a weekly budget, a monthly budget, an annual budget and a budget for a full degree course of three years' duration. It is also useful to have a payment calendar that details when large payments have to be made so that you can budget for these costs through the three years of a degree course.

The following budgets have been produced by four students studying at different universities in the United Kingdom. As you will see from the tables presented below, budgets vary, depending on a number of factors such as type and place of course, type of accommodation and the interests and activities of students.

Weekly budget

Students find that there are certain costs that they have to pay every week. These will vary, depending on the week of the year and whether additional, one-off costs have to be paid. However, as a general guide to weekly budgeting, a second-year student, in her fourth week of the second term at a university in London, was asked to keep a record of her weekly income and expenditure. This is presented in Table 7.1 below.

Table 7.1 Weekly university budget

Course costs	Weekly expenditure
Books	£21.99
Photocopying	60p
Laser printing	£1.20
Stationery	£2.30
Living costs	
Rent	£75
Telephone	£5.20
Laundry	£3.00
Transport/travel	£6.80
Leisure/entertainment	£25.00
Food and drink	£32.00
Sports and hobbies	£7.30
Sub-total, course and living costs	£180.59
Source of income	**Weekly income**
Employment	£56.70
Student loan	£62.00
University bursary	£57.89
Sub-total	£176.59
Total weekly profit/loss (ie income minus living and course costs)	–£4

During the week outlined in Table 7.1 the student used her income from her student loan and university bursary to pay for everything she needed during that week, finding that she spent only £4 more than her income. However, she pointed out that as the end of the year approached she had run out of money from her loan and bursary and had to cut her spending considerably, to make ends meet. As you can see from the above table, her largest weekly expense was accommodation. However, she was a student in London and felt that, if she had studied elsewhere in the United Kingdom, her accommodation costs could have been reduced (see Chapter 2).

Monthly budget

Some students find it easier to work out their university costs on a monthly basis, especially in cases where accommodation and meals are paid for by monthly direct debit. Table 7.2 below is from a student studying in the south of England. The month that he chose to record was the second month of the autumn term, although he felt that his monthly budget did not differ too much, from month to month. This student did not take advantage of the tuition fee loan, instead paying his tuition fees in 8 monthly instalments.

Table 7.2 Monthly university costs

Item	Cost
Tuition fees	£393.12 (8 monthly instalments)
Accommodation	£440 (includes 2 meals a day, 5 days a week)
Additional food	£15.00
Alcohol	£20.00
IT equipment	£50.00 (includes paper and printing)
Telephone	£14.99
Petrol and parking	£28.00
Total	**£961.11**

Most of the income to pay for this monthly expenditure came from the student loan and parental contribution, as this student did not qualify for a university bursary. By the end of the first year the student's parents had had to 'help me out a little, you know, with food packages and a bit of extra money'.

Annual budget

A student who completed his second year at a university in Northern Ireland in June 2008 was asked to produce an annual budget, which he has been able to do, basing it on his bank statements. Other items, such as food, drink and social activities have been estimated by the student and all figures have been rounded up. This student had to pay the variable fee

of £3,070 (2007/08), but was able to receive a maintenance grant because he was from a low-income family. However, he neglected to take up his university bursary because he hadn't realised that it was available for him. His budget is presented in Table 7.3.

Table 7.3 Annual university budget

Expenditure	Cost
Tuition fees	£3,070
Accommodation costs	£2,310 (£55 × 42 weeks)
Utilities	£235
Telephone	£160
Broadband	£714 (£16.99 × 42 weeks, rounded up)
Clothes	£310 (estimate)
Food	£1,000 (estimate)
Drink (including alcohol)	£840 (estimate)
Course materials and books	£600 (estimate)
Sports and leisure	£57 (sports card)
Evening entertainment	£400 (estimate)
IT equipment and gadgets	£927
Things for the house	£38
Travel	£300 (train and buses, estimate)
Total expenditure	**£10,961**

Income	Amount
Student loan for tuition fees	£3,070
Student loan for maintenance	£4,510
Maintenance grant	£3,265
Part-time job (from April, 2008)	£696
Total income	**£11,541**

This student began to run out of money as the year progressed. He realised that he had to take a part-time job from Easter onwards, which meant that he finished the academic year with £580 in his bank account. If he had not taken this part-time job he would have been overdrawn by the end of the year. He worked through the summer of 2008, starting his course in October 2008 with £3,000 in his bank account, before he

received any other income from loans and grants. He believes that this will see him through his final year and that he will not have to take a part-time job and can, therefore, concentrate on his studies.

Payment calendar

As you can see from Tables 7.1, 7.2 and 7.3, the biggest costs are for tuition fees and accommodation. There are different ways that you can pay for these, depending on how you like to budget and when the income that you will receive is paid. For example, some people prefer to pay their tuition fees in one sum at the start of their course, especially if the university offers a discount for doing so. Others prefer to pay in instalments, usually because they cannot afford to pay the whole amount in one go. This is often the case with accommodation; again, some universities will offer a discount if accommodation is paid for in advance, yet other students cannot afford to do this so they have to pay in instalments instead. (You should note, however, that if you choose to take out a student loan for tuition fees, this will automatically be paid up-front straight to your university at the start of term, and you will not have the option of paying your fees in instalments.)

Tables 7.4 and 7.5 present two different payment calendars so that you can get an idea of the different schemes that are available and the effect these will have on your finances. The tables have been based on the full cost of tuition fees (£3,145 for 2008/09) and on average accommodation cost (catered halls, all bills included). Prices and dates differ from university to university, and some will require larger booking fees or a guarantor, so you will need to check specific costs and dates with your chosen university.

Tables 7.4 and 7.5 illustrate that you can save £172.66 at this university, if you choose to pay both accommodation and tuition fees at the start of your course. This is a little more than you would be able to earn on interest, even if you were to place your funds in a high-interest bank account, which would be difficult given the current economic conditions and low interest rates.

Table 7.4 University payment calendar (instalments)

Date	Expenditure	Cost
May (prior to arrival)	Accommodation booking fee	£175
August (prior to arrival)	Accommodation damage deposit	£200
1 September	Instalment for accommodation	£1,453.20
1 October	Instalment for tuition fees	£1,575
2 January	Instalment for accommodation	£1,453.20
2 January	Instalment for tuition fees	£1,570
3 April	Instalment for accommodation	£726.60
Total		£7,153

Table 7.5 University payment calendar (lump-sum payments)

Date	Expenditure	Cost
May (prior to arrival)	Accommodation booking fee	£175
August (prior to arrival)	Accommodation damage deposit	£200
October	Accommodation (in full – 2 per cent discount)	£3,560.34
October	Tuition fees (in full – £100 discount)	£3,045
Total		£6,980.34

Summary

The cost of university varies, depending on the course and university, the type of accommodation and the interests, needs and activities of the student. Some people find it easier to budget weekly, others monthly and some annually. This chapter has presented budgets from students at different stages of their course so that you can understand how much university is likely to cost. A payment calendar has also been presented so that you can understand when the two most significant costs (accommodation and tuition fees) need to be paid.

Now that you understand how much university will cost it is important to consider what funds are available to students to help you to pay for university. These issues are discussed in the next section of this book.

Useful websites

www.ucas.com

UCAS is the organisation responsible for managing applications to higher education courses in the UK. On this website you can find all the information you need about applying for higher education and there is a useful student budget calculator available. This enables you to enter your monthly income and expenditure, and calculates the figures for you. There is also information about the cost of study and sources of funding available for students in all parts of the United Kingdom.

www.ukcosa.org.uk

This is the website for the UK Council for International Student Affairs. If you are an international student visit this site for comprehensive information about sources of funding for international students and for information about how to pay for university. There is also a section for UK students who intend to study abroad.

Part Two

What funds are available?

8 *Government funding (England)*

The previous section of this book has outlined the various costs involved in going to university. This section moves on to discuss the different types of statutory (government) funding that are available to help with these costs.

There are various government schemes available to help students pay for their university education, and these vary depending on which part of the United Kingdom you live in and where in the United Kingdom you decide to study. This chapter provides information on government funding for students from England.

Knowing about the types of funding

There are various types of funding that students may be eligible to receive from the government, if they live and study in England. These are described below.

Maintenance grant

The government offers a maintenance grant of up to £2,906 for students from low-income families (2009/10 figures). This grant is intended to help you cover the costs of course materials, accommodation, food, clothes, travel and so on. The full maintenance grant is available for students with a household income of up to £25,000. If your household income is between £25,000 and £50,020, you will receive a partial maintenance grant, on a sliding scale. No grant is available for students with a household income above £50,020.

Interestingly, this figure has been reduced from a household income of £60,005 the previous year. This could lead to 10 per cent of students

(around 35–40,000) losing grants altogether. Also, the income thresholds have changed so that students who receive a partial grant will actually receive less than students received last year. For example, a student with a family income of £40,000 will get an annual grant of £711 rather than £1,023, while for a household income of £30,000 it falls from £2,053 to £1,906. It is possible that these reductions could affect up to another 90,000 students, according to figures obtained by the BBC (reported on 2 December 2008).

Student loans

Maintenance loans

All full-time students in higher education in England can apply for a student loan for maintenance to cover costs such as living expenses, course materials, accommodation and travel. The maintenance loan rates are based on where you live and study, your household income and the amount of maintenance grant to which you are entitled (your loan entitlement will be reduced slightly if you receive a grant over a certain amount). Maximum rates of maintenance loan for 2009/10 are as follows:

- studying in London and living away from your parents' home: up to £6,643 a year;
- studying outside London and living away from your parents' home: up to £4,745 a year;
- living at your parents' home (either in or outside London): up to £3,673 a year.

These amounts will be slightly lower in the final year, to allow for the course finishing at the end of the summer term.

Tuition fee loans

Students studying in England can also apply for a student loan to pay for tuition fees. The tuition fee loan will be enough to cover tuition fees (up to £3,225 in 2009/2010) and will be paid direct to your university at the start of each year (see Chapter 1 for more information about tuition fees).

Interest rates and repayment

Student loans are not like commercial loans, but instead are subsidised by the government and attract a low interest rate. The interest rate payable on income-based student loans has been reduced following the latest change to the Bank of England rate in January 2009. The new rate for income-based student loans is 2.5 per cent, effective from 9 January 2009 until further notice. Interest is applied to loans from the date that you receive the money until they are repaid in full.

You begin to repay your loan only once you have finished studying and are earning over the repayment threshold of £15,000 per year (this figure may rise in the future). When you are required to repay your loan, your employer will be notified about your loan repayment and it will be taken from your earnings at the same time as tax and National Insurance Contributions (NICs) are deducted (see Chapter 23 for more information about income tax and NICs).

Special Support Grant

A Special Support Grant is available for students who are eligible to receive income support or other means-tested benefits. Assessment and payment procedures for this grant are the same as they are for the maintenance grant. However, unlike the maintenance grant, if you receive the maximum Special Support Grant, you will still be able to apply for the full maintenance loan. Students who are in receipt of the maintenance grant will not be eligible for the Special Support Grant.

Additional grants

There are additional grants available for students from England, including a Childcare Grant, an income-assessed Parents' Learning Allowance and an Adult Dependants' Grant. These grants are discussed in more detail in Chapter 15. Also, students with disabilities can apply for extra grants (see Chapter 13).

Access to Learning Fund

The Access to Learning Fund is allocated to universities by the government to provide selective help to students who have serious financial difficulties. This fund is available for both full-time and part-time students to help with course-related costs such as books, equipment, childcare and general living costs. Each applicant is assessed individually by the university: you may be required to show evidence of your income when you make an application. Payment is usually made as a one-off grant that you do not have to pay back, although some universities may also offer emergency loans from this fund. There is no automatic entitlement to money from these funds and competition can be strong.

Knowing about eligible courses

The following full-time courses are eligible for student support if they take place in a UK institution:

- Higher National Diploma (HND);
- Higher National Certificate (HNC);
- foundation degree;
- undergraduate degree (BA, BSc, BEd, BMus);
- Diploma in Higher Education (Dipl HE);
- Postgraduate Certificate in Education (PGCE) or other postgraduate courses of initial teacher training leading to the award of qualified teacher status or a specified equivalent qualification.

If you are intending to study part time, there are grants available to help you to pay your tuition fees and maintenance costs. If you are in receipt of certain benefits, you will qualify automatically for the maximum support available for your course's intensity (see Chapter 1 for more information about this). You cannot apply for a student loan if you study part time because it is assumed that you will be able to meet your costs through work and savings.

Applying for government support

From spring 2009 students studying in England should be able to apply for all their financial support through a new service: Student Finance England (details below). Using this service you can apply for grants, bursaries, student loans and other types of financial support. An online calculator will help you to work out how much financial support you could receive and view information about the amount and number of bursaries available at your chosen university. At time of writing this service is being developed so it is unclear whether it will be up and running on time and whether there will be any teething problems.

Keeping your information secure

When you register with Student Finance England you are asked to provide a username, password and secret answer. These should not be disclosed to anyone: if you think you have accidentally given someone else this information you can use the online service to change your password and secret answer at any time.

Recently, a number of bogus e-mails pertaining to be from Student Finance England have been sent to students, asking for personal financial information. Student Finance England will never send e-mails to you asking for login details, usernames or any personal financial information. If you receive one of these e-mails, you are requested to forward them to security@slc.co.uk.

When you log in and access your student finance online account, you are protected by a secure encrypted session. You will see the web address starting 'https' rather than just 'http' and a small padlock icon in the status bar at the bottom of your browser window. If these do not appear you will be on a fraudulent site. As with all secure sites, you should type the URL address into your browser, rather than follow a link, as this ensures you are going to the correct site and not a spoof or fraudulent one. Also, make sure that you always log out of the site and close the browser window, when finished.

Applying for access funds

Once you have taken up your place with your chosen university contact the student funding office or welfare department as soon as possible to find out about additional hardship funds. Your students' union or university welfare officer will be able to offer you further advice.

Application forms for the Access to Learning Fund can be downloaded from university websites or you can request an application form from the student funding office. Once you have completed the form, you will need to return it to the relevant department along with the supporting documentation required. If you are intending to apply for funding from hardship funds while at university you must show that you have applied for the full student loan and any other relevant government support.

To be successful in obtaining funds you will need to demonstrate genuine financial hardship. Priority is given to certain types of student, such as those with disabilities or with children, care leavers, mature students, those from low-income households or final-year students.

Summary

There are various sources of finance available for students who intend to study at university in England. These include a maintenance grant, student loans for tuition fees and maintenance, Special Support Grants and hardship funds. Funding tends to be prioritised for students from low-income families and those who struggle financially during their course. When applying for any type of financial support, you must make every effort to keep your information secure, as recently there have been a number of fraudulent websites and e-mail campaigns trying to obtain personal financial information from students and parents.

Funding arrangements for students in Wales differ from those described above and are therefore described in detail in the following chapter.

Further information

Information about government grants can be obtained from the student support office of your local authority. The telephone number will be in

your local telephone book or can be obtained from www.dfes.gov.uk/studentsupport. Ask for an application form and a copy of *A Guide to Financial Support for Higher Education Students in 2009/10*. Alternatively, the guide can be obtained by telephoning (0800) 731 9133.

Useful websites

www.studentfinanceengland.co.uk

All the information that students require about financial support in England should be available on this website. This site will also contain an online application service for the year 2009/10, although this wasn't up and running at the time of writing. There should also be useful information for parents and partners of students on this site.

www.studentsupportdirect.co.uk

This is a comprehensive service for students applying for a range of student support products. At this time of writing this service was still live and available for continuing students. However, it may be replaced by Student Finance England in the near future.

www.direct.gov.uk

More information about all aspects of education and learning, including financial support, can be obtained from this government information website.

do you live in wales
and want to know about funding
for your higher education?

wyt ti'n byw
yng nghymru
ac am gael gwybod
am yr arian sydd ar
gael ar gyfer cyrsiau
addysg uwch?

student finance wales

cyllid mytyrwyr cymru

0845 602 8845

www.studentfinancewales.co.uk
www.cyllidmyfyrwyrcymru.co.uk

or speak to your Local Authority
neu siarada â dy Awdurdod Lleol

invest in your future
buddsodda
yn dy ddyfodol

Llywodraeth Cynulliad Cymru
Welsh Assembly Government

9 Government funding (Wales)

In the previous chapter the funding arrangements for English students were discussed. If you live in Wales there are various government schemes available to help you to pay for your university education, but some of these differ from those offered in England and in other parts of the United Kingdom. This chapter, therefore, provides information about these schemes, including details of tuition fee payments, application procedures and eligibility criteria.

Knowing about the types of funding

There are various types of funding that students may be eligible to receive from the Welsh Assembly Government and Student Loans Company (SLC), if you live and study in Wales or elsewhere in the United Kingdom. These are described below.

Assembly Learning Grant

In Wales you can apply for a maintenance grant of up to £2,906, on a sliding scale, if your household income is below £39,329 (2009/10 figures). Your permanent home must be in Wales but you may be entitled to receive the grant if you study elsewhere in the United Kingdom. This is similar to the maintenance grant offered in England, although household income levels, on which the grant is calculated, are lower in Wales (see Chapter 8).

Special Support Grant

Some full-time students, including single parents and those eligible for certain benefits, may be eligible for the Special Support Grant (SSG). The amount available through the SSG is the same as the Assembly Learning

Grant. However payment made through the SSG will not affect a student's entitlement to Department of Work and Pensions benefits.

The Tuition Fee Grant

The 2009/10 tuition fee rate is £3,223. A Tuition Fee Grant is available for students who normally live in Wales and choose to study at university in Wales. In 2009 the fee grant will be worth £1,940 and is paid irrespective of family income, direct to the university. Welsh students who choose to study in other parts of the United Kingdom, or other UK students studying in Wales, will not be entitled to the Tuition Fee Grant. This grant is also available for non-UK EU/EEA students who choose to study in Wales. A student loan can be taken out to cover the rest of the tuition fees not covered by the tuition fee grant.

New funding arrangements from 2010/11

In March 2009, an announcement was made by the Minister for Children, Education, Lifelong Learning and Skills confirming arrangements for new students entering higher education in 2010/11. The key changes are as follows:

- the level of a full Assembly Learning Grant will be £5,000;
- the household income threshold for a partial Assembly Learning Grant will rise by about £10,000 to £50,000;
- no Tuition Fee Grant;
- an enhanced Tuition Fee Loan to ensure no full-time undergraduate students have to pay up front fees;
- all new Welsh domiciled students who take out a maintenance loan from the academic year 2010/11 will receive up to £1,500 debt relief when they enter repayment.

Entry in September 2009

Welsh students entering higher education in the academic year 2009/10 will not be affected by the 2010/11 changes, although students taking out new maintenance loans from the academic year 2010/11 may be eligible for debt relief.

Continuing Welsh Students

Continuing students will be entitled to the same student finance arrangements as they were in previous years (including the tuition fee grant if studying in Wales), although continuing students taking out new maintenance loans from the academic year 2010/11 may be eligible for debt relief.

Student loans

Loans for living costs

All full-time students in higher education in Wales can apply for a student loan for living costs to cover items such as living expenses, course materials, accommodation and travel. The loan for living costs rates are based on where you live and study, your household income and the amount of Assembly Learning Grant to which you are entitled (your loan entitlement will be reduced slightly if you receive a grant over a certain amount). Maximum rates of loan for living costs for 2009/10 are as follows:

- living away from your parents' home: up to £4,745 a year;
- living at your parents' home: up to £3,673 a year;
- studying overseas: up to £5,658;
- studying in London: up to £6,648 (your local authority will decide whether you will be entitled to the London loan rates on the basis of the postcode of your place of study).

These amounts will be slightly lower in the final year to allow for the course finishing at the end of the summer term. Also, if you course is longer than 30 term-time weeks (plus the short holidays), there is an extra weekly loan available.

Tuition fee loans

As we have seen in the previous chapter, students studying in England can also apply for a student loan to pay for tuition fees, up to £3,225 (2009/10 levels). This full tuition fee loan may also be available for Welsh students who decide to study elsewhere in the United Kingdom. Welsh students who choose to study in Wales can receive a tuition fee grant from the Welsh Assembly Government and therefore do not need to apply for the full tuition fee loan (see above). The tuition fee loan will be paid direct to your university at the start of each year (see Chapter 1 for more information about tuition fees).

Interest rates and repayment

Student loans are not like commercial loans, but instead are subsidised by the government and attract a low interest rate. The interest rate payable on income-based student loans has been reduced following the latest change

to the Bank of England rate in January 2009. The new rate for income-based student loans is 2.5 per cent, effective from 9 January 2009 until further notice. Interest is applied to loans from the date that you receive the money until they are repaid in full.

You begin to repay your loan only once you have finished studying and are earning over the repayment threshold of £15,000 per year (this figure may rise in the future). When you are required to repay your loan, your employer will be notified about your loan repayment and it will be taken from your earnings at the same time as tax and National Insurance Contributions (NICs) are deducted (see Chapter 22 for more information about income tax and NICs).

Financial Contingency Fund

This fund is for students studying in Wales and is administered by your university. It is allocated to universities by the Welsh Assembly Government to provide selective help to students who have serious financial difficulties. This fund is available for both full-time and part-time students to help with course-related costs such as books, equipment, childcare and general living costs. Each applicant is assessed individually by the university and you may be required to show evidence of your income when you make an application (see quotation below). Payment is usually made as a one-off grant that you do not have to pay back, although some universities may also offer emergency loans from the Fund. There is no automatic entitlement to money from these funds.

Childcare Grant

A Childcare Grant of up to £161.50 per week is available to full-time students with have one child and £274.55 per week for those with two or more children (2009/10 figures). The amount you receive will be dependent upon your household income and is based on 85 per cent of your actual childcare costs (see Chapter 15).

Parents' Learning Allowance

An income-assessed Parents' Learning Allowance is available for full-time students with children; in 2009/10 the amount payable will be between £50 and £1,508 (see Chapter 15).

Adult Dependants' Grant

If you are a full-time student and have an adult who is financially dependent on you, it is possible to receive an Adult Dependants' Grant of up to £2,647 (2009/10 figures). The amount that you can receive depends on your household income (see Chapter 15).

Travel grants

Full-time students on eligible courses may be able to apply for a travel grant if, for example, they are required to attend an institution other than their normal one as part of the course.

Disabled Students' Allowance (DSA)

Any student who has a disability and is studying a designated course can apply for a DSA. The DSA can provide additional help with costs incurred on your course as a direct result of your disability. These grants are discussed in detail in Chapter 13.

Welsh Bursary Scheme

Eligible full-time education students, regardless of where they come from in the United Kingdom, will be considered for a means-tested Welsh Bursary of a minimum of £319 a year (2009/10 figures).

Knowing about eligible courses

The following full-time courses are eligible for student support if they take place in a UK institution:

- Higher National Diploma (HND);
- Higher National Certificate (HNC);
- foundation degree;
- undergraduate degree (BA, BSc, BEd, BMus);
- Diploma in Higher Education (DipHE);
- Postgraduate Certificate in Education (PGCE) or other postgraduate course of initial teacher training leading to the award of qualified teacher status or a specified equivalent qualification.

Part-time study

If you intend to study part time there is a fee grant available to help you to pay for your course. The amount that you can receive depends on the intensity of your study, and is up to a maximum of £955 (2009/10 figures). You can also apply for financial help towards course-related costs, up to a maximum of £1,075.

Part-time and distance-learning students with dependants may be eligible to apply for additional support through the Part-time Childcare Grant, Part-time Adult Dependants' Grant and Part-time Parents' Learning Allowance. The amount of support you may be eligible to receive will depend upon your household income and the intensity of study level of your part-time course. Further information is contained in the guide: *A Guide to Financial Support for Part-time Students in Higher Education,* which can be downloaded from the Student Finance Wales website (details below).

Applying for government support

From spring 2009 students studying in Wales can apply for all their financial support through Student Finance Wales (details below). Using this service you can apply for grants, bursaries, student loans and other types of financial support. An online calculator will help you to work out how much financial support you could receive and to view information about the amount and number of bursaries available at your chosen university.

Keeping your information secure

When you register with Student Finance Wales you must take security seriously, by adhering to the following:

- Keep your username, password and secret answer secret. Do not disclose this information to anyone. Recently a number of bogus e-mails pertaining to be from student finance sites have been sent to students, asking for personal financial information. Genuine organisations will never send e-mails to you asking for login details, usernames or any personal financial information.
- When you log in and access your student finance online account, you are protected by a secure encrypted session. You will see the web address starting 'https' rather than just 'http' and a small padlock icon

in the status bar at the bottom of your browser window. If these do not appear you will be on a fraudulent site.

- As with all secure sites, you should type the URL address into your browser, rather than follow a link, as this ensures you are going to the correct site and not a spoof or fraudulent site.
- Make sure that you always log out of the site and close the browser window when finished.
- Remind your parents of these security issues, if relevant.

Applying for contingency funds

Once you have taken up your place with your chosen university, contact the student funding office or welfare department as soon as possible to find out about additional contingency funds. Your students' union or university welfare officer will be able to offer you further advice.

Application forms for the contingency fund are available from the student funding office at your university, and may also be available as a download from the university website. Once you have completed the form, you will need to return it to the relevant department along with the supporting documentation required. If you are intending to apply for funding from contingency funds while at university, you must show that you have applied for the full student loan and any other relevant government support.

To be successful in obtaining funds you will need to demonstrate genuine financial hardship. Priority is given to certain types of student, such as those with disabilities or with children, care leavers, mature students, those from low-income households or final-year students (see the case study below).

Julie, 24, Bristol

Yes, well, I was studying at Newport on a photography degree. It all went well... the course was great. But then I started to run out of money and it can be expensive doing that course, you know, what with buying film and travelling about for projects. So I went to the welfare office in the students' union and the lady there told me about hardship funds... filled in the form and waited and then I got a grant... it was quite easy really... it meant I could carry on in my final-year project.

Summary

There are various sources of finance available for students who intend to study at university in Wales. This includes an Assembly Learning Grant, Tuition Fee Grant, student loans for tuition fees and living costs, Childcare Grant, Parents' Learning Grant, Dependants' Grant and hardship funds. Funding tends to be prioritised for students from low-income families and those who struggle financially during their course. When applying for any type of financial support, you must make every effort to keep your information secure, as recently there have been a number of fraudulent websites and e-mail campaigns trying to obtain personal financial information from students and parents.

Funding arrangements for students in Scotland differ from those described above, and are therefore described in detail in the following chapter.

Further information

Information about government grants can be obtained from the student support office of your local authority. The telephone number will be in your local telephone book or can be obtained from www.dfes.gov.uk/studentsupport. Ask for an application form and a copy of *A Guide to Financial Support for Higher Education Students in 2009/10*. Alternatively, the guide can be downloaded from the website below.

Useful websites

www.studentfinancewales.co.uk

If you are a Welsh student more information about student finance can be obtained from this website. Online applications can be made here and there is a useful budget calculator so that you can work out how much money you could receive as a university student.

10 Government funding (Scotland)

In the previous chapter the funding arrangements for Welsh students were discussed. If you live in Scotland there are various government schemes available to help you to pay for your university education, but some of these differ from those offered in England and Wales. This chapter, therefore, provides information about these schemes, including details of tuition fee payments, application procedures and eligibility criteria.

Knowing about the types of funding

There are various types of funding that you may be eligible to receive if you are from Scotland. These are described below. To find out how much you may be entitled to, visit the Student Awards Agency for Scotland (SAAS) website and use their online calculator (details below).

Tuition fees

If you are a Scottish student and you intend to study at a Scottish institution, the SAAS will pay your tuition fees. If you are Scottish and you intend to study elsewhere in the United Kingdom you will have to pay up to £3,225 each year towards your tuition fees. If you don't have the money to pay your fees at the start of your course, you can apply to SAAS for a student loan to pay part or all of them (see below).

The SAAS will not normally pay the standard tuition fee for periods of study you have to repeat, or for any extension to the minimum length of the course, unless there are medical or strong compassionate reasons such as the death or serious illness of a close relative. Also they will not usually pay your tuition fees if you have previously been on a full-time

HIGH£R £DUCATION?
H£LP AVAILABL£

If you are a student considering Higher Education, you could benefit from a range of financial support from the **Student Awards Agency for Scotland**.

This funding can include help with your tuition fees, a living costs loan and even travel expenses.

You might also be able to take advantage of a Young Students Bursary or a Disabled Students Allowance.

For more information or to apply online go to

www.saas.gov.uk

The Scottish Government

SAAS

higher education course at HNC, HND, degree or equivalent level, and had help from public funds for your study (see Chapter 1).

Student loans

All full-time students in higher education in Scotland can apply for a student loan to help with living costs. Students can receive a maximum loan for living costs of £4,625 if they live away from the parental home and a maximum of £3,665 if they live in the parental home (2009/10 figures). The amount of loan will be reduced in the final year to reflect the shorter year.

To be eligible for a loan for living costs you must meet the following conditions:

- be studying on a full-time course that qualifies for a loan;
- meet the residence criteria (details are available on the SAAS website);
- not be in breach of any obligation to repay the loan;
- be under 50 on the first day of the first academic year of the course, or be aged 50 to 54 on that date and plan to return to employment when you finish your studies;
- have a valid National Insurance Number (see Chapter 22).

If you are entitled to receive the Young Students' Bursary your loan will be reduced because part of it will be replaced by this bursary, although there is an additional loan available for you (see below).

Loans to cover the full amount of tuition fees, up to £3,225 in 2009/2010, will be available for students who choose to study in other parts of the United Kingdom. If you apply for a loan, the SAAS will pay the fees directly to your university on your behalf. If you do not take out a loan to pay your fees, you will have to make your own arrangements to pay direct to your university. Discounts are available for students who choose to pay their fees in full at the start of the course (see Chapter 1).

Students' Outside Scotland Bursary

Young and mature students studying outside Scotland can apply for an income-assessed bursary if they are studying a full-time higher education course at a UK institution outside Scotland and are eligible for help with tuition fees (see above). However, you may not be eligible for this bursary if you have received support from UK public funds for a course of higher education before or you have to repeat a year of your course.

The maximum amount of bursary you can receive is £2,150 a year if your family income is £19,310 or less a year (2009/10 figures). The bursary will go down to £1,761 a year for a family income of £22,000, and is not available for families with incomes over £35,000 a year. If you receive this bursary, the amount of loan that you can receive for living costs will be reduced.

Young Students' Bursaries

These bursaries are only available for young people under the age of 25 who choose to study in Scotland. To receive this bursary you must be taking a full-time course of higher education and be eligible to receive help with your tuition fees (see above). However, you will not be eligible to receive the bursary if you are married, in a civil partnership or live with a partner, or you have supported yourself from earnings or benefits for any three years before the first day of the first academic year of your course, and you do not have a dependent child. All students under the age of 25 who have a child that is dependent on them can apply for the bursary.

The maximum bursary is worth £2,640 a year if your household income is £19,310 or less per annum. The bursary will go down to £2,163 a year for a household income of £22,000 and then down to zero for a household income over £35,000 a year (2009/10 figures). If you do not qualify for this bursary you will need to find out whether you are eligible for a student loan (see above).

Students who qualify for this bursary will have the amount of student loan reduced. However, if you are eligible to receive the Young Students' Bursary, you may also be eligible for an additional loan of £605 for a household income of £18,000 or less a year. This loan will not be available for students with a household income over £23,000.

Travel expenses

If you are on a low income the SAAS may help with your travel expenses to and from university. They will only pay for the most economical fare and will not pay if you live within easy walking distance of your university.

How much support you will get depends on your family income (see quotation below). For example, if you are a dependent student living in your parents' home while you study, you can claim up to £811 a year for a standard 30-week course. If you live away from your parents' home you can claim up to £462 a year for daily travel costs and the cost of one trip between your home and your university at the start and end of each term (2009/10 figures). Travel expenses will not normally be paid if they are less than £159, or £82 if you are studying one of the allied health professions.

Pete, second-year student, Glasgow

I'd heard travel expenses were available so I applied for them. But my mum and dad earned too much so I couldn't get help with my travel to uni. But it did cost a lot going in every day and all that… So I told my parents so they bought me a travel pass each term. It really helped me 'cos I could use it all the time, even when I went out with my mates. Mind you, travel isn't as expensive here as it is at home.

Knowing about eligible courses

The following full-time courses are eligible for student support if they take place in a recognised institution:

- Higher National Diploma (HND);
- Higher National Certificate (HNC);
- foundation degree;
- undergraduate degree (BA, BSc, BEd);
- Diploma in Higher Education (DipHE);

- courses leading to Advanced Diploma and some one-year Diploma courses;
- Postgraduate Certificate in Education (PGCE) and Postgraduate Diploma in Community Education (PGDipCE);
- courses leading to a qualification in the allied health professions;
- courses leading to certificates and diplomas in social work taken as a first course;
- certain advanced courses of study at theological colleges;
- certain courses at privately funded institutions including those chosen for support by the Department for Innovation, Universities & Skills (DIUS) at institutions in England and Wales.

This support is not available for part-time courses, correspondence and distance-learning courses, including those the Open University offer. If you are studying a part-time higher education course or a distance-learning course, you may be eligible for a fee grant of up to £500. Applications can be made by contacting ILA Scotland on (0808) 100 1090. You may also be eligible to apply for the Disabled Students' Allowance: visit the SAAS website for more details (see Chapter 13).

Applying for government support

You must apply for financial support as soon as you have received an unconditional or conditional offer of a place at a university. You can apply for financial support from the April before your course starts and the SAAS will provide a date by which your forms should be returned. Late applications may result in late payments.

Applications for financial support are made through the SAAS (contact details below). Help text boxes are available throughout the application to help you fill it in. However, if you experience any difficulties completing the form you can call the SAAS General Enquiries Team on 0845 111 1711 and they will be able to resolve any problems you have with it. The SAAS will process your form and send you an award notice outlining the amount of support you are to receive and the amount of parental contribution required. If you have applied for a loan, your application will be sent to the Student Loans Company (SLC) and they will send details of how and when your loan will be paid. You should normally expect to

receive your payment schedule about six weeks before the start of your course.

The Graduate Endowment

The Graduate Endowment used to be paid by some Scottish students who had finished their course and who had been awarded a degree. However, the fee was scrapped by the Scottish Parliament when it approved the Graduate Endowment Abolition (Scotland) Bill on 28 February 2008. This means that all current and future students, as well as those who graduated on or after 1 April 2007, will not have to pay the Graduate Endowment.

Summary

There are various government support schemes available for Scottish students who wish to study in Scotland or elsewhere in the United Kingdom. These schemes include payment of tuition fees, student loans, young students' bursaries, outside-Scotland bursaries and help with travel costs. Applications are made from April onwards through the SAAS, either online or by downloading an application form. A useful calculator is available on the SAAS website to help you to work out how much support you could receive. Most of the support outlined above is available for full-time study: if you intend to study part time you should contact the SAAS or the university at which you intend to study for more information.

Funding arrangements for students in Northern Ireland differ from those described, and therefore are described in detail in the following chapter.

Useful organisations

More information about all aspects of student financial support in Scotland can be obtained from the SAAS. Applications can be made online or by downloading a form from their website.

The Student Awards Agency for Scotland
Gyleview House
3 Redheughs Rigg
Edinburgh EH12 9HH
Tel: (0845) 111 1711
Fax: (0131) 244 5887
e-mail: use the online form found on the website
www.saas.gov.uk

11 *Government funding (Northern Ireland)*

In the previous chapter the funding arrangements for Scottish students were discussed. If you live in Northern Ireland there are various government schemes available to help you to pay for your university education, but some of these differ from those offered in other parts of the United Kingdom. This chapter, therefore, provides information about these schemes, including details of tuition fee payments, loans, grants, support funds, application procedures and eligibility criteria.

Knowing about the types of funding

There are various types of funding that students from Northern Ireland may be eligible to receive from the government. These are described below. A calculator is available on the Student Finance NI website to help you to work out your student support entitlement (details below).

Student loans

All full-time students in higher education can apply for a student loan. This includes a loan for maintenance and a loan for tuition fees. In 2009/10 the maximum amount of loan for maintenance that you could receive is:

- London: £6,643;
- elsewhere: £4,745;
- overseas: £5,653;
- living with parents: £3,673.

The loan for living costs is usually paid in three instalments, one at the start of each term, directly into your bank account. Student Finance NI

DO YOU NEED HELP PAYING FOR UNIVERSITY?

IF SO, CONTACT US!

If you live in Northern Ireland, there are various Government schemes available to help you pay for your University education.

If you wish to study in the UK or Republic of Ireland as a full-time or part-time student, there are a number of ways we can help:

- Student loans
- Maintenance grants
- Special support grants
- Supplementary grants
- Support funds
- Tuition fees
- Travel expenses
- Eligibility criteria and application procedures

Students can get more info on student support by contacting Student Finance Northern Ireland on 0845 600 0662 or by logging onto www.studentfinanceni.co.uk

Department for
Employment and Learning
www.delni.gov.uk

will issue a payment-schedule letter to you that will explain what amounts will be paid and when.

Loans for tuition fees of up to £3,225 a year are available for courses for new students (2009/10 rates). These loans are paid direct to your university at the start of your course. Both loans will start to be repaid by you once you have left university and are earning over £15,000 a year.

Loans for extra attendance

If your course is longer than normal, you may be able to receive an additional loan to cover the extra weeks at the following maximum rates (2009/10 figures):

- London: £106;
- elsewhere: £83;
- overseas: £115;
- living with parents: £54.

Maintenance grant

The government is offering a maintenance grant for students from low-income families at the following rates (2009/10 figures):

- a household income of £18,820 or less will receive a full grant of £3,406;
- a household income between £18,821 and £40,238 will receive a partial grant, on a sliding scale;
- a household income of over £40,238 will not receive a grant.

The maintenance grant is usually paid in three instalments, one at the start of each term, along with any other financial support to which you are entitled. You should note, however, that up to £1,792 of the maintenance grant will be paid in substitution for an element of the student loan for maintenance. This means that your eligibility for the student loan will be reduced by up to the amount of grant you are paid.

Special Support Grant

This is available for students who are eligible to receive certain benefits such as income support or housing benefit, and could be up to £3,406 a year (2009/10 figures). However, this grant is not available to students in receipt of the maintenance grant or gap-year students. The grant is intended to cover additional course costs such as books, equipment, travel or childcare that result from attending a course. Payment arrangements and income assessment procedures are the same as they are for the maintenance grant described above.

Supplementary grants

There is a range of extra help available for full-time students who have children or adult dependants (see Chapter 15 for more information about these grants).

The Childcare Grant is available to students with dependent children in prescribed childcare. You could receive up to 85 per cent of your actual childcare costs in term-time and during holidays, up to £148.75 a week for one child and up to £255 a week for two or more children. This grant is means-tested but you will not be eligible for it if you or your husband, wife or partner receives the childcare element of the Working Tax Credit from HM Revenue & Customs.

The Parents' Learning Allowance helps with course-related costs for students with dependent children. This allowance is means tested and you could receive up to £1,508 per year.

The Adult Dependants' Grant is for students who have a partner or another adult, usually a member of their family (but not any children), who depends on them financially. This grant is means-tested and you could receive up to £2,642 per year.

Support funds

These are funds that are provided by the government and administered through your university. The amount of money you may receive depends upon available funds, your financial circumstances and family income. Funds may be available for full-time and part-time students on undergraduate and postgraduate courses. Students must have explored all other

avenues of assistance before applying to the support funds, and these funds are not available to students who are repeating courses/modules.

More information about these funds, including eligibility criteria and application procedures, can be obtained from the student finance officer or students' union once you have begun your course.

Travel expenses

Travel expenses may be available only in the following circumstances:

- if you are attending a course in medicine or dentistry, and you have to attend for clinical training at a place in the United Kingdom or Republic of Ireland other than your normal place of attendance;
- if you have to attend an educational institution outside the United Kingdom for at least 50 per cent of each term (you may also be able to receive some financial help towards the cost of your medical insurance, in these circumstances).

All travel expenses are income-assessed and you will have to pay the first £303 towards the expense.

Funding for part-time students

Part-time undergraduate students who are studying at least 50 per cent of an equivalent full-time course can apply for a grant. How much you receive will depend on your household income and intensity of study, at the following levels (2009/10 figures):

- equivalent to 59 per cent or less of the full-time course: £805;
- equivalent to 60 per cent to 74 per cent of the full-time course: £970;
- equivalent to 75 per cent or more of the full-time course: £1,210.

Part-time students can also apply for an income-assessed course grant of up to £260 to cover the cost of books, travel and other course-related expenses. Fee grants are paid direct to your university, whereas course grants are paid direct to you. Both are paid as a single payment.

Knowing about eligible courses

The following full-time courses are eligible for student support if they take place in a recognised institution:

- a first degree (BA, BSc, BEd);
- Higher National Diploma (HND);
- Higher National Certificate (HNC);
- foundation degree;
- Diploma in Higher Education (DipHE);
- Postgraduate Certificate in Education (PGCE) or other postgraduate course of initial teacher training leading to the award of qualified teacher status or a specified equivalent qualification;
- NVQ level 4 where this is awarded along with a first degree, DipHE or HND.

Equivalent and lower qualifications (ELQs)

From the academic year 2009/10, most new eligible Northern Ireland-domiciled students applying for student support for a second full-time, part-time or full-time distance learning course that is equivalent to or lower in level than their first higher education course will be excluded from further fee and maintenance (grant and loan) support. This will apply if a student has a degree from a UK or overseas institution.

A number of exceptions to this policy will continue to apply to certain categories of students. Eligible students may be entitled to further student support for:

- Postgraduate Certificate in Education courses (fee and maintenance support);
- first-degree Bachelor of Education courses (maintenance loan);
- medicine, dentistry, veterinary science, architecture and social work (maintenance loan);
- courses that attract means-tested National Health Service bursaries (reduced rate maintenance loan).

Applying for government support

Students applying for university courses that start on or after 1 September 2009 will also be able to apply for their student finance at the same time. Your Education and Library Board (ELB) will provide a date by which your forms should be returned. Late applications may result in late payments.

Online applications and contact details for the ELBs can be obtained from Student Finance NI (details below). Complete and return your form, filling in all the answers required. Your ELB will let you know whether you are eligible to receive financial help and, if so, will send you a financial assessment form that must be completed and returned by the specified deadline. You will be sent a financial notice outlining the amount of support you are to receive and the amount of parental contribution required (see Chapter 17 for more information about the parental contribution). All forms should be returned as soon as possible to avoid delays.

Summary

There are various government support schemes available for students from Northern Ireland who wish to study in the United Kingdom or Republic of Ireland. These schemes include maintenance grants, student loans, special support grants, supplementary grants and support funds. Applications for funds should be made as soon as possible, although you can only apply for support funds once you have started your course and find that you are facing serious financial hardship.

Universities in Northern Ireland, Wales and England must provide bursaries for students from low-income families if they wish to charge higher variable fees for their courses. These bursary schemes are discussed in the following chapter.

Further information

A Guide to Financial Support for Higher Education Students in 2009/10 can be obtained from your local ELB or downloaded from the Student Finance NI website. A guide called *Higher Education Student Finance: How you are assessed and paid* can also be downloaded from this site.

Useful organisations

Education and Library Boards

ELBs provide information about all aspects of study for students from Northern Ireland. You can contact them using the details below or, if you are unsure of which ELB to contact, visit the Student Finance NI website and enter your postcode to be directed to the right ELB.

If you live in Belfast, contact:

Student Awards Section
Belfast Education and Library Board
40 Academy Street
Belfast BT1 2NQ
Tel: (028) 90 564000
e-mail: student.awards@belb.co.uk

If you live in Antrim, Ballymena, Ballymoeny, Carrickfergus, Coleraine, Larne, Magherafelt, Moyle or Newtownabbey, contact:

Student Awards
North Eastern Education and Library Board
182 Galgorm Road
County Hall
Ballymena BT42 1HN
Tel: (028) 2565 5025
e-mail: student.awards@neelb.org.uk

If you live in Ards, Castlereagh, Down, Lisburn or North Down, contact:

Student Awards Section
South Eastern Education and Library Board
Grahamsbridge Road
Dundonald
Belfast BT16 2HS
Tel: (028) 9056 6200
e-mail: info@seelb.org.uk

If you live in Armagh, Banbridge, Cookstown, Craigavon, Dungannon or Newry & Mourne, contact:

Student Awards Section
Southern Education and Library Board
3 Charlemont Place
The Mall
Armagh BT61 9AX
Tel: (028) 37 512432
e-mail: student.support@selb.org

If you live in Fermanagh, Limavady, Londonderry, Omagh or Strabane, contact:

Student Awards Section
Western Education and Library Board
1 Hospital Road
Omagh
Co Tyrone BT79 0AW
Tel: (028) 82 411411 / 411499
e-mail: student.awards@welbni.org

Useful websites

www.studentfinanceni.co.uk

You can find out all the information you need about funding for students from Northern Ireland on this website. Also, you can apply online for funding or download applications from this site. There is a useful budget calculator available to help you to work out how much financial support you could receive.

12 University bursary scheme funding

Since the introduction of variable tuition fees in England, Wales and Northern Ireland, all universities intending to charge the higher fees must have a bursary scheme in place to help students from low-income families. Each university must produce an 'access agreement' that provides details of their bursary scheme. These agreements can be obtained from www.offa.org.uk or from individual university websites.

English, Welsh and Northern Irish universities have bursary schemes for students. However, Scottish universities are not charging variable fees and therefore do not have this type of bursary scheme in place. If students from other parts of the United Kingdom want to study in Scotland, they may be eligible for the minimum bursary. This chapter describes the type of university schemes that have been put in place and discusses eligibility criteria, application procedures and administration.

Knowing about bursaries and scholarships

Most institutions have split their financial support packages into two types: bursaries and scholarships. In general, bursaries are non-repayable cash or fee-remission awards based on criteria such as income, background, under-representation and area of abode. Most bursaries are awarded for the duration of the course, although some may be awarded for the first year only.

Scholarships that are offered as part of the bursary package tend to be cash or fee-remission awards based on academic merit and/or family income and background. Some scholarships are awarded on entry while others are awarded at selected progression points throughout the course. They may be linked to academic, sporting, music, community and/or

voluntary achievement. Some scholarships are not income-assessed while others are awarded specifically to under-represented groups and students from low-income households. You should note that all universities offer other types of scholarship that are separate from the bursary package and usually awarded on academic merit; consult individual university websites for more information about this type of scholarship, or use the Hot Courses scholarship search (details below).

A minority of institutions have chosen to offer additional incentives such as free laptop computers, accommodation vouchers, travel passes and sports cards as part of their bursary package. Others have created or enhanced existing discretionary hardship funds to which students can apply if they face financial hardship at any time during their studies.

EU Students

In their access agreements some universities specifically mention EU students and point out that they are included in the bursary schemes, whereas others have developed bursary schemes only for UK students. If you are a non-UK EU student you should check with your chosen university to find out whether you are included in the bursary package as this could make a big difference to the financial support that is available to you.

Knowing about bursary levels

Each university decides the amount of bursary it will pay, although there is a minimum amount that universities must pay to students from low-income households who pay the full tuition fees. In 2009/10 this minimum amount is £319.

Table 12.1 shows the maximum amount that each university in England, Wales and Northern Ireland will pay, and the household income level under which this maximum will be paid. Some universities specify that students must meet certain additional criteria, such as being from the local area or mature students. If this is the case, it has been highlighted in Table 12.1. As most universities had not announced their figures for 2009/10 at time of writing, the figures for 2008/09 have been presented as a guide. Some of these figures will rise for the next year, others will remain

ACCESS BURSARIES

**Applying for a place at The University of Edinburgh?
Concerned about how to finance university study?**

THEN APPLY FOR
AN ACCESS BURSARY

Over 180 bursaries are available for degree programmes for
2010 entry, each worth a minimum of £1,000 per year of study.

Apply for a bursary online now.
Closing date for applications is 1 April 2010.

www.scholarships.ed.ac.uk/bursaries
email: financial.aid@ed.ac.uk   tel: 0131 651 4778

THE UNIVERSITY *of* EDINBURGH

Within Scotland there are no variable top-up fees. Students who are Scottish-domiciled undertaking a first degree are eligible to have their tuition fees covered by the Scottish Government and are required to complete an online application by the required deadline with the Student Awards Agency for Scotland (SAAS). Students from England, Wales and Northern Ireland pay a flat-rate tuition fee for each year of their programme, and although these fees will be payable upfront, students will have access to a fee loan from the Student Loan Company (SLC) to cover this. Further details on student loans and grants provided by the government can be found at www.scholarships.ed.ac.uk/undergraduate

The University of Edinburgh has a long tradition of offering undergraduate entrance bursaries and offers over 180 bursaries each year to UK students from schools or colleges in the UK who are experiencing financial difficulties in taking up their place of admission at the University. In considering applications the main criterion is significant financial need, but the University also takes into account personal and family circumstances which might make it difficult for students to take up a University place. In awarding these bursaries no account is taken of academic merit, since it is assumed that those who receive an offer of a place have fully demonstrated their ability and potential to benefit from Higher Education.

The minimum value of each award is £1,000 per annum which will be paid at the start of each academic session towards maintenance costs and will be tenable for the duration of the undergraduate programme of study subject to satisfactory academic progress. Please visit our website at www.scholarships.ed.ac.uk/bursaries and watch our bursary video to see how Access Bursaries have benefited some students who have received an award. Candidates can apply online at www.scholarships.ed.ac.uk/bursaries/apply.htm

Some feedback from University of Edinburgh bursary recipients:

"As a mother of two children I am in no doubt that I could not have continued in my studies without the assistance I received from the bursary." (Amanda Steven)

"The bursary has helped me by removing some of the stress and financial worries that I would have otherwise experienced. It allowed me to give up my weekend job to concentrate on my degree, to the extent that I was able to achieve a first class honours degree." (Charlene McRobbie)

"The key thing about the Access Bursaries is that they provide an opportunity to those who might not have been able to attend university due to financial constraints, to go and realise their potential. Thanks to my bursary I have benefited in so many different ways. Thank you! (Callum Gillespie)

The University also offers 90 Accommodation Bursaries to first year undergraduate UK students who choose to live in University accommodation. Each bursary has a value of £1,000 which is paid directly to Accommodation Services towards the costs of accommodation and is tenable for one academic session. Applicants should be UK students entering their first year of an undergraduate degree and be expecting to receive the full Young Students bursary for Scottish students, or full maintenance grant for English and Northern Ireland students, or full Assembly learning grant for Welsh students. Further details are available at www.scholarships.ed.ac.uk/bursaries/accom.htm

Sports Bursaries are available for outstanding student athletes who make major contributions to student sport within the University and who are seeking to achieve elite standards of performance. These are offered under three headings: multi-sport, team, and golf. Individual multi-sport bursaries include an education programme (including sports psychology; nutrition; time management), sports medicine care from FASIC (the University's specialist Fitness Assessment and Sports Injury Centre), gym membership, financial support up to £400, supervised strength and conditioning, branded sports kit and mentoring support from the Centre for Sport and Exercise staff. A commensurate though slightly scaled Team Bursary programme

is also offered to students who are members of the University's leading high performance sports clubs. A limited number of Golf bursaries are also available for outstanding golfers who wish to develop their academic and golfing talents to the fullest potential. The golf bursaries are sponsored by the Royal and Ancient Golf Club of St Andrews. Further details on Sports Bursaries can be obtained from the Centre for Sport and Exercise, the University of Edinburgh, 46 Pleasance, Edinburgh, EH8 9TJ or at www.sport.ed.ac.uk

Some feedback from University of Edinburgh Sports Bursary recipients:

"I first heard of the bursary while at school and so I applied because I thought it would make it that little bit easier for me to pursue my sporting career alongside my academic aspiration. The bursary has encouraged me to compete at the British University Championships and has given me the confidence to pursue my love of athletics along with a medical career." (Nony Mordi)

"I chose Edinburgh because it is close to my home and therefore my Volleyball Club. The Sports Bursary has enabled me to have access to physical training twice a week with expert coaches who plan a strength and conditioning programme specific to my needs." (Colin McNab)

The University also provides a number of Industrial Scholarships with a value of around £1,000 for each year of study and provides an opportunity to undertake a paid placement with a company during the summer months. Eligible candidates studying chemistry, engineering or informatics can apply. Scholarship opportunities also exist for those who have achieved the best entrance qualifications in physics.

A number of KEYCOM Industrial Scholarships are also available to full-time undergraduate students studying within the The Business School, The School of Engineering, The School of Informatics, and The School of Mathematics. Each scholarship has a value of £1,000. Further details on these and other scholarships offered by the University of Edinburgh can be found at www.scholarships.ed.ac.uk

the same; contact individual universities for specific figures. The bursaries are paid in cash, unless otherwise stated.

Table 12.1 University bursaries in England, Wales and Northern Ireland (2008/09)

University	Maximum bursary	Household income level for maximum bursary
A		
Aberystwyth University	£1,000	Up to £18,370
Anglia Ruskin University	£310	Up to £25,000
Arts Institute at Bournemouth, The	£310 + £150 at end	Up to £25,000
Arts, University of the	£310	Up to £25,000
Aston University	£800	Up to £18,000
B		
Bangor University	£1,000	Up to £25,000
Bath Spa University	£1,200	Up to £16,299
Bath, University of	£1,200	Up to £25,000
Bedfordshire, University of	£820	Up to £18,360
Belfast Metropolitan College	£310	Up to £18,360
Birmingham, City University	£525	Up to £25,000
Birmingham, University College	£1,050	Up to £25,000
Birmingham, University of	£840	Up to £34,600
Bishop Grosseteste University College	£1,050	Up to £39,250
Bolton, University of	£320	Up to £25,000
Bournemouth University	£1,310	Up to £25,000
Bradford, University of	£500	Up to £40,000
Brighton, University of	£1,050	Up to £25,000
Bristol, University of	£1,160	Up to £25,000
Brunel University	£1,000	Up to £25,000
Buckinghamshire New University	£500	All students qualify
C		
Cambridge, University of	£3,150	Up to £25,000
Canterbury Christ Church University	£820	Up to £25,000

University	Maximum bursary	Household income level for maximum bursary
Cardiff University	£1,050	Up to £25,000
Cardiff, University of Wales Institute	£750	Up to £18,370
Central Lancashire, University of	£1,000	Up to £60,000
Central School of Speech and Drama	£310	Up to £25,000
Chester, University of	£1,000	Up to £25,000
Chichester, University of	£1,050	Up to £25,000
City University, London	£750	Up to £25,000
Conservatoire for Dance and Drama	£1,650	Up to £25,000
Courtauld Institute of Art	£300	Up to £25,000
Coventry University	£310	Up to £60,005
Creative Arts, University for the	£310	Up to £25,000
Cumbria, University of	£1,260	Up to £25,000
D		
De Montfort University	£400	Up to £60,000
Derby, University of	£800	Up to £25,000
Durham University	£1,285	Up to £18,500
E		
East Anglia, University of	£600	Up to £25,000
East London, University of	£310	Up to £25,000
Edge Hill University	£500	Up to £25,000
Education, Institute of	£310	Up to £25,000
Essex, University of	Top-up on HE grant	Up to £32,690
Exeter, University of	£1,500	Up to £25,000
F		
Falmouth, University College	£850	Up to £25,000
G		
Glamorgan, University of	£310	Up to £25,000
Gloucestershire, University of	£310	Up to £25,000
Glyndwr University	£500: Welsh, £1,400: UK	Up to £18,370
Goldsmiths, University of London	£1,000	Up to £19,000
Greenwich, University of	£500 (mature students)	Up to £60,005

University	Maximum bursary	Household income level for maximum bursary
H		
Harper Adams University College	£1,000	Up to £17,910
Hertfordshire, University of	50% of HE grant	Up to £40,000
Huddersfield, University of	£500	Up to £25,000
Hull, University of	£1,000	Up to £25,000
I		
Imperial College London	£3,000	Up to £25,000
K		
Keele University	£310	Up to £25,000
Kent, University of	£1,000	Up to £25,000
King's College London	£1,250	Up to £25,000
Kingston University	£1,000	Up to £1,000
L		
Lampeter, University of Wales	£310	Up to £18,370
Lancaster University	£1,315	Up to £18,360
Leeds College of Music	£1,055	Up to £18,360
Leeds Metropolitan University	Low tuition fees	All students pay low fee
Leeds, University of	£1,500	Up to £25,000
Leicester, University of	£1,310	Up to £20,000
Lincoln, University of	£600	Up to £25,000
Liverpool Hope University	£800	Up to £17,500
Liverpool Institute for Performing Arts	£500	Up to £25,000
Liverpool John Moores University	£1,050	Up to £25,000
Liverpool, University of	£1,400	Up to £25,000
London Metropolitan University	£1,000	Up to £18,000
London School of Economics	£2,500	Up to £3,000
London South Bank University	£500	All students paying full fees
London, University College	50% of HE grant	Up to £60,005
Loughborough University	£2,720 (mature students)	Up to £25,000
M		
Manchester Metropolitan University	£1,000	Up to £20,460

University	Maximum bursary	Household income level for maximum bursary
Manchester, University of	£1,000	Up to £27,810
Middlesex University	£310	Up to £25,000
N		
Newcastle upon Tyne, University of	£1,240	Up to £18,360
Newman University College	£1,100	Up to £17,910
Newport, University of Wales	£1,000	Up to £20,000
Northampton, University of	£1,000	Up to £25,000
Northumbria University	£310	Up to £25,000
Norwich University College of the Arts	£567	Up to £25,000
Nottingham Trent University	£1,050 + £260 local	Up to £25,000
Nottingham, University of	£1,050	Up to £33,500
O		
Oriental and African Studies, School of	£740	Up to £25,000
Oxford Brookes University	£1,800	Up to £4,999
Oxford, University of	£4,000	Up to £17,999
P		
Plymouth, University of	£815	Up to £25,000
Portsmouth, University of	£900	Up to £25,000
Q		
Queen Mary, University of London	£1,050	Up to £25,000
Queen's University Belfast	£1,025	Up to £17,910
R		
Ravensbourne College	£310	Up to £25,000
Reading, University of	£1,350	Up to £25,000
Roehampton University	£500	Up to £60,005
Rose Bruford College	£310	Up to £25,000
Royal Academy of Music	£630 (fee remission)	Up to £25,000
Royal Agricultural College	£1,500	Up to £25,000
Royal College of Music	£1,000	Up to £25,000
Royal Holloway, University of London	£750	Up to £60,005

University	Maximum bursary	Household income level for maximum bursary
Royal Northern College of Music	£1,050	Up to £25,000
Royal Veterinary College	Depends on course	Up to £25,000
Royal Welsh College of Music and Drama	£310	Up to £18,370
S		
Salford, University of	£310	Up to £25,000
Sheffield Hallam University	£700	Up to £40,000
Sheffield, University of	£680	Up to £16,785
Southampton Solent University	£1,050	Up to £18,360
Southampton, University of	£1,000	Up to £25,000
St George's, University of London	£1,230	Up to £25,000
St Mark and St John, Plymouth	Reduced fees, free laptop	All students qualify
St Mary's University College, Belfast	£1,230	Up to £17,910
St Mary's University College	£700 + £305 all students	Up to £20,000
Staffordshire University	£1,000	Up to £20,817
Stranmillis University College	£1,050	Up to £18,360
Sunderland, University of	£525	Up to £39,305
Surrey, University of	£2,000	Up to £10,000
Sussex, University of	£1,000	Up to £25,000
Swansea Metropolitan University	£310	Up to £18,370
Swansea University	£310	Up to £18,370
T		
Teesside, University of	£1,000	Up to £25,000
Thames Valley University	£1,030	Up to £25,000
Trinity and All Saints	10% of HE grant	Up to £60,005
Trinity Laban Conservatoire	£700 + £300 for transport	Up to £25,000
Trinity College, Carmarthen	£310	Up to £18,370
U		
Ulster, University of	£1,040	Up to £18,360
W		
Warwick, University of	£1,800	Up to £36,000

University	Maximum bursary	Household income level for maximum bursary
West of England, University of the	£1,250	Up to £18,360
Westminster, University of	£310	Up to £60,005
Wimbledon College of Art	£1,000 (non-trad students)	Up to £60,005
Winchester, University of	£820	Up to £25,000
Wolverhampton, University of	£500	Up to £25,000
Worcester, University of	£750 (£500 all students)	Up to £60,005
Writtle College	£300	Up to £25,000
Y		
York St John University	£1,570	Up to £18,360
York, University of	£1,400	Up to £25,000

Household income levels

Most universities work out bursary entitlement on the basis of the household income levels set by the government for assessing student entitlement to financial support (see Chapters 8, 9, 10 and 11). As Table 12.1 is based on the year 2008/09 these income levels, in most cases, will change for 2009/10. In England the new levels are:

● household income level for claiming maximum support: £25,000;
● household income level for claiming partial support: £25,001–£50,020.

The income levels for 2009/10 in Northern Ireland are:

● household income level for claiming maximum support: £18,820;
● household income level for claiming partial support: £18,821–£40,238.

The income levels for 2009/10 in Wales are:

● household income level for claiming maximum support: £18,370;
● household income level for claiming partial support: £18,371–£39,329.

Bursaries – There is help out there!

The University of York provides financial assistance to students through a variety of bursaries. The York Undergraduate Bursary is most frequently accessed as students are automatically assessed for this using information they provide on their student finance application form.

The York Undergraduate Bursary, of up to £1,436 per year, supports those students whose residual household income is less than £41,040 per year. Support is assessed on a sliding scale, with students from households where income is less than £25,000 receiving the full amount.

Current Biochemistry undergraduate, Shiraz Ziya (right), said "After deciding to pursue my choice of university course, I was worried about financial support. The advice given to me by the Student Welfare Office enabled me to receive a bursary. This has allowed me to focus on my course. Now in my second year, I have received more support than I could possibly have imagined. I advise anyone wanting to pursue the career of their choice not to be deterred by finance."

Financial support is available through a number a channels; first and foremost the state student support package, but also a number of funds administered by the University itself including the University of York Undergraduate Bursary, University of York Foundation Year Bursary, Access to Learning Fund, York Annual Fund Bursary, and the Accommodation Bursary.

The University also has a Student Financial Support Unit which offers advice and guidance to current and prospective University of York students. An online money guide is also available. More information about financial support at the University of York, and contact details for Student Financial Support Unit, can be found at www.york.ac.uk/studentmoney.

THE UNIVERSITY *of York*

Most universities will use these income levels as maximum amounts when working out bursary entitlement. However, some will have higher levels and some will decide to base their bursary entitlement on lower household income levels, as you can see in Table 12.1.

Bursary administration

For the academic year 2009/10 all students should be able to apply for financial support from Student Finance England (www.studentfinanceengland.co.uk), Student Finance Wales (www.studentfinancewales.co.uk) and Student Finance Northern Ireland (www.studentfinanceni.co.uk). Using these services you can apply for university bursaries at the same time that you apply for grants and student loans. You can also access an online calculator that will help you to work out how much financial support you could receive.

In most cases, when you apply for government financial support you will be assessed automatically for financial support from your university. However, when you complete the application form you must *not* tick the 'data sharing consent' opting out box on the 'Student's Declaration' page of the application form (PN1). If you do this it will not be possible for the university to use your household income details to work out whether you are eligible for a bursary.

If you are eligible for a bursary, universities have varying payment methods. All will pay the money direct into your bank account if you have provided details before the start of your course (see quotation below). Some will pay the money up-front, in one instalment at the start of the academic year. Others pay in two instalments, perhaps mid-way through the first and second term, while others will pay in three instalments, sometimes at the beginning, or perhaps mid-way through each term. Some universities will only pay the money at the end of the academic year, once you have successfully completed the year. You will need to find out which method is adopted by your chosen university and make sure that this will enable you to meet your financial commitments.

Chris, second-year student, University of Portsmouth

I'd applied for my loan and bursary and everything in April, well around that time I think… When I finally got to university I'd already changed my bank because I'd had a bit of trouble with my bank going overdrawn… Well unfortunately I forgot to give the university my new banks details and I wondered why my bursary hadn't gone into my bank. I'd told the student loans place, but forgot to tell the university. My bursary finally got paid when I realised what I'd done, but it was three months late. My mum and dad had to help me with my hall fees 'cos I was going to use some of the bursary to help pay for them.

Bursary take-up rates

Recent statistics produced by the Office for Fair Access (OFFA) illustrate that universities have spent less on bursaries than they initially thought they would. A variety of reasons have been put forward for this lower take-up:

- Universities over-estimated the amount they would need to pay out in bursaries.
- The system was too complicated and stopped eligible students applying for bursaries.
- Middle-class students are better at applying for financial support than working-class ones, and since most bursaries were aimed at working-class students from low-income households, take-up was lower than predicted.
- Students failed to tick the box that enabled the sharing of their information, because they didn't trust the system, they misunderstood the importance of agreeing to share information or didn't notice the tick box on the form.
- Students managed to tick the box, but failed to claim their bursary for a variety of reasons, such as lack of knowledge/information or forgetfulness.

To try to address some of these problems, from 2009/10 you will have to opt out of sharing your information on the application form, rather than opt in. Also, you should make sure that you fully understand what bursaries are available for you, and ensure that you take up these bursaries throughout your course.

You can find out what bursaries are available at each university by visiting the government information website bursary map (http://bursarymap.direct.gov.uk). If you are in any doubt, contact the student financial support office or students' union at your university for more information.

Summary

All universities in the United Kingdom intending to charge variable tuition fees must have a bursary scheme in place to help students from low-income families. Each university must produce an 'access agreement' that provides details of their bursary scheme. The amount of money available and the type of scheme on offer vary between institutions, and the government has requested that information about what is available should be made easily accessible by universities on their websites and in their prospectuses.

Some universities offer extra funding through their bursary schemes for people with disabilities. If you have any type of disability you may qualify for an additional bursary, so contact your chosen university for more information. You can also apply for Disabled Students' Allowances, which are discussed in the following chapter.

Useful organisations

Office for Fair Access (OFFA)

The Office for Fair Access (OFFA) is an 'independent, non departmental public body which aims to promote and safeguard fair access to higher education for under-represented groups in light of the introduction of variable tuition fees in 2006/07'. On the website you can access individual university agreements.

Office for Fair Access
Northavon House
Coldharbour Lane
Bristol BS16 1QD
Tel: (0117) 931 7171
Fax: (0117) 931 7083
e-mail: enquiries@offa.org.uk
www.offa.org.uk

Useful websites

www.scholarship-search.org.uk

This website provides a comprehensive guide to student finance and has been developed by Hot Courses in association with UCAS. There is a useful budget planner and funding database available on this site.

Further reading

A book called *University Tuition Fees and Bursary Schemes* is available from www.studentcash.org.uk. This book has an alphabetical listing of all universities in England, Wales and Northern Ireland, providing a comparative table of tuition fee levels, maximum and minimum bursaries, eligibility criteria, application procedures and contact details.

13 Funding for students with disabilities

The Disabled Students' Allowances (DSAs) are funds set up by the government to help you with extra costs you may have to pay as a result of a disability. The funds will pay for non-medical personal help, major items of specialist equipment, travel and other course-related costs. DSAs are not dependent on your income or that of your parents. Students with disabilities are also eligible to apply for other forms of government funding, such as student loans, Special Support Grants and hardship funds (see Chapters 8, 9, 10 and 11).

Broadly similar arrangements for DSAs are in place in Scotland, England, Wales and Northern Ireland. However, to check your specific circumstances contact your local authority (LA) (England and Wales), your local Education and Library Board (ELB) (Northern Ireland) and the Student Awards Agency for Scotland (SAAS) (Scotland). This chapter discusses the funds that are available through DSAs, along with information about eligibility criteria and application procedures.

Knowing about the type and amount of funds

Funds are available to help students with a high level of need. Maximum amounts are discussed below, but you will not receive the full amount unless you have this high level of need. In 2009/10 the maximum amounts for undergraduate students are as follows:

- *Specialist equipment allowance*: up to £5,161 for the whole of your course, for part-time and full-time students (£5,166 in Wales). This allowance can be used to pay for, or rent, major items of equipment

such as computers. It can also be used to pay for repair, insurance or warranty costs.

- *Non-medical helper's allowance*: up to £20,520 a year. This maximum amount will be reduced to £15,390 if you are studying part time. This allowance can be used for human support such as readers and note-takers. It is not intended to help with personal assistance costs as these are usually the responsibility of your local social services department.
- *General Disabled Students' Allowance*: up to £1,724 a year (£1,729 in Wales). This maximum amount will be reduced to £1,293 if you are studying part time. This allowance is for general expenditure, such as tapes and Braille paper, or can be used to top up the other two allowances, if necessary.
- *Travel costs*: no upper limit.

If you are intending to enter university at postgraduate level you can receive one allowance of up to £10,260 to help with the extra costs you incur as a direct result of your disability while you study.

Eligibility criteria

To qualify for DSAs you need to meet the following criteria:

- You intend to study on a full-time or part-time course and are personally eligible to receive government financial support (see Chapters 8, 9, 10 and 11).
- You have been living in the United Kingdom, the Channel Islands or the Isle of Man for the three years immediately before the start of the academic year in which the course begins. You must be living in England, Scotland, Wales or Northern Ireland on the first day of the academic year in which your course starts. (In certain circumstances you may still be eligible to apply for DSAs even if you do not meet the residency criteria so consult your LA, ELB or SAAS for more information.)
- You can provide proof of your disability and satisfy the LA, ELB or SAAS of your entitlement to financial help.

Eligible courses

If you are studying on the following types of course you are eligible to apply for DSAs:

- full-time higher-education and distance-learning courses;
- part-time higher-education and distance-learning courses;
- postgraduate courses;
- Open University courses.

If you are a postgraduate student in receipt of a Research Council or NHS Bursary you will not be entitled to apply for a DSA. Instead you should contact your bursary provider to find out what support is available for students with disabilities. Most will provide extra support if you can supply proof of your disability.

Making an application

You should apply as soon as you can before the start of your course, even if you have not received confirmation of a place. This will ensure that payments are made promptly and will be ready for the start of the academic year. However, you can apply for DSAs at any time during your course.

If you are applying for an undergraduate higher education course you should follow the steps outlined below.

Step 1

Find out if your LA employs a named officer who deals specifically with applications for DSAs. If there is such a person, contact them for advice and guidance. They will be able to help you with the application procedure. Students in Northern Ireland should contact their local ELB (see Chapter 11 for contact details) and students in Scotland should contact the SAAS (see Chapter 10 for contact details).

Step 2

Apply for government financial support through your LA, ELB or SAAS, or online through the relevant Student Finance website (details below). You

can download an application form for DSAs from these sites. It may speed up your application if you can send proof of your disability with the form.

Step 3

Receive confirmation of your entitlement to DSAs. If your application is turned down you can appeal against the decision.

Step 4

You will be asked to have a needs assessment carried out to find out what kind of help you need on your course. Once this assessment had been completed, suitable assistance will be arranged for you while you are studying.

The application process for part-time and postgraduate students is similar to that outlined above, although you should make sure that you request and fill in the appropriate forms. Application forms for part-time students and for postgraduate students can be downloaded from the relevant Student Finance website (details below). All application forms and booklets are available in alternative formats, including large print, Braille and audio versions.

Supplying evidence of your disability

In general you will be required to provide one or more of the following:

- Medical proof of your disability such as a letter from your doctor or specialist.
- If you have a specific learning difficulty, you will need to provide any full diagnostic assessment that has been carried out since you were 16.
- You may be asked to have an independent assessment to establish your disability and eligibility for DSAs. You will have to pay for the test yourself although you may be able to apply for assistance with this payment through your university. Contact the university disability officer for more information.

Obtaining help after enrolment

When you start your course, make contact with the disability officer/ adviser at your university. They are employed to help you with the following:

- DSA applications;
- assessment of needs appointments;
- learning support, specialist tuition and IT support;
- accommodation;
- training for support workers;
- special examination arrangements.

Many universities have a disability support unit in which trained staff act as a useful resource for students and staff (see quotation below). If you require any additional help, contact your students' union and ask to speak to the person responsible for disability issues.

Julie, third-year student, Sheffield Hallam University

I am deaf. I needed help with lectures. What the university disability support unit did was arrange for me to have a note-taker. This meant that she went with me to all my lectures and took notes. I can lip read sometimes but if the lecturer turns away or it is too dark or there is a window behind, I can't see to lip-read. So a note-taker is really useful. The university trains them to take notes and they get paid. They are all students as well, but they are usually from a different course. I didn't know that this service was available until I spoke to the disabilities officer. It makes life much easier for me.

Completing your course

All equipment bought with DSAs becomes your property and you can keep it once you have finished your course. However, some students decide to donate the equipment to their university when they leave so that other students can benefit.

Summary

DSAs are available to help students with extra costs they may have to pay because of a disability. Funds are available for specialist equipment, non-medical helpers, travel costs and other general expenses that may be incurred as a result of disability. In addition to financial support, universities will provide specialist help and advice, usually from a disability adviser employed by the university. This person will be able to offer help and support throughout your degree course.

DSAs are available specifically for students with disabilities. Other funding is available for specialist courses, for both disabled and able-bodied students. This funding is discussed in the following chapter.

Useful organisations

Skill: the National Bureau for Students with Disabilities

Skill is a national charity that promotes opportunities for young people and adults with any kind of impairment in post-16 education, training and employment. It has published a booklet called *Disabled Students' Allowances*, which gives guidance on the evidence needed from applicants.

Skill: the National Bureau for Students with Disabilities
Chapter House
18–20 Crucifix Lane
London SE1 3JW
Tel: (0800) 328 5050
Textphone: (0800) 068 2422
e-mail: info@skill.org.uk
www.skill.org.uk

Further information

A booklet called *Bridging the Gap* answers most questions about DSAs, and can be downloaded from the relevant Student Finance website:

England: www.studentfinanceengland.co.uk
Wales: www.studentfinancewales.co.uk
Northern Ireland: www.studentfinanceni.co.uk
Scotland: www.saas.gov.uk

Alternatively, it can be obtained from your LA or by telephoning (0800) 731 9133. The booklet is available in Braille, large print and on audio tape.

14 *Funding for specialist courses*

Chapters 8, 9, 10 and 11 outlined the various government schemes available to help students to pay for their university education. In addition to these schemes, there are other funds available for students who wish to study on a specialist course. This type of course includes teacher training, healthcare, dance and drama, social work, fine and performing arts and study abroad. These funding schemes, along with their eligibility criteria and application procedures, are discussed in this chapter.

Funding for teacher training

The funds available for teacher training depend on which part of the United Kingdom you come from and the route by which you plan to enter teaching. Some people decide to enter the profession through the undergraduate route, studying for a teaching degree such as a Bachelor of Education (BEd). This route enables you to study for your degree and complete your initial teacher training (ITT) at the same time (see quotation below). All BEd graduates receive qualified teacher status (QTS) in addition to their degree.

Others decide to enter through the postgraduate route, studying first for a degree and then enrolling on a postgraduate course that leads to QTS, such as a Postgraduate Certificate in Education (PGCE) or a Professional Graduate Diploma in Education (PGDE). An alternative route is to study first for a degree and then train while working as a teacher through a scheme such as School-Centred Initial Teacher Training (SCITT).

Change the
world become
a civil engineer

The ICE QUEST Undergraduate
Scholarship offers up to £12,000
and top industry work placements

With QUEST your career in civil
engineering starts when term does

To apply visit **ice.org.uk/questundergrad**

QUEST – a scholarship to change your world

Are you looking for a challenging and an exciting career where you could literally build a better world? A scholarship from the Institution of Civil Engineers (ICE) could set you on your way to a rewarding career in civil engineering and place you at the heart of society.

Over £1 million in scholarships has been awarded in previous academic years as part of the QUEST awards, which are designed to encourage and support education in civil engineering.

The QUEST Undergraduate Scholarship was set up in 1977 to give help to outstanding students that demonstrate real potential to become leaders in the profession. Hundreds of civil engineering students have benefited from the scholarship since then.

QUEST works with some of the UK's leading civil engineering and construction companies to offer students financial support of up to £3,000 a year, mentoring, and sought-after industry work experience placements.

Emma Kent is one of the many scholars who benefited from a QUEST scholarship and is now a graduate engineer at Buro Happold.

"The financial support was incredibly useful. It made the difference between needing a part-time job to get by and being able to concentrate full time on university. With the support, I could buy up-to-date copies of text books, rather than fighting over the library copies."

QUEST scholars will typically undertake an eight week work placement with a leading company over the summer months as part of the scholarship. Scholars will meet a wide range of people across the industry and work on real life projects. They will experience first-hand how the knowledge and skills they have gained at university can be applied in the day to day work of civil engineering. Each scholar will also receive guidance from a mentor within the industry and advice from colleagues on work placements.

"Summer placements were a great way to supplement my learning at university. It helped put the topics I was studying into an industrial context. I was assigned to a graduate engineer who helped me settle into the company and answer any queries I had", says Emma.

The companies involved with the scholarship believe it's an excellent programme that provides access to top students who will shape the future of civil engineering. BAM Nuttall, a prominent contractor, have been involved in the scholarship since 2003.

Nicola Dobson, student liaison officer for BAM Nuttall said, "The scholarship has allowed us to work and build relationships with the scholars during their work placements. Our scholars show us their commitment to the company and we support and encourage their development."

ICE is a global membership organisation that promotes and advances civil engineering around the world. ICE believes in fostering and developing young people within civil engineering.

The QUEST Undergraduate Scholarship is open to anyone who wants to study a civil engineering undergraduate degree. To find out how to apply, visit ice.org.uk/questundergrad.

Collective **inspiration**

THE IET
AWARDS
AMBITION

As an engineer, you'll make the world a **better place.**
Consider this your first paycheque.

Apply for an IET scholarship and you could get up to £3,000 a year to take an engineering or technology related degree course.

You're eligible if you:

- Expect to achieve at least 300 UCAS points
- Plan to take any IET accredited degree course at a university in the UK or Ireland
- Apply by 30 June each year.

For an application form and more information, go to:

www.**theiet**.org/undergradawards

As an engineer, you'll make the world a better place.

Consider this your first paycheque.

Calling all engineering and technology undergraduates: financial help is at hand from the IET!

Budding engineers and technologists are being invited to apply for a prestigious scholarship from one of the world's leading engineering and technology organisations.

Every year, the Institution of Engineering and Technology (IET) awards a series of scholarships to those who are studying (or considering studying) an engineering or technology degree course in the UK or Ireland.

The IET offers a range of undergraduate scholarships of up to £3,000 per annum, every year to students who are in need of financial support for the duration of the degree course.

You can apply for an IET scholarship if you are about to commence any IET accredited BEng or MEng degree course and expect to achieve a minimum of 300 UCAS points in your A Levels (or equivalent).

If you are starting the second, third or fourth year of an IET accredited degree course in October 2009 and expect to obtain 60% or more (i.e. a 2.i or above) in your end of year exams, then why not apply for an IET Grant worth £1,000?

Previous scholars have found the financial assistance has really given them a boost as well as enriching their CVs. William Cobern says, "The money was obviously useful and I think it is a very prestigious award to have on one's CV."

Amin Nobakhti says, "I would say more than the financial benefits, it is important as it showed my achievements were recognised by an independent body."

Agnes Segal, Manager, Membership Services says, "As one of the world's leading organisations for engineering and technology

professionals, and a registered charity, one of our main aims is to advance science, engineering and technology.

"These awards and scholarships are part of our annual investment of £3m to ensure that our young people continue to study science, engineering and technology subjects.

"Without them we won't have the next generation of engineers and technologists who will conceive and deliver the solutions to everyday problems that will affect us all."

All successful applicants also receive free IET membership which offers a range of benefits including:

- Award winning publications, including the Engineering and Technology magazine
- Access to over 65,000 books, 3,000 periodicals and full text collections of electronic articles
- 37 technical and professional networks which will enable you to connect with your peers in your specific area of interest
- Wherever you are in the world, you will not be far from one of our Local Networks. There are 100 Local Networks globally
- Over 1,500 global networking events every year to which you will receive discounted registration
- A range of online tools, including IET Discover, a dedicated social bookmarking website which will enable you to share your links with the rest of the IET community and to create specialist global networks with colleagues

In addition to all this, you can network from your desk with IET.tv – an online resource showing live footage of events which will allow you to participate and ask questions during live streaming.

For further information telephone 01438 767272, email awards@theiet.org or visit www.theiet.org/undergradawards

John, primary school teacher, Liverpool

I knew I wanted to be a primary school teacher so I knew it would be best to do a BEd. The course was for four years and there was plenty of teaching practice involved. I was able to get a full grant because my parents didn't earn a lot, and I got a loan. It sort of helped, but I did leave uni with a big debt. I don't know whether it was because I am a man and not many men go into primary school teaching… I was the only man on my course, but I got a job as soon as I left uni and because I got an extra training grant I was able to sort out my debts really quickly.

Funding through the undergraduate route

If you decide to train to be a teacher through the undergraduate route you must apply to your LA (England: see Chapter 8; Wales: see Chapter 9), ELB (Northern Ireland: see Chapter 11) or the SAAS (Scotland: see Chapter 10). Your position is assessed in a similar way to all prospective undergraduate students, which means that you could receive the grants, loans and bursaries described in the relevant chapter for your country. You may also be eligible for a university bursary (see Chapter 12).

If you are training to teach secondary priority subjects in Wales you may also be eligible to receive a Higher Education Funding Council for Wales grant during your school-based placement, currently worth £1,000. Visit www.hefcw.ac.uk for more information.

Funding through the postgraduate route

There are a number of schemes available for students who decide to enter the teaching profession through the postgraduate route:

● *Help with tuition fees*: if you live in Scotland, you will have your tuition fees paid for you if you are studying for a PGDE and have not previously received funding for a vocational undergraduate or postgraduate course. If you live in Wales you may be able to receive some help with your tuition fees.

- *Maintenance grant*: if you are starting a postgraduate ITT course (for example a PGCE course) in England, Wales or Northern Ireland and are studying for 10 or more weeks in the academic year, you will be able to receive a £1,106 maintenance grant no matter what your household income. Students with lower household incomes may qualify for the full maintenance grant. If your course is between six and 10 weeks you will receive a maintenance grant of at least £553.
- *Training bursaries*: as a teacher trainee in England or Wales you may be entitled to a tax-free bursary from the Training and Development Agency for Schools (TDA). The size of the bursary depends on when you start training and what subject you train to teach. For up-to-date figures visit www.tda.gov.uk. You usually apply for your tax-free bursary from your university or SCITT provider as part of your course induction. To be eligible for a training bursary, you must be a home or EU trainee on a TDA-funded course and be eligible for student support.
- *Golden hellos*: home and EU students in England could also be eligible to receive a payment of either £2,500 or £5,000 from the TDA if they complete a postgraduate ITT course and take up a permanent position teaching the subject in which they trained. A similar 'teaching grant' scheme is offered to Welsh students.
- *Welsh medium incentive supplement*: additional financial help is available for students taking secondary ITT postgraduate courses and training through the medium of Welsh. Decisions on eligibility for the supplement are made by individual ITT providers involved in the scheme. Visit www.tda.gov.uk for more information.
- *Bursaries and supplementary grants*: in Scotland you may be entitled to a bursary and any supplementary grants that apply to you, if you have not previously received funding for a vocational or postgraduate course. If you study for a PGDE in a priority subject area, however, this previous study rule does not apply and you will receive your full entitlement to a bursary, supplementary grants and help with tuition fees.

Funding for healthcare courses

NHS bursaries are available for medical and dental students and for full-time and part-time students on health professional courses. A bursary is

an annual payment awarded to cover day-to-day living costs while studying. There are two types of NHS bursary:

- *Non-income-assessed bursary*: this provides a basic maintenance grant and your income, or that of your parents, is not taken into account. These bursaries are available for nursing and midwifery diploma courses, operating-department-practice diploma courses and accelerated/postgraduate nursing diploma courses only. The bursaries are offered as an incentive to increase recruitment in these areas. Extra allowances may be payable if you have to attend for more than 45 weeks a year and if you have a practice placement in London.
- *Income-assessed bursary*: for these bursaries your income, or that of your parents, is taken into account when working out how much money you will receive. This is available for degree-level students (including graduate-entry medical and dental degree students) and postgraduate diploma courses.

To receive funding you must be accepted on an NHS-funded place on a full or part-time course that leads to professional registration in the following occupations:

- doctor or dentist;
- chiropodist (including podiatrist), dietician, occupational therapist, orthoptist, physiotherapist, prosthetist, orthotist, radiographer, audiologist or a speech and language therapist;
- dental hygienist or dental therapist;
- nurse or midwife (degree course);
- nurse, midwife or operating-department practitioner (diploma course).

Making an application

Students intending to study in England can download the relevant forms from www.nhsstudentgrants.co.uk. Students from elsewhere in the United Kingdom should contact the relevant organisation listed below to obtain an application form and guidance notes.

Funding for dance and drama courses

Dance and drama awards are available for talented students who wish to become professional dancers, actors or stage managers. The awards offer greatly reduced tuition fees and help with living and learning costs. Dance and drama awards are available from accredited providers and there are only a limited number each year. A list of accredited providers can be obtained from www.direct.gov.uk/danceanddrama.

You should note, however, that dance and drama awards are offered only at further education level and lead to National Certificates or National Diplomas. If your course is at higher education level you should contact your LA, ELB or the SAAS for information about funding (see Chapters 8, 9, 10 and 11). Courses may last between one and three years and can be in the following subjects:

- professional acting;
- professional dance;
- professional music theatre;
- professional production skills;
- professional classical ballet.

Funding is available for students in England, Wales and Scotland. If you live in Northern Ireland you should contact your local ELB for more information. Students from a non-UK EU country can apply for help with tuition fees only.

Amount of funding

The level of funding depends on your family income. At time of writing the figures for 2009/10 had not been announced so the figures for 2008/09 have been presented below as a general guide. These figures represent the maximum amount students received towards their fee contribution and maintenance if their family income was below £21,000:

- students living at home: £2,242;
- students living in lodgings outside London: £4,711;
- students living in lodgings in London : £5,333.

If their family income was over £33,000 they did not receive any help towards their fee contribution or maintenance costs. It is expected that these figures will rise slightly for 2009/10.

Making an application

You should apply to the dance and drama training provider in which you are interested. Once you have applied, you will be invited to attend an audition and interview and you should inform the college at this time that you wish to apply for an award. The awards will be allocated according to talent displayed at the audition. However, if applicants are thought to be of equal talent, funds will be allocated according to individual financial circumstances.

Funding for social work courses

Most social work undergraduate students receive the same help as other undergraduate students (see Chapters 8, 9, 10 and 11). However, there are extra schemes available to help encourage people to train for, and work within, shortage areas. Some of these are available at undergraduate level, whereas others are available at postgraduate level, as discussed below.

The Social Work Bursary in England

The NHS Business Services Authority (NHSBSA) administers a non-means-tested bursary to all students studying on an approved degree or diploma-level course (a list of approved courses can be obtained from www.gscc.org.uk). This bursary is paid in addition to any help received through the LA or SLC. The Social Work Bursary includes a basic grant, a fixed contribution towards expenses related to practice learning opportunities, and tuition fees if you are not subject to variable fees. It is available for full-time and part-time courses. Additional funds may be available for postgraduate study. Application forms and guidance notes for all types of social work funding can be downloaded from www.nhsbsa.nhs.uk/Students.

The Social Work Bursary in Wales

A non-income-assessed Social Work Bursary is available for Welsh students studying on undergraduate or postgraduate degree courses in social work in Wales. The bursary includes tuition fee support, a practice learning opportunity allowance and an additional graduate bursary for postgraduate students. To be eligible you need to be ordinarily resident in Wales, not receiving financial support from an employer and be studying on an approved course. For more information about the bursary, for a list of approved courses and for application information, visit www.ccwales.org.uk.

Student Incentive Scheme (Northern Ireland)

A non-means-tested incentive grant is offered to students from Northern Ireland who study on an approved course in Northern Ireland. A contribution towards expenses for work based learning is also available. Applications are made through your chosen university. For more information about the scheme and to find out current levels of funding, visit www.niscc.info.

Scottish Social Services Council Bursaries

A limited number of bursaries are available for students from Scotland who intend to study on a full-time postgraduate social work course in Scotland. The bursary includes payment of tuition fees, a means-tested maintenance allowance and additional grants for expenses, dependants and childcare. To find out about the postgraduate bursary policy and for more information about the scheme, visit www.sssc.uk.com.

Funding for fine and performing arts

The Leverhulme Trust offers a limited number of scholarships and bursaries for students in the fine and performing arts (details below). These are available for talented students who wish to continue their professional development and training in these areas. Funds are normally offered for a maximum of three years and the amount you will receive depends on your personal financial circumstances.

To be eligible for funding you must be engaged in a programme of studying or professional development in the fine or performing arts and you must not already have embarked on a professional career. Applications must be made through the institution to which you have applied for your course. When you apply, ask whether they have funds available. If they do not, they can make an application on your behalf by contacting the Trust. Applications from individual students will not be accepted.

Obtaining financial help for study abroad

There are a variety of schemes available for students who wish to study abroad, as described below.

European Region Action Scheme for the Mobility of University Students (ERASMUS)

Through ERASMUS students can spend between three and 12 months studying in another European country. To be eligible you need to meet the following criteria:

- You must be a citizen or permanent resident of the EU or one of the European Free Trade Association Countries.
- You must be a student enrolled on a formal programme of higher education study.
- You must have completed at least one year of study at university.

Student grants are available through ERASMUS. These are intended to help cover the extra costs involved in studying abroad, but will not meet all costs. The amount offered under this scheme depends on the country in which you intend to study. Details about ERASMUS can be obtained from www.britishcouncil.org/erasmus. Alternatively, you can e-mail them at erasmus@britishcouncil.org or contact them on (029) 2039 7405.

International exchange programmes

Some universities take part in exchange programmes with other universities from all around the world. These tend to be open to third-year students who are chosen for these schemes on the basis of their academic achievements and their 'ambassadorial' qualities. The number of grants available and the amount of money provided will vary between institutions. Contact the international office of your chosen university for more information.

Departmental exchanges

Some university departments run their own exchange programmes with similar departments in other universities around the world. Eligibility criteria will vary, but in general will be based on academic record and subject relevance. Contact your department administrator for more information.

The Association of Commonwealth Universities

This organisation offers a variety of scholarships, fellowships and bursaries for students who wish to study in another Commonwealth country. Eligibility criteria and funding amounts vary considerably between the different schemes and competition can be strong. More information can be obtained from www.acu.ac.uk.

University scholarships, fellowships, grants and awards

Throughout the world many universities offer funding to overseas students who wish to study at their institution. Funding levels and eligibility criteria vary according to the university, country and nature of the scheme. Details of these schemes can be accessed through the International Education Financial Aid website: www.iefa.org.

Summary

Funding is available through specialist schemes for courses in teacher training, healthcare dance and drama, social work, fine and performing

arts and study abroad. The amount of funding available, eligibility criteria and application procedures vary, depending on where you live and study. Therefore, if you are interested in any of these specialist schemes you should contact the relevant organisations listed below for more information and advice specific to your circumstances.

Most of the funding discussed in this section of the book is also available for adult students, unless they are taking a second degree. However, there are additional sources of funding available for adult students, depending on their specific circumstances. These schemes are discussed in the following chapter.

Further information

Teacher training

Further information about funding for teacher training can be obtained from the Student Support free information line (0800 731 9133), or from the Teaching Information Line (0845 6000 991). Your LA, ELB or SAAS will also provide you with information about student support and additional supplementary grants available to trainee teachers.

Healthcare

The Department of Health booklet *Financial Help for Healthcare Students* explains NHS funding in more detail and can be obtained from www. nhsstudentgrants.co.uk. Information about financial support for childcare while you are studying can be obtained from this website, along with information about the other types of grants that may be available.

Dance and drama

More information about dance and drama awards can be obtained from www.direct.gov.uk/danceanddrama. Alternatively, you can e-mail the Dance and Drama Awards helpdesk: dada@lsc.gov.uk.

Useful organisations

Healthcare

For enquiries concerning NHS financial support in England contact:

Student Grants Unit
Hesketh House
200–220 Broadway
Fleetwood
Lancashire FY7 8SS
Tel: (0845) 358 6655
Fax: (01253) 774490
e-mail: bursary@nhspa.gov.uk
www.nhsstudentgrants.co.uk

For enquiries concerning NHS financial support in Wales contact:

The NHS Wales Student Awards Unit
3rd floor
14 Cathedral Road
Cardiff CF11 9LJ
Tel: (029) 2019 6167 (bursary enquiries)
Tel: (029) 2019 6168 (childcare enquiries)
e-mail: use the contact form found on the website:
www.nliah.com

For enquiries concerning NHS financial support in Scotland contact:

The Student Awards Agency for Scotland
3 Redheughs Rigg
South Gyle
Edinburgh EH12 9HH
Tel: (0845) 111 1711
Fax: (0131) 244 5887
e-mail: use the contact form found on the website:
www.saas.gov.uk

For enquiries concerning NHS financial support in Northern Ireland contact:

Central Services Agency
Bursary Administration Unit
Nursing Board NI
2 Franklin Street
Belfast BT2 8 DQ
Tel. (028) 9055 3661
e-mail: use the contact form found on the website:
www.centralservicesagency.com

Dance and drama

Advice about careers and funding in dance and drama, and tips for passing auditions, can be obtained from the following organisations:

Council for Dance Education and Training (CDET)
Old Brewer's Yard
17–19 Neal Street
London WC2H 9UY
Tel: (020) 7240 5703
Fax: (020) 7240 2547
e-mail: info@cdet.org.uk
www.cdet.org.uk

National Council for Drama Training
249 Tooley Street
London SE1 2JX
Tel: (020) 7407 3686
e-mail: info@ncdt.co.uk
www.ncdt.co.uk

Social work

Welsh students should contact the Care Council for Wales:

Student Funding Team
7th Floor
South Gate House
Wood Street
Cardiff CF10 1EW
Tel: (0845) 070 0249
e-mail: studentfunding@ccwales.org.uk
www.ccwales.org.uk

Scottish students should contact the Scottish Social Services Council:

Compass House
11 Riverside Drive
Dundee DD1 4NY
Tel: (0845) 60 30 891
e-mail: enquiries@sssc.uk.com
www.sssc.uk.com

Students in Northern Ireland should contact the Northern Ireland Social
Care Council (NISCC):

Northern Ireland Social Care Council (NISCC)
7th Floor
Millennium House
19–25 Great Victoria Street
Belfast BT2 7AQ
Tel: (028) 9041 7600
Fax: (028) 9041 7601
e-mail: info@nisocialcarecouncil.org.uk
www.niscc.info

Further information about bursaries and working in social work in England
can be obtained from the following address (social work bursaries are

now administered by the NHS Business Services Authority on behalf of the Department of Health):

NHS student bursaries
Hesketh House
200–220 Broadway
Fleetwood
Lancashire FY7 8SS
Tel: (0845) 358 6655
Fax: (01253) 774490
e-mail: bursary@nhspa.gov.uk
www.nhsstudentgrants.co.uk

Fine and performing arts

Further details about the funds can be obtained from:

The Leverhulme Trust
1 Pemberton Row
London EC4A 3BG
Tel: (020) 7822 5220
e-mail: enquiries@leverhulme.ac.uk
www.leverhulme.ac.uk

Useful websites

www.tda.gov.uk

This is the website of the Training and Development Agency for Schools. On this site you can obtain further information about all aspects of teacher training.

www.teachertrainingwales.org

This is a useful site for anyone who is thinking about teacher training in Wales, and includes useful links to Welsh university sites and relevant funding sites.

www.socialworkcareers.co.uk

More information about becoming a social worker and obtaining funding for social work courses can be obtained from this website.

15 *Funding for adult students*

If you are an adult student, in most cases you are able to apply for all the government and university funds outlined in the previous seven chapters, unless you are studying for a second degree. In addition to these sources of funding, there is other cash available for adults who are hoping to study at college or university. This type of scheme includes additional government funding, such as for childcare and adult dependants, adult education bursaries, the adult education allowance scheme, trade union funding, tax credits and certain benefits. All these schemes are discussed in this chapter.

Government funding for adult students

There are additional grants available for students who have children and/ or adult dependants. These are described below.

Government funding for childcare in England, Wales and Northern Ireland

If you have children you may be able to receive support through one or more of the following schemes.

Childcare Grant

This is available for full-time students in higher education with dependent children in registered or approved childcare. You cannot receive this grant if you or your partner are in receipt of the childcare element of the Working Tax Credit from HM Revenue & Customs (see below). The amount you will receive in 2009/10 depends on your income and that of your depend-

Hillcroft
The Educational
Charity for Women

STAY AND STUDY

RESIDENTIAL COURSES EXCLUSIVELY FOR WOMEN

Want to get back into education, employment or gain access to University? Are you wondering where to start?

Hillcroft, is a vibrant and innovative National Residential College for adult women aged 19 and over, specialising in helping to change lives through learning. Its unique residential environment enables Women to get away from their everyday routine. On-site child care and additional learning support allows women to become more focused and realise their potential. Hillcroft College is situated in 3 acres of secluded gardens and woodland and only 15 minutes from London Waterloo.

Please call us   020 8399 2688
Email us   enquiry@hillcroft.ac.uk
Or simply visit   www.hillcroft.ac.uk

Reg. Charity 312825

Hillcroft College part of the educational charity for women.

The National Residential College for Women
www.hillcroft.ac.uk

Hillcroft is a vibrant and innovative residential college for adult women of 19 and above with no upper age limit. Since 1920 the college has been helping women change their lives through learning. So if you are looking for a new skill or just want to improve your talents, Hillcroft can help you.

- No entrance qualifications are required. You can come and do any course at Hillcroft providing you meet the eligibility criteria. Please call Admissions for further details
- Special attention is always paid to the needs of individual learners and the college is proud of the amount of learning support it is able to offer to students
- An OFSTED registered Crèche and a dedicated Learning Resource Centre.
- Two innovative study programmes for women who want to prepare for university and boost their confidence and learning skills
- A range of personal development and skills boosting courses which run over weekends, half-terms and holidays. These include courses to help women prepare for work, or women who wish to set up their own business, social enterprise or community group.
- Eligible students can apply for grants and adult learner bursary's to cover course fees and accommodation, with many fees covered by the LSC.
- The college also specialises in building links with community groups across the country on education and training programmes.

Hillcroft residential college sits in 3 acres of woodland. The peaceful and secluded atmosphere this creates is ideal for study, making new friends and a welcome break from the pressures of everyday life and yet central London is close by, only 15 minutes from Waterloo.

For more information - Please call: 020 8399 2688 or Email: enquiry@hillcroft.ac.uk

Hillcroft College, South Bank, Surbiton KT6 6DF Registered Charity 312825 Funded by LSC

ants, up to a maximum of £148.75 for one child and £255 for two children (England and Northern Ireland). In Wales the amounts are £161.50 per week for one child and £274.55 per week for two or more children. The Jobcentre Plus or Housing Benefit office should not take account of any payments you receive through this scheme. The money is paid in three instalments by the SLC and is available during term-time and vacations.

Parents' Learning Allowance

This is available to help with course-related costs for full-time students in higher education with dependent children. It is available for those people who are in receipt of the Childcare Grant or for those with partners or spouses who are on a low income. How much you get will depend on your income and that of your spouse or partner, up to a maximum of £1,508 (2009/10 figures). The grant should not be taken into account when benefits are calculated. The money is paid in three instalments from the SLC.

Child Tax Credit

Students with dependent children may be eligible for the Child Tax Credit from the HM Revenue & Customs (details below).

Government support for childcare in Scotland

If you live in Scotland and you have children, there are three schemes available to help with your university costs.

Lone Parents' Grant

This is available for single students bringing up children and covers 52 weeks from the first day of your course.

Childcare Grant for Lone Parents

If you are in receipt of the Lone Parents' Grant, you may also qualify for an additional grant to help pay for the cost of registered or formal childcare. If you think you may be entitled to this support, you should indicate

this on your application form and the SAAS will send you another form to complete (see Chapter 10).

Childcare fund

Your university may have a childcare fund that provides money for registered or approved childcare. You need to apply to your university as soon as possible as funds are limited.

Government funding for adult dependants

The Adult Dependants' Grant is available in England, Wales and Northern Ireland if you have an adult dependant who depends on you financially (see quotation below). It is available only for full-time students and is paid by the SLC. The amount you will receive depends on your income, up to a maximum of £2,642 in England and Northern Ireland, and £2,647 in Wales (2009/10 figures).

In Scotland the Dependants' Grant is available for students and you can claim this income-assessed grant for your husband or wife if you are legally married. It is not available for children.

Carla, graduated from Bournemouth University in 2007

I have a son who is autistic. I get various benefits for him and I get a carer's grant, but when I wanted to go to university I was worried that I would lose some of my money. But it turned out because he was an adult I got an extra grant which was just over £2,000 and I was able to keep claiming some of my benefits because they weren't affected by the grant. I think I would have still gone to university because it's the best thing I've ever done, but certainly the grants helped me to pay for my studies.

Adult education bursaries

In the United Kingdom there are six colleges that specialise in providing long-term residential courses for adults (details below). A bursary scheme

has been set up for adults who enrol on a full-time course of at least a year in length at one of these colleges. A similar scheme is also available for students from Scotland (see below). Grants are given to students to cover the tuition fees and to provide a suitable amount of money on which to live for the year. Also a dependants' allowance is given for those who need extra financial support. Additional grants are available for students with disabilities.

The bursaries are available to students attending certificate and diploma courses. They are not available for students who are studying on a course that leads to a professional qualification or for students who are studying on courses at first-degree level.

Eligibility criteria

To be eligible for funding you need to meet the following criteria:

- You must be at least 19 years old before the start of the academic year in which the course begins. Some colleges may request a higher age limit, so you will need to check before you apply.
- You must be resident in England or Wales. Scottish students can apply for the Adult Education Allowance Scheme (details below).
- You must have been ordinarily resident in the United Kingdom, the Channel Islands or the Isle of Man throughout the period of three years immediately preceding your bursary application. During this period you must not have been resident solely for the purposes of receiving full-time education. There may be additional rules concerning residence that can be complicated so, if in doubt, you should contact your chosen college for more information.
- You must have 'settled status', which means that you must be settled in the United Kingdom within the meaning of the Immigration Act of 1971 at the date you apply for a bursary.
- You must have been offered a place at one of the colleges listed below and been recommended for a bursary.
- You should not have received an Adult Education Bursary on a previous occasion.
- You should not have attended a course at a UK higher education institution and received public funding to do this on a previous occasion.

EU nationals

If you are an EU national or the child of an EU national, you may be able to receive help with your tuition fees but not with your maintenance costs. However, if you are an EU national and you have lived in the United Kingdom for more than three years, you may qualify for support with both tuition fees and maintenance. Contact your chosen college for information specific to your circumstances (details below).

Amount of bursary

The Adult Education Bursary covers the following:

- a personal maintenance grant and certain additional allowances where applicable (for example: Childcare Grant, Parents' Learning Allowance, Adult Dependants' Grant, Disabled Students' Allowance);
- in most cases, approved travel expenses in excess of £80 a year;
- tuition and other fees (for example examination fees).

The personal maintenance grant is means-tested, so how much you will receive depends on your family income. It is paid to the college at the start of term and usually distributed to students in the autumn, spring and summer terms. The standard rate of personal maintenance grant for full-time attendance of 30 weeks plus the vacations at Christmas and Easter in 2008 was as follows (2009 figures had not been announced at time of writing):

- students living in college in the London area: £4,545;
- students living in college elsewhere: £3,585;
- students living in the family home: £2,710.

If the normal term-time exceeds 30 weeks, an additional weekly rate may be paid (2008 rates):

- students living in college in the London area: £94;
- students living in college elsewhere: £72;
- students living in the family home: £43.

Making an application

Once you have been offered a place at your chosen college you will be sent an application form and an *Adult Education Bursary Guide* with your offer letter. Complete the form and return it to the college, which will forward it to the awards officer. If your application is approved, the awards officer will write to you confirming this and will send you a further form to complete. This is called a 'statement of financial circumstances' and enables the awards officer to assess how much grant you should receive.

Once your grant has been assessed you will be sent a 'notification of bursary'. This shows you how much you will be paid and when instalments are due. You may need to provide additional information if requested. If your application is not successful the awards officer will contact you to explain why. You have the right to appeal if you think the decision is wrong.

Adult Education Allowance Scheme

This scheme is similar to that described above but is available for Scottish-domiciled students attending a course at one of the colleges of adult education in the United Kingdom. Through this scheme you can receive help with tuition fees and an income-assessed maintenance grant, plus other supplementary grants, if these apply to your circumstances. For more information about the scheme and to apply online, visit www.saas.gov.uk.

Trade union funding

In 1998 the government set up the Union Learning Fund (ULF) as a source of funding available for trade unions to help them promote and organise learning opportunities for their members. There are a variety of schemes run by trade unions, some of which are supported by the ULF. Some of these may provide free education and training for their members, or for union representatives and officers. Others provide small grants for their members to enrol on various types of education programme. The main schemes are listed below.

The General Federation of Trade Unions (GFTU)

This is the federation for specialist unions. Affiliated unions cover a wide range of jobs and industry from clothing and textiles to youth services, from ceramics and pottery to probation services. A full range of courses is offered through the Educational Trust, aimed at union members, representatives and officers. The Trust also awards grants and prizes to students (details below).

The GMB

This was originally known as the General Municipal Boilermakers, but is now simply known as the GMB. It is a general union covering a variety of trades and the service and production sectors. The GMB promotes and supports the education and training of officers, representatives and members. Each region has its own regional education officer who will be able to offer advice and guidance about the opportunities available. Contact details can be found on the GMB website (details below).

Unite

Unite used to be called Amicus. This union has trained union learning representatives available to offer advice and guidance to members and colleagues in the workplace about the range of learning and training opportunities available through the union. Their lifelong learning department aims to improve access to education and training, and provides careers guidance to members (details below).

Unison

This union has a Learning and Organising Service that co-ordinates education and training for activists and members. Regional education officers and lifelong-learning advisers can help members to access education opportunities and will be able to provide advice on financial support for education and training (details below).

Receiving tax credits

If you are a part-time student and you have a part-time or vacation job, or you have children, you may be entitled to apply for tax credits. The Working Tax Credit and the Child Tax Credit were set up in April 2003 and have been designed to provide extra help for childcare and for working people on low incomes. Within the Working Tax Credit there is a child-care element that helps provide financial support for registered childcare.

The amount of tax credit you will receive depends on your family income, the number of children you have, their ages and whether or not they have any disabilities. You can obtain an estimate of how much you might receive by consulting www.taxcredits.inlandrevenue.gov.uk.

Eligibility criteria

To be eligible to apply for the Child Tax Credit you need to be over 16 years of age and must usually live in the United Kingdom, although there may be exceptions to this rule. You must be the parent or carer of a child (or children) under the age of 16 or still in full-time education or a speci-fied training programme, such as Entry to Employment. You do not have to be in paid work to receive the Child Tax Credit.

The Working Tax Credit is available for people on low incomes with or without children. You must be employed or self-employed and meet the following criteria:

- usually work 16 hours or more a week;
- are paid for that work;
- expect to work for at least four weeks.

Also, you must be:

- aged 16 or over and responsible for at least one child, or
- aged 16 or over and disabled, or
- aged 25 or over and usually work at least 30 hours a week (this includes mature students).

To be eligible for the childcare element within the Working Tax Credit, a lone parent must work at least 16 hours a week and, for couples, both members must work at least 16 hours a week.

Students with children are entitled to make a claim if they meet the eligibility criteria. If you are a student and you receive the maximum amount of Child Tax Credit (and no Working Tax Credit), you will be entitled to free school meals for your children.

Tax credits and student grants

As a student, you cannot receive the Childcare Grant if you are in receipt of the childcare element of the Working Tax Credit (see above). However, you do not have to apply for the childcare element of the Working Tax Credit, so it is advisable to see whether this or the Childcare Grant would provide you with more money before making your application.

Most elements of student support should not influence your entitlement to tax credits. However, if you are in receipt of the Adult Dependants' Grant, this will count as income for Tax Credit purposes (see above). If you are in any doubt you should consult your local tax office.

Receiving benefits

Full-time students

Most full-time students are not entitled to claim social security benefits. However, students from certain vulnerable groups such as lone parents or student couples with dependent children may be able to claim some benefits.

If you are already claiming benefits and want to study full time, you should check with your Jobcentre Plus office to find out how your benefits might be affected. Students who are eligible for social security benefits may be able to get a Special Support Grant of up to £2,906 a year in England or £3,406 a year in Northern Ireland (2009/10 figures: see Chapters 8 and 11 for more information about this grant).

Part-time students

If you intend to study part time and you are on a low income, you may be eligible to claim some benefits, as the part-time grant is not considered to be enough to affect your entitlement. The benefits that you could claim include:

- Income Support;
- Income-based Jobseeker's Allowance;
- Disability Living Allowance;
- Incapacity Benefit;
- Maternity Benefit;
- Housing Benefit;
- Council Tax Benefit.

If you are intending to study on a part-time course you should check with your Jobcentre Plus office, as your benefits may be affected by some of the income you receive as a student (see below).

Benefits and student grants

If you are claiming benefits and decide to study, the Jobcentre Plus office will take into account any income you receive through the following:

- student loans;
- Adult Dependants' Grant;
- maintenance grant.

However, the following grants should not count as income and therefore should not affect your benefits:

- Childcare Grant;
- Parents' Learning Allowance;
- Access to Learning Fund (and other hardship fund) payments that are not meant for general living costs;
- Special Support Grant.

Summary

Adult students can apply for a variety of government grants, including Childcare Grants, Adult Dependants' Grants and adult education bursaries. Funds may also be available through your trade union. It is possible for certain groups of students to claim tax credits and benefits while they study, but you should check how any benefits you receive could be affected by your student grants and loans.

If you are a student facing financial hardship it is vital that you apply for, and take up, all the funds to which you are entitled. To do this you need to understand what funds are available and know how and when to apply, so that you do not miss any important deadlines. These issues are summarised in the next chapter.

Further information

A copy of *A Guide to Childcare Grant and Other Support for Full-time Student Parents* can be downloaded from www.direct.gov.uk. Contact your Local Authority for a fact sheet called *Applying for the Childcare Grant: What you need to know*.

For information about registered or approved childcare in your area visit www.childcarelink.gov.uk, or telephone the National Childcare Information Line on (0800) 096 02 96.

Adult education bursaries

A booklet called *Adult Education Bursaries: A guide for applicants for courses at the long-term residential colleges* is available from the address below:

Awards Officer
Adult Education Bursaries
c/o Ruskin College
Walton Street
Oxford OX1 2HE
Tel: (01865) 556 360
e-mail: awards@ruskin.ac.uk

Useful organisations

Adult residential colleges

The six adult residential colleges are:

Coleg Harlech
Harlech
Gwnedd LL46 2PU
Tel: (01766) 781 900
Fax: (01766) 817 621
e-mail: use the enquiry form shown on the website
www.harlech.ac.uk

Fircroft College
1018 Bristol Road
Selly Oak
Birmingham B29 6LH
Tel: (01214) 720 116
Fax: (01214) 725 481
e-mail: use the contact form shown on the website
www.fircroft.ac.uk

Hillcroft College (for women)
South Bank
Surbiton
Surrey KT6 6DF
Tel: (020) 8399 2688
Fax: (020) 8390 9171
e-mail: use the enquiry form shown on the website
www.hillcroft.ac.uk

Newbattle Abbey College
Dalkeith
Midlothian EH22 3LL
Tel: (0131) 663 1921
Fax: (0131) 654 0598

e-mail: office@newbattleabbeycollege.ac.uk
www.newbattleabbeycollege.ac.uk

Northern College
Wentworth Castle
Stainborough
Barnsley
South Yorkshire S75 3ET
Tel: (01226) 776 000
Fax: (01226) 776 025
e-mail: courses@northern.ac.uk
www.northern.ac.uk

Ruskin College
Walton Street
Oxford OX1 2HE
Tel: (01865) 554 331
Fax: (01865) 554 372
e-mail: enquiries@ruskin.ac.uk
www.ruskin.ac.uk

Trade unions

The General Federation of Trade Unions can be contacted at:

GFTU Educational Trusts
Central House
Upper Woburn Place
London WC1H 0HY
Tel: (0207) 387 2578
Fax: (0207) 383 0820
e-mail: gftuhq@gftu.org.uk
www.gftu.org.uk

The GMB can be contacted at:

GMB National Office
22/24 Worpole Road
London SW19 4DD
Tel: (020) 8947 3131
Fax: (020) 8944 6552
e-mail: info@gmb.org.uk
www.gmb.org.uk

Unite can be contacted at:

Unison Education Department
Hayes Court
West Common Road
Hayes
Bromley BR2 7AU
Tel: (020) 8462 7755
Fax: (020) 8315 8234
e-mail: education@unitetheunion.com
www.unitetheunion.org.uk

Unison can be contacted at:

Unison Learning and Organising Services
1 Mabledon Place
London WC1H 9AJ
Tel: (0845) 355 0845
Fax: (0207) 535 2105
e-mail: use the contact form shown on the website:
www.unison.org.uk

Useful websites

www.entitledto.co.uk

This website provides a free web-based calculator to help people work out their entitlement to benefits and tax credits.

16 *Taking advantage of government and university funding*

It may surprise you to know that some students do not claim the money to which they are entitled. There are a variety of reasons for this non-take-up of funds; some people lack knowledge about what is available, or believe that funds are available for others but not for them; some find the application procedure difficult and are unwilling to share financial data with third parties (from students and/or parents). Others miss the deadlines for applications and are unable to backdate their claim for funds.

As we have seen previously, the cost of a university education is rising quickly, so it is important that you take advantage of all the funds that you are entitled to. The different types of funding that may be available have been discussed in detail earlier in this part of the book. This chapter sums up the pertinent points, illustrating how to find out what is available, helping you to know when and how to apply, and offering advice about raising your levels of success. An overview of funding available in different parts of the United Kingdom is also provided for quick reference.

Knowing what is available

Now that you have read Part Two of this book you should be more familiar with the type of funding that is available to you, depending on where you intend to study in the United Kingdom. You should also contact the student finance section of your local authority to find out information specific to your locality. Most LAs will run briefing sessions for parents and students in local schools, and you should make sure that you attend one of these sessions. You will be able to find out all the information relevant to your circumstances and can pick up application forms and information packs.

The University Of Sheffield.

Cash You Don't Pay Back.

Loads of our students get bursaries* of between £250 and £3,225 every year.

Find out how much you could get right now with our online bursary calculator:
www.sheffield.ac.uk/bursaries

*Bursary amounts are current for 2009/10 academic years.

The
University
Of
Sheffield.

The University of Sheffield Bursary Scheme

What's available?

As well as any government loans and grants you're entitled to, you could also get a University of Sheffield bursary to help with your living costs. It's exactly the same as a grant – the money doesn't have to be paid back. The maximum available in 2009 is £3,225.

There is no cap on the number of bursaries we give out. If you're eligible for a bursary, however big or small, you will get it, provided you have registered for assessment with the relevant student finance authority in England, Scotland, Northern Ireland or Wales.

To find out how much you could get, try our online calculator:

www.sheffield.ac.uk/bursaries

Who's eligible?

Any full-time UK student can get a University of Sheffield bursary. The scheme is designed to help students from lower-income families, but it also rewards academic achievement, regardless of how much your family earns.

You're entitled to an award for every A grade you get at A Level. This still applies to equivalent qualifications such as Scottish Highers or International Baccalaureate. One A could earn you £265.

Beth applies to study Architecture. Her household income is £14,340 and her grades are AAA. She receives the maximum income bursary of £700, plus a prior achievement bursary of £1,665. Total: £2,365 per year.

If you're studying a priority subject (below), or entering the University through one of our outreach schemes, these factors can also increase the amount you're entitled to. Priority subjects are courses in these departments:

Faculty of Engineering	School of Mathematics
Chemistry	Physics and Astronomy
Computer Science	Information Studies
School of Health and Related Research	Archaeology

How to apply

When you register with your student finance authority to be assessed for government loans and grants, the information you give becomes linked to your UCAS application, so the University can see if you're eligible for a bursary and how much you should get. If you're eligible, we'll contact you to let you know.

Jamie applies for Chemical and Process Engineering. His household income is £50,046 and his grades are AAB. He doesn't qualify for an income bursary, but CPE is a priority subject, so his two As make him eligible for a prior achievement bursary of £535 per year.

Don't miss out

Our bursaries are not all means tested. Even if your family's income is relatively high, you could still be eligible for hundreds of pounds that will really come in handy when you start your course. If for any reason you don't register with your student finance authority when you apply for a place you could miss out on cash that we want you to have.

Speak to your careers teacher to find out when these sessions take place (see quotation below). If you are an adult student, contact your local authority direct for more information about local events.

You may also find it useful to consult the student finance section of the government information website (www.direct.gov.uk) as this provides additional, up-to-date information about funding for students.

Jeanette, 42, Northampton

I saw a session advertised in the paper at the local sixth-form school. It made me wonder whether Mark's school was doing anything... He's useless and hadn't told me anything... so I contacted his teacher and he put me in touch with the careers teacher. They were having a session but Mark hadn't bothered to tell me about it. Parents were invited and a man came from the council to talk about what was available... It was really useful for me as a parent because as I say, Mark is useless at passing any information onto me.

Knowing when and how to apply

The date by which you must make your application and the way in which you apply varies, depending on the type of funds.

Student loans and grants

Students can now apply for these funds online. In most cases, you can register your details in the autumn term prior to the start of the next academic year (you do not have to wait until you have received an offer of a university place). Once you have registered, you will receive updated information about the application process so that you do not miss any deadlines. Once you have created an account you can check the progress of your application at any time and your parents/partner can provide household income details to support your application. Visit the relevant Student Finance website listed in Chapters 8, 9, 10 and 11 to register.

University bursaries

Once you have been offered a place at a particular university, it will send you information about its bursaries. Most universities have an automatic assessment procedure, based on the information you have supplied for your government funding.

From 2009/10 there will be an opt-out procedure, which means that you will have to tick a special box if you do not want your financial information shared with the university. If you do not tick this box your information will be shared automatically and you will receive the bursary to which you may be entitled (see Chapter 12). However, some universities require that you also fill in a separate application form for your university bursary, so you must check whether this is the case before you begin your course (application forms are usually sent with your student pack, or can be downloaded from the university website). In most cases universities will require you to fill in all relevant forms, or have applied for statutory support, before the start of term.

Hardship funds

You can only apply for hardship funds once you have started your course, and you can make your application at any time during your course. You must display serious financial hardship, and prove that you have applied for all the statutory funding, such as loans and grants, before you apply for hardship funds. More information about these funds is provided in Chapters 8, 9, 10 and 11.

Raising levels of success

You can increase your chances of success in obtaining all the funds to which you are entitled by taking notice of the following points:

- Become familiar with all types of funding that are available and make sure that you are clear about all the application deadlines. Complete and send forms in good time, allowing for possible delays.
- Read all instructions and guidelines before you fill in the form so that you know what is required. If you do not understand anything, seek

advice from a student finance officer at your local authority, or from your careers teacher if you are still at school. Any mistakes or omissions will delay your application and may lead to an unfavourable response from funding staff and/or a delay in funding.

- Make sure that your parents/partner understand what is required of them and that they have all the relevant financial details to hand and fill in the relevant forms on time (see quotation below).
- Print or save your completed form so that you have a record of what you have included.
- Monitor the progress of your application by using the online facility at the relevant student finance website.

Liz, 52, Weymouth

We are both self-employed and we don't know how much we have earned until the end of the tax year. When our son asked us to fill in all the financial details we couldn't do it on this year, well, it turned out that you had to do it on the previous year anyway, so it worked out OK... The only problem was we had earned much more the year before so we needed to do it on this year, which they will let us do, I think, but the problem is we were delayed getting all the information on time... This has caused us a few problems and his teacher thinks it might delay his payments, but fingers crossed it will work out OK.

Overview of funding in the United Kingdom

Table 16.1 below provides an easy reference to the types of funding that are available to university students in the United Kingdom.

CALLING ALL BRIGHT SPARKS

A BRUNEL DEGREE = A BRIGHTER FUTURE

- teaching that reflects today's industry needs
- great employability
- up to £1,000 non-repayable Brunel Bursaries available
- first class on-campus accommodation
- exceptional student support
- easy access to Central London

Find out more:

Come to an Open Day in June or September:
www.brunel.ac.uk/courses/sro/open_days

Amanda Hall of Brunel University offers advice:

Funding your university study can seem like a daunting prospect especially if you are going to be living away from home for the first time. However, fear not, there is a lot of financial help available. You should not be thinking that you can't go to university because you can't afford it.

There are two main costs you will need to meet: **Tuition Fees** and **Living Costs**.

Tuition Fees: most universities charge approx £3,200 per year with exceptions for Foundation years, NHS courses and Sandwich Placement years.

However, **you don't have to pay your fees upfront**, you can take a Government **Tuition Fee Loan** who pay the fees on your behalf and you pay them back when you're earning

Living Costs: if you learn to manage your money then university life will be far easier! You should always have an idea of your bank balance, income and what you can afford to spend. The majority of income tends to come from a Government **Maintenance Loan** and many will also have access to a **Maintenance Grant**.

There is also help from University **Bursaries** and **Scholarships**. These can range from a few hundred pounds to a few thousand. Generally money that comes as a Grant, Bursary or Scholarship does not have to be repaid so it's free money.

You may also need to supplement your income by taking a **part-time job**, using the perks of your **student bank account** like an interest-free overdraft, or getting some **help from parents and family**.

Top tips from Brunel students:

- Pay accommodation costs first. This is by far your biggest expense.
- Get a good quality part-time job that pays well. Jobs that pay around £10 per hour are often based on campus.
- Don't blow your loan/grant on expensive items like a plasma TV or designer shoes!
- Remember to buy a TV Licence; the fine is quite hefty if you get caught without one!
- Learn to cook. This will help you avoid pricey fast-food.
- If parents/family can help, ask for money on a monthly basis.
- Always ask for student discount and socialise in university bars/cafes.

Table 16.1 Easy reference to government and university funding

Type of funding	England	Scotland	Wales	NI
Student loans	✓	✓	✓	✓
Maintenance grant	✓	✗	✗	✓
Special Support Grant	✓	✗	✓	✓
Assembly Learning Grant	✗	✗	✓	✗
Tuition Fee Grant	✗	✗	✓	✗
Students' Outside Scotland Bursary	✗	✓	✗	✗
Young Students' Bursaries	✗	✓	✗	✗
Travel Expenses/Grant	✗	✓	✓	✓
University bursaries	✓	✗	✓	✓
NHS bursaries	✓	✓	✓	✓
Social work bursaries	✓	✓	✓	✓
Disabled students' allowances	✓	✓	✓	✓
Access to Learning Funds	✓	✗	✗	✗
Hardship Funds	✗	✓	✗	✗
Financial Contingency Funds	✗	✗	✓	✗
Support Funds	✗	✗	✗	✓
Childcare Grant	✓	✗	✓	✓
Parents' Learning Allowance	✓	✗	✓	✓
Adult Dependants' Grant	✓	✗	✓	✓
Dependants' Grant	✗	✓	✗	✗
Lone Parents' Grant	✗	✓	✗	✗
Childcare Grant for Lone Parents	✗	✓	✗	✗
Childcare Fund	✗	✓	✗	✗
Adult Education Bursary	✓	✗	✓	✗
Adult Education Allowance Scheme	✗	✓	✗	✗

Summary

Perhaps surprisingly, some students fail to claim the financial support to which they are entitled. This can be for a variety of reasons, including lack

of information, missing deadlines and not realising that funds are available. However, the cost of university is rising quickly so it is becoming all the more important for students to make sure that they receive all the funds they can. This chapter has summarised the funds that are available for students in different parts of the United Kingdom.

Part Two of the book has outlined the different types of funds that are available to school leavers and adults who wish to study at university. The next part goes on to consider the different methods that parents can use to fund their children's university education, starting with the various ways through which they can offer financial support to their children.

Part Three

How can I pay, as a parent?

17 *Providing financial support for your child*

There are various ways that you can provide financial support for your child when he or she goes away to university. If your child is financially dependent on you and your income is over a certain amount, the government expects you to make a contribution towards tuition fees and living costs while the child is studying at university. In addition to this parental contribution there are other ways that you can help your child financially, such as providing gifts and loans, helping with living costs and encouraging the take-up of statutory support. These issues are discussed in this chapter.

Understanding the parental contribution

All parents earning over a certain amount are expected to make a contribution towards their child's university education. To work out how much parental contribution you have to make, your residual income for the previous financial year is taken into account. If your income has fallen significantly over the last financial year you can ask that the current year is taken into account instead. Your residual income is worked out by taking your gross income (before tax and national insurance) and taking off the following allowances (2009/10 figures):

- £1,130 for each financially dependent child;
- pension scheme payments that qualify for certain specified tax relief;
- £1,130 if you, as a parent, are also a student.

Once the right amounts have been taken away and your residual income has been worked out, your contribution is calculated according to the following (2009/10 levels):

- Income less than £50,778: no contribution;
- Income over £50,778: £1 for each £5 of total income over this amount, until 72 per cent of the full maintenance loan remains (72 per cent of the student loan for maintenance is an automatic entitlement, whereas 28 per cent of the loan is means-tested on household income. Therefore, you would need to make a contribution at this rate until you had paid the equivalent of 28 per cent of the full maintenance loan). For more information about the student loan for maintenance, see Chapters 8, 9, 10 and 11.

If your children are not financially dependent on you they will be classed as independent students and there will be no requirement for you to pay a parental contribution, although they (and/or their partner/spouse, if relevant) will have to pay a household contribution if they earn over a certain amount. They will also have to supply proof that they are financially independent. They will not be able to claim independent status just because they do not get on with you or because they do not live with you. Also, they will not be able to claim independent status simply because you do not want to give details of your income or refuse to provide financial support.

Your children will qualify as independent students if they meet *one* of the following conditions:

- They are 25 or over before the start of the academic year for which they are applying.
- They have been married or entered into a civil partnership before the start of the academic year for which they are applying for support.
- They have supported themselves for at least three years before the start of the academic year of their course.
- They are permanently estranged from you.

Cases of separation and divorce

If you are separated, the income of the parent considered to 'be appropriate in the circumstances' will be assessed. If you have remarried, entered into a civil partnership, or live with a partner (of the same or opposite sex), the partner's income will also be taken into account when your parental contribution is worked out.

Making financial gifts to your child

If you choose to make a financial gift to your child to help with university costs, you will need to be aware of the inheritance tax (IHT) implications. Inheritance tax is paid on the estate of a person who has died if the taxable value of their estate is above £325,000 (2009/10 figures). The tax is only paid on the part of the estate that is above this limit: if your estate is worth less than this amount there is no IHT to pay. Currently, the rate of IHT is 40 per cent.

IHT rules state that where a gift has been made within seven years before the date of your death the gift must be added to your estate when calculating whether IHT is due, unless the gift is exempt from IHT (see below). Therefore, your child, as the recipient of your gift, may be liable to IHT on the gift if you should die within seven years of having given the money.

However, there are exemptions available and if you make a financial gift to your child that is exempt, he or she will not have to pay IHT if you die within seven years. The three most relevant exemptions are:

- Small gifts of up to £250 can be made to as many people as you wish in any one tax year, which can include your children, although this small gift exemption cannot be used in conjunction with the annual exemption described below.
- An annual exemption of £3,000 per year can be given to your child. However, this cannot be used in conjunction with the small gift described above. This exemption can be carried forward for one year, meaning that you can give £6,000 in one tax year if you did not use your annual exemption in the previous year. As parents you should both remember to make use of your annual exemption. This could

provide a significant amount of money to help fund your child's university course, and can help you to reduce IHT liability on your death.

- Maintenance gifts of a 'reasonable amount'. Although exact amounts aren't specified, you could not give away more than what would be considered necessary for maintenance purposes to your children, including adopted or stepchildren, if they are under the age of 18 or in full-time education. This is a useful exemption for parents who have children studying full time at university. However, rules can be complex, so if in doubt you should seek advice from a professional who is experienced in IHT rules and regulations (see useful websites below for details of how to find a professional in your area).

When making any of the above gifts you will need to keep careful records that can be given to the tax office to prove that the gifts have been made in a manner that is exempt from IHT.

Potentially exempt transfers

If you want to make larger financial gifts to your child, such gifts will not be exempt so you will need to take a gamble that you will not die within seven years of having made the gift if you want to avoid IHT. This type of gift is called a 'potentially exempt transfer' (PET) because it has the potential to be exempt from IHT if you survive the gift by seven years.

Regular gifts out of income

In addition to the exempt gifts mentioned above, it is possible to make regular gifts to your children that are part of your normal expenditure. These gifts must be made from your after-tax income and should be part of your regular expenditure. You can give these sums away monthly, annually or as frequently as you wish, and they will not be counted as part of your estate when you die. This type of gift could be used to help your child to pay rent or tuition fees, for example. After making such gifts you must be left with sufficient income to maintain your normal standard of living. The money must be surplus to your requirements and these gifts must not impoverish you in any way.

As the taxpayer, the onus is on you to prove that you have met the required conditions. It is advisable to start giving as soon as possible so

that a regular pattern can be put in place. Standing orders from bank accounts over a period of three or more years should be enough to convince the tax officer. These gifts can be made in addition to the exempt gift described above.

Loaning money to your child

As we have seen in Part Two of this book, your child can apply for a student loan to cover the cost of tuition fees and maintenance while studying at university. However, you may choose to loan the money to your children yourself, rather than take advantage of the student loan, or you may choose to loan them additional money on top of their student loan. This may be for a number of reasons:

- You do not wish to declare your income to the Student Loans Company.
- You prefer to maintain control over your child's finances (and your child is happy for you to do this).
- You feel the student loan is inadequate and needs to be topped up.
- Student loan payments are late and you need to provide an interim loan.

If you choose to loan money to your child you need to make sure that he or she understands that you have made a loan rather than a gift. It is advisable to draw up a contract that is understood by your child, which clearly lays out the conditions of the loan and the repayment terms. Also, you should note that, if your child is still repaying your loan and wants to take out a mortgage once he or she has left university and is in paid employment, the mortgage company may take the loan into account when assessing your child's application. They may request to see a copy of the contract and reduce the amount that they are willing to lend.

Ensuring take-up of statutory support

You can help your children financially by making sure that they take up all the financial support that is available to them. There are a variety of

reasons why students miss out on the support that they are entitled to, which can include:

- People may fail to read/fill in the forms correctly.
- Forms are too complicated.
- Students/parents don't trust the system.
- Students apply too late.
- Students fail to collect their money, even though they have applied.
- Students forget to open a bank account, or supply the wrong bank details.

It may seem odd that students don't claim the money to which they are entitled, but it is quite common. For example, in 2007/08 it was discovered that universities had spent less on bursaries than the amount for which they had budgeted. One of the main reasons for this was that students had failed to claim the bursaries to which they were entitled. You can help your children financially by making sure that they are clear about, and apply for and collect, all money due to them.

Part Two of this book provides comprehensive information and advice about all the funds that may be available to your child, including university bursaries. In addition to this information, individual university websites and prospectuses contain financial advice and you can contact the student finance office or the students' union at your child's preferred university for advice tailored to their needs.

Helping with costs

There are a variety of ways that you can help your child with the cost of university, as outlined below:

- Find out whether your household insurance will cover your children's possessions while they are at university. Some household policies will include this insurance, and it may be cheaper for you to include your children on your policy rather than them taking out their own insurance. Also, it will give you peace of mind to know that their possessions are safe while they are studying.

- Although students don't need their own IT equipment while they are studying, most find it convenient to do so. You can help with costs by agreeing to buy their computing equipment for them. Take advantage of educational discount schemes or consider second-hand equipment when making your purchases (see Chapter 6).

- In the present economic climate, more and more students are finding it cheaper to live at home while they are studying. However, you will need to discuss this with your child to make sure that it is the best option for all of you. One of the benefits of going away to university is learning how to live independently and students will not get the chance to do this if they live at home while studying. However, if they are happy to live in the parental home you can help with their costs, perhaps by not charging for rent, utilities and food. As this provides significant savings for students, living at home is likely to become more common as the costs of university study rise.

- If you, or your child, think that it is better to study away from home you can still help with costs by providing free accommodation and food through the vacations. Many university halls of residence will provide accommodation for term-time only. If students can return home through the vacations, and you are willing to provide their food and accommodation, they can reduce their costs significantly (see Chapter 2).

- You can help with living costs by consulting the university website or prospectus to find out exactly what is required by your child before arrival at university. Most household items that students will require, such as bedding, cooking utensils and cleaning products, can be supplied by you, usually at very little cost because you already have them available. Most universities will provide a list of what is required prior to arrival. If your child is moving into halls of residence, check the list of prohibited items so that you don't waste money buying equipment that cannot be used. For example, most halls will not allow students to use kettles, irons, cooking appliances, freezers and electric fires in the bedrooms. If certain equipment is allowed, universities will insist that it complies with relevant standards and that it has been tested recently.

Tips from parents

Parents were asked to give their tips on providing financial support and ways to help their children to save money while they were studying at university:

I sent regular food parcels, you know, the basics, back with her when she went back after she had been home. I probably sent about 10 parcels a year. I have a Cash and Carry card, so I could go and get things that would last, you know, like boxes of Cup a Soups, Pot Noodles, rice, pasta, tins of beans, tea, coffee and so on. She said it really helped her as she only had to go and buy fresh fruit and veg. *Angela, 45, Bournemouth.*

I didn't get annoyed when he brought all his washing home. I would just do it, and pack it and send it back with him... He said the laundrette was really expensive and I was doing his brother's anyway. Mind you, he didn't live too far away so he was home every other week... I also agreed to buy all his books. I thought it would be good because I thought he might not buy books if I didn't get them. *Joan, 52, Southampton.*

Denise lived at home while she studied, so it was easy to carry on as normal, treat her like she was still at school... So I didn't ask for any rent and I cooked for both of us, like I always did... All her friends went to the same place and still lived at home, so she didn't miss any of her friends... I think she spent less money because she was still at home... It worked well really, but I realise it wouldn't work for everyone, but then Denise and me have always been very close. *Kate, 38, Northampton.*

I gave Adam the family computer. We didn't need it. I also gave him lots of stuff from his gran's house when she moved into a home. And he had his gran's car... Mind you, he stopped running it in the second year because it was too expensive and he didn't really need it... So my tip would be don't run a car and give your children everything they need to live with. *Jenny, 45, Weymouth.*

Summary

As a parent there are several ways that you can help children financially while they are at university. This includes paying the parental contribution, making gifts or loans, encouraging them to apply and collect money to which they are entitled, and helping with costs such as accommodation, IT equipment and living expenses. If you choose to give money to your child you need to be aware of IHT implications and make sure that you take advantages of IHT exemptions.

Some parents want to plan early for their child's university education, so that they have the necessary finances in place to help out financially when required. Today there are a variety of specialist savings plans available to help parents to do this. These schemes are discussed in the following chapter.

Further information

A guide called *Talking Money: A parent's guide to student finance* can be downloaded from www.direct.gov.uk.

Useful websites

www.thepfs.org

The Personal Finance Society (PFS) is the largest professional body for individual financial advisers and those in related roles in the United Kingdom. You can use their online service to find a financial adviser in your area, and access useful information on getting the most out of your adviser and choosing the right person, in particular somebody who understands IHT rules and regulations.

www.step.org

The Society of Trust and Estate Practitioners (STEP) is a professional body for professionals specialising in trusts, estates and related taxes. You can find a practitioner in your area by visiting this website. This person will be

able to offer advice on all aspects of trust and estate planning, including IHT rules and regulations.

www.lawsociety.org.uk

This is the website of the Law Society. Through 'solicitors online' you can search the database by firm name, postcode or location, country or area of law to find a suitable solicitor for your needs. This is useful if you need to draw up a legally binding contract with your child.

18 *Making use of children's savings plans*

Some parents decide that they would like to start saving for their child's university education well before the child reaches university age. Two popular ways to do this are through children's savings plans and through general investment opportunities. Chapter 19 discusses the general investment opportunities that are available to parents. This chapter looks at children's savings plans, including Child Trust Funds, children's savings accounts and children's bonds. If you choose to follow this route it is important to maximise your investment, protect your money and understand the tax issues. These issues are discussed in this chapter.

You should note, however, that only financial advisers who are authorised by the Financial Services Authority (FSA) are able to give financial advice, so you should contact a professional in your area for advice suited to your circumstances and needs. Comparative tables for various types of investment product can be viewed on the FSA website (www.fsa.gov.uk/tables).

When to start investing

The general rule is that the sooner you start investing, the more money you will be able to provide when your child starts university. For example, if you feel that you can survive financially without spending your child benefit, you can choose to invest the money for your children to help pay for their university education. From January 2009 child benefit is £20 a week for the eldest (or only) child. If you saved this money from birth until your child reaches the age of 18, you would have a sum of £18,720. Any interest that you earn would be on top of this figure. If you invested wisely

you could earn enough from your child benefit to pay for every year of your child's university course so that your child could leave university debt-free.

If you could afford to put aside more than your child benefit each week/ month, you could save considerably more, which would not only pay for your child's university education, but could help him or her to put down the money for a deposit on a house, for example.

Investing in Child Trust Fund accounts

If your child was born after 31 August 2002 you will have received a voucher from the state that must be invested on his or her behalf. In 2009 this voucher is worth £250. Also, if you are in receipt of the Child Tax Credit (CTC) and you have a household income not greater than the CTC threshold of £15,575 for 2009, you will receive an extra payment. In addition to this, all eligible children will receive a further payment of £250 into their CTF account at age seven, with children from lower-income families receiving an additional £250. These payments will be paid around the children's seventh birthday direct into their account.

Money cannot be taken out of the Child Trust Fund (CTF) once it has been put in, and when children reach the age of 18 they will be able to decide how to use the money. If you would like them to use the money to help to pay for their university course, you should discuss this with them before they are able to access the money.

Types of account

There are three types of account that you can choose, depending on the level of risk you are prepared to take and how you wish the money to grow:

- A savings CTF account that works like a normal savings account. This is a safe option but the returns may not be as great as they may be as when the money is invested in shares, especially over the long term.
- A stakeholder CTF account where the money is invested mainly in the stock market, perhaps through unit trusts, but there are controls in

place to reduce the amount of risk. Also, there is a limit to the amount of fee that can be charged by the company managing the investment.

- Stock-market-linked CTF accounts. These do not meet the conditions of the stakeholder account described above and therefore contain a higher element of risk, but have the potential to earn more on the investment over the long term. This type of account has to be viewed as a long-term investment (current economic conditions have shown us that the value of such investments can be reduced considerably over the short term).

The type of account that you choose is your decision and it is possible to choose ethical accounts, or sharia accounts that are based on Islamic moral values. You can top up the account each year, to a maximum of £1,200 per year (2009 figures). The start date for contributions is your child's birthday and it is not possible to carry forward any unused contribution to the following year.

Comprehensive information and advice about CTFs can be obtained from www.childtrustfund.gov.uk. On this site you can find a useful 'account chooser' tool that helps you to choose the right account for your circumstances. Further information and advice about investing in CTFs can be obtained from the Investment Management Association (details below).

Investing in children's savings accounts

Some banks and building societies offer savings accounts for children that have higher interest rates than other types of savings account. In most cases the interest rate is variable and will fluctuate according to the bank's policy and/or the Bank of England base rate, although it is possible to obtain a fixed rate savings account. The current base rate can be obtained from www.bankofengland.co.uk. The banks or building societies may also offer vouchers, tokens or other perks when an account is opened.

Children's savings accounts operate like ordinary savings accounts although before the age of seven the account must be in your name with your child's initials attached. The account can be opened in your child's name if they are over seven, but they will have control over the account and can spend the money any way that they wish.

Children's accounts with higher interest rates tend to have greater restrictions, such as a limit to the amount that can be withdrawn, or longer periods of notice before cash is withdrawn. However, this type of savings account is a low-risk option and your money is safe as it is protected by the government's deposit guarantee scheme (see below).

Investing in children's bonds

Children's bonds are different from children's savings accounts in that when you buy a savings bond you are, in effect, lending money to the bank or building society, or to the government. In return, they agree to pay back the original sum you invested, along with an agreed amount of interest within an agreed period of time. Bonds can be bought with a lump sum or on a monthly basis; there will be restrictions on how much you can invest, whether as a lump sum or each month, so check that the scheme meets your requirements before buying the bond. Bonds can be useful if you have a lump sum to invest over a number of years as interest rates can be higher than they are on savings accounts. This is useful if you are setting aside a lump sum for your child's university education, as the money can be tied up safely until your child reaches university age.

Some bonds are linked to the performance of the stock market, so the amount your child will receive at the end of the term depends on the performance of the stock market and the company's investment management. This type of bond is therefore more risky, but you can make sure that it is a 'guaranteed' bond so that you will not lose your original investment at the end of the term.

Baby bonds

Friendly societies provide tax-free savings plans in children's own names. It is possible to buy baby bonds for your children from these organisations. These plans tend to run for a minimum of 10 years and are unit-linked stock-based investments. They are open to any UK resident child under 16 and can be opened on behalf of the child by anyone. In particular, grandparents find them a useful way to invest money for their grandchildren. When the plan matures it provides a lump sum for your child/grandchild. More information about friendly societies and a list of links to

individual websites can be obtained from the Association of Friendly Societies website (www.afs.org.uk).

University bonds

University bonds, on the other hand, are designed to pay out three or four years in succession to match the academic year. They are a low-risk investment and you will be guaranteed to receive back the amount you have paid along with a certain amount of interest. Policies are written in the child's name, which means that you can't access the savings. It is for this reason that this type of saving can be of interest to grandparents who wish to put aside some money that is protected. When you open a building society account in your child's name, it can be registered to receive gross interest (free of 20 per cent savings tax) by completing form R85 (see below).

National Savings Children's Bonus Bonds

Anyone aged 16 or over can buy Children's Bonus Bonds for children under 16. You can invest a lump sum and interest is added each year, along with a bonus every five years until your child's 21st birthday. You can invest in as many issues as you like, up to £3,000 per issue for each child, in units of £25.

Children's Bonus Bonds are owned by your child, but until their 16th birthday the Bond is controlled by you as the parent, regardless of who bought it. This means that, although the money belongs to your child, only you can cash in the bond. However, once children reach the age of 16, they control the Bond themselves, so you would have to discuss the issue of paying for university with them before they access the money.

Maximising your investment

As an investor you will want to maximise your return on income, capital growth or both. However, you will also want to make sure that your finances are protected. When you invest your money, risk and return are two of the issues you need to consider. In general, the higher the risk, the more potential there is to earn more, especially over the long term.

However, greater risk also means that there is the potential for greater loss. As a general guide you should consider the following points:

- Savings accounts offer low risk and low returns.
- Bonds are seen to be medium risk. Corporate bonds may offer slightly higher returns than government bonds.
- Shares carry higher risk, but may offer greater returns, especially on long-term investments. Risks can be reduced if you hold a number of different shares, spread your investment and purchase through an experienced fund manager.

Protecting your investment

Investing money for your child's university education will be a long-term investment strategy, during which time you cannot predict what will happen to the financial market. As we have seen recently, the market can experience significant fluctuations where huge amounts of money can be lost overnight. You need to make sure that your savings are protected so that your child has enough money available for university. There are several ways that you can help to protect your finances, as detailed below.

The deposit guarantee scheme

As a consequence of the recent financial crisis, the government has introduced a deposit guarantee scheme that guarantees savings up to £50,000 (from 7 October 2008). If you are a couple and you hold a joint account, your savings will be protected up to £100,000. However, if your savings are above this amount there is no guarantee that you will get your money back should the financial institution in which you have deposited your money fail. Also, the deposit guarantee scheme only applies to authorised institutions (see below).

Using authorised firms

You can protect your finances, therefore, by making sure that you only use authorised institutions. The FSA Register has information on all authorised

firms currently doing business in the United Kingdom. It also includes firms that are authorised in another European Economic Area (EEA) state and that also conduct business in the United Kingdom. You can search the register by firm reference number, or firm name and postcode. The register can be accessed at www.fsa.gov.uk/register. If you want to find out more about how a bank or building society is authorised, contact the Financial Services Authority Consumer Contact Centre on (0845) 606 1234.

Spreading your investment

Another way to protect your money is to spread your investment between different institutions. For example, you could choose to deposit up to £50,000 in a high-interest savings account with one authorised bank. You know that this money is protected if the bank should collapse. Any money above this amount can be invested elsewhere, perhaps in another bank or building society. Although the scheme only guarantees deposits up to £50,000, you would be very unlucky indeed to have both banks collapse at the same time.

It may be prudent, also, to spread your investment across different types of investment, such as cash and share investments. This is known as 'diversification'. It will offer protection and may also provide the opportunity for greater returns. However, as we have seen previously, it tends to be the case that the higher returns you are promised, the greater the risk. If the offer seems far too good to be true, you must approach the investment with extreme caution. Check that the firm is authorised (see above) and seek independent financial advice if in doubt.

Accessing your money

One final point to note is that if you put investments in your children's names, when they reach the age of 18, 21 or 25 (depending on the type of investment) the money will be theirs to spend on whatever they choose, regardless of your intentions. It is important that you discuss this issue with your child, so that you both understand why the money has been set aside. However, as a parent you might need to acknowledge that a university education does not suit everyone, and that your child might have other plans in mind.

Understanding tax issues

Children have their own personal allowance for tax in the same way as adults do. This means that, in most cases, it is unlikely that an investment taken out in your child's name will generate enough income for your child to have to pay tax. When you open an account you should fill in HMRC form R85 as this will ensure that no tax will be deducted from the interest earned on funds in the account. This form can be obtained from the bank or building society or downloaded from www.hmrc.gov.uk.

One point to note is that if you, as a parent, make contributions to a child's account that generates an income of more than £100 in a year, that income will be treated as a parental income and you will have to pay tax on that income. This rule, however, does not apply if contributions are made to your child's account by other relatives or friends. Also, with the Children's Bonus Bonds from National Savings and Investment, the interest and bonuses are all free of UK Income tax and capital gains tax. Even if your child starts work and becomes a taxpayer before cashing in the bonds, he or she won't have to pay tax on the interest from the bond.

Summary

There are several ways that you can choose to invest your money in children's savings plans to help to pay for your child's university education. This includes Child Trust Funds, children's savings accounts and children's bonds. The type of plan that you choose depends on the amount of risk you are happy to take and the level of return you would like. If you are to protect your finances and achieve a higher return, it might be best to diversify your investment and seek the advice of experienced professionals.

One of the problems with investing your money in your children's names is that they are able to control the money when they reach a specific age, depending on the type of investment. You might find that they want to spend the money on something other than university, which may go against your wishes. To overcome this problem you could decide to make use of more general investment opportunities, where the investment is made in your name instead of your child's. These issues are discussed in the following chapter.

Useful organisations

Financial Services Compensation Scheme (FSCS)

The FSCS is an independent body set up under the Financial Services and Markets Act 2000 (FSMA) to pay compensation to customers of authorised financial services firms in cases of default. This may be when an institution has collapsed or where cases of dispute have arisen. You can search the database on the website to see if the firm you are making enquiries about has already been declared in default by the FSCS.

Financial Services Compensation Scheme
7th floor, Lloyds Chambers
Portsoken Street
London E1 8BN
Tel: (020) 7892 7300
Fax: (020) 7892 7301
e-mail: enquiries@fscs.org.uk
www.fscs.org.uk

Useful websites

www.investmentuk.org

This is the website of the Investment Management Association, which is the trade body for the asset management industry. On this website you can find useful advice and guidance about investing your money and a comprehensive fact sheet on investing in a child trust fund. You can find authorised investment fund managers by using the search facility on this site.

19 Making use of general investment opportunities

The different ways of investing in savings plans for children were discussed in the previous chapter. However, it was pointed out that one of the drawbacks to this kind of investment is that the children take control of the money when they reach a certain age (this age depends on the type of investment). They may choose to spend the money for something other than their university education, which may go against your wishes. You can overcome this problem by making use of general investment opportunities, investing your money in your name instead of theirs, so that you can keep control of your finances. While there may be certain tax disadvantages to this type of investment, you can make sure that your child does not fritter away your savings. These issues are discussed in this chapter.

Again, you should note that only financial advisers who are authorised by the FSA are able to give financial advice, so you should contact a professional in your area for advice suited to your circumstances and needs.

When to start investing

As with investments that you take out in your child's name, the sooner you start investing, the more money you are likely to make for your child's university education. Consider the following examples:

- According to the Association of Investment Companies (www.theaic. co.uk), investing £50 a month in the average investment company over the last 18 years would have resulted in a sum of £29,330 for your child's university education. This would pay for their whole

course and accommodation, enabling them to leave university debt-free, without a student loan to have to pay back. However, the performance of your investment depends on the performance of the stock market with this type of investment, so you will have to monitor your investment carefully, making sure that your money is accessed at the right time. It is also important to spread, or diversify, your investment (see below).

- According to the Investment Management Association (www.invest mentuk.org), if you had started saving £20 a month in August 1998 into the average UK All Companies investment fund savings plan, then by August 2008 you would have built up a sum of £3,050. Making the same monthly payments into a building society account over 10 years would have resulted in a sum of £2,596. Not only does this example show that investment plans can work better than building society accounts, it also demonstrates that you would have enough money to pay for your child's tuition fees or accommodation costs in their first year of study by saving only £20 a month over 10 years (based on 2009/10 tuition fees). If you were to save a little more than £20 a month, you would be able to help with tuition fee costs in the second and third years as well.

Investing in National Savings and Investments

National Savings and Investments offer a variety of other investment opportunities for parents, in addition to the Children's Bonus Bonds described in the previous chapter, and some of these are tax free (see below). More information about all these savings methods can be obtained from www.nsandi.com. You can apply for National Savings and Investment products online, by telephone or by picking up an application form from your local post office. The different types of products that may be of interest to you are described below.

Premium bonds

These can be bought by anyone aged 16 or over and can also be bought on behalf of someone under the age of 16 by parents and grandparents. However, if you buy the bonds in your children's names they can choose what they wish to do with them after they reach the age of 16, so you might prefer to buy the bonds in your own name. The minimum purchase is £100 and the maximum purchase is £30,000. Instead of paying interest, bonds are entered into monthly prize draws, with a top prize of £1 million. There is no limit to the investment term, although the true value of your money will reduce over time.

Index-linked Savings Certificates

These enable you to invest your money so that it increases in line with inflation as measured by the Retail Prices Index (RPI). You can invest £100 to £15,000 in each issue of each term. Unlike ISAs, Index Linked Savings Certificates aren't tied to the tax year so you can invest up to another £15,000 tax-free whenever a new issue goes on sale. This is a lump-sum investment and is available for three or five years. However, you will not know how much your investment will make until the end of the term. You can buy Savings Certificates on behalf of children if they are under the age of seven, but they then become responsible for them on their seventh birthday, so you may feel that it is better to buy them in your name. To get the maximum return from your investment, you need to keep your Savings Certificates for the full term

Fixed Interest Savings Certificates

These are lump-sum investments that earn guaranteed rates of interest over set periods of time. You can invest £100–£15,000 in each issue and this doesn't count towards your allowance for Index-linked Savings Certificates or cash ISAs. To get the maximum benefit from your Savings Certificate, you need to keep your money invested for the full length of the term you choose. At this present time you can invest for two years, five years or both. There is a calculator available on the website to help you to work out how much your investment would be worth at the end of the term.

Investing in unit trusts, open-ended investment companies or investment trust savings plans

If you want to save regularly for your child's university education over the long term, you could consider unit trust or investment trust companies. These enable private individuals to pool their contributions with others, which combine to form a large fund. The fund or investment trust company invests in a range of different assets to minimise the risk of loss. The success of the fund depends on the skill of the fund manager and the performance of the stock market, so you should seek independent financial advice or conduct comprehensive research to find out about the best-performing funds.

You can choose to invest a lump sum or invest regularly each month. Many parents find that it is preferable to invest each month, because once a standing order has been set up the money goes directly from their account each month and is not frittered away. In most cases you can invest as little as £10 a month, although this minimum value will vary, depending on the fund or company.

Set-up costs and annual charges vary considerably, so you should shop around for the best deal in addition to choosing a fund that performs well. For unbiased, comprehensive information about unit trusts and open-ended investment companies (OEICs), visit www.which.co.uk. You can find a fund or fund manager by using the online search facility of the Investment Management Association website (www.investmentuk.org).

Investing in individual savings accounts

If you want to have more flexibility and control over the money that you are investing for your child, you could choose to invest in an individual savings account (ISA). These are savings schemes that were introduced in 1999 to encourage people to save by offering tax incentives. In 2007, the Government announced that the ISA scheme is to continue indefinitely into the future, so this could be a useful long-term investment opportunity for your child's university education (see quotation below).

Mr and Mrs Young, Northampton

We pay £50 a month into an ISA. Sam is only five at the moment, but we hope to continue paying this for at least the next 12 years. We reckon it will be enough to see him through university and because it goes straight from our account we don't even notice it anymore. Obviously we don't know how much the investment will be worth by then. At the moment we've paid in more than it's worth because of the terrible mess the world is in at the moment. But we're going to hold our nerve. We reckon the cycle will be high by the time he's old enough to go to university and we cash in the ISA.

An ISA is not an investment in itself, but rather the regulatory and taxation framework in which eligible investments sit. Eligible investments can be cash, equities (stocks and shares), some life insurance products, or a combination of these. The type of ISA that you choose will depend on how much you wish to invest and for how long, so you should seek specialist advice if you wish to follow this route. If your children are under the age of 15, the ISA will have to be taken out by you in your name as children under this age cannot have an ISA. You may prefer this option as you maintain control of the ISA. However, if you prefer, children aged 16 and 17 can have a cash ISA and the subscription limits are the same as for savers who are over 18, currently up to £3,600 in each tax year. Subscription limits for stocks and shares ISAs are currently £7,200 per tax year.

It is possible to invest a lump sum, a series of lump sums or regular savings into an ISA. The types and minimum amount of investment vary, and are set by individual providers. Broadly, ISAs should be treated as longer-term investments. If you choose to take money out of an ISA during the year, it is still considered to have counted towards the maximum annual investment limit. Therefore, it cannot be replaced in the same tax year if the full subscription limit has been used. However, you can now transfer money from cash to stocks and shares ISAs and it will not count as part of the £7,200 annual allowance. You cannot move money from a stocks and shares ISA to a cash ISA in the same way.

More information about investing in ISAs can be obtained from HMRC (ISA helpline: (0845) 604 1701; website: www.hmrc.gov.uk/isa) or from your financial adviser.

Maximising your investment

In Chapter 18 we saw that, where investment plans for your children are concerned, a general rule is that the more risk attached to your investment, the higher your returns are likely to be. This is also the case with the type of investments discussed in this chapter. However, the recent financial crisis has illustrated that stocks and shares can fall by huge amounts, and you have to hold your nerve if you have decided to invest in a regular stocks and shares savings plan (see quotation above).

The key, however, is to consider the investment over the long term: if you continue to buy stocks and shares when prices are very low, you will be able to buy more at this time for the same monthly contribution. This means that your investment has the potential to grow considerably once the economy recovers.

Protecting your investment

You can protect your investment by taking note of the following points:

- Make sure that you only use an authorised firm by checking the FSA register (www.fsa.gov.uk/register). If you want to find out more about how a bank or building society is authorised, contact the Financial Services Authority Consumer Contact Centre on 0845 606 1234.
- If the company in which you have deposited your money goes bust, or you wish to seek compensation against it for financial mismanagement, contact the FSCS for more information (details in Chapter 18).
- Spread your investment over a number of different types of investment and within different authorised firms.
- Conduct comprehensive research and/or seek the services of a professional.
- Seek advice about protecting your investment from your financial adviser.
- Monitor the market on a regular basis. If there is significant change, speak to your financial adviser to find out if there is any action you should take to further protect your investment.

Professional investors 'de-risk' investments as they approach maturity and you need to monitor the market to find out whether you should adopt this approach. This is a process where the total risk to the investment is identified, prioritised and managed appropriately. In terms of your investment this would involve a careful assessment of market conditions prior to the expected disposal date, which will probably be the time that your child intends to enter university. This assessment might indicate that it is better to cash in your investment if there is a chance that the market will slump just before the date you originally had in mind. The cash can be placed into something more secure, such as a high-yield account until you wish to pay for your child's university education. Alternatively, some investors choose to wait until the value of their investment reaches a pre-defined amount, and once this occurs, they go ahead and sell, again investing the proceeds until their children are about to start university.

Understanding tax issues

If you choose to invest in National Savings and Investment products, you can invest up to £93,600 tax free. A 'tax-free investment calculator' is available on their website (www.nsandi.com) to help you to work out how much money you can invest tax free. Investments with National Savings and Investment are also free from capital gains tax (CGT).

If you decide to take out an ISA and it is in your name, you do not have to pay income tax or CGT on the profit earned. However, if you give money to your child (aged 16 or 17) to invest in an ISA in his or her name, and the total income earned from the investment exceeds £100 in any tax year, it will be treated as part of your income for tax purposes. Note that this is only the case if your children have taken an ISA in their own names and if you have contributed the capital.

Although the IHT position can be complicated, in most cases savings that you hold in your name on behalf of your children while they are under the age of 18 will be added to your estate for IHT purposes (see Chapter 17).

Summary

There are various ways to invest your money for your child's university education. Taking an investment out in your name, rather than your child's, enables you to keep control of your money and spend it in the way that you want. There are inheritance tax implications to consider if the investment is in your name, but there are investments available that are free of income tax and capital gains tax. If you are to maximise the potential of your investment you need to conduct comprehensive research and/or seek the advice of a professional.

Many parents see that it can be both lucrative and interesting to invest their money in property, which they can either sell to help to pay for their child's university education, or as a place in which their child can live while studying. These issues are discussed in the following chapter.

20 *Investing in property to pay for university*

A strategy that parents can use to help to pay for their children's university education is to invest in property. This tends to be done in two ways. The first is to buy a second property well in advance of children starting their university education. This property can be let to tenants or used as a holiday home until the children begin university, at which time it can be sold to raise cash for their education. The second method is to buy a property for the children to live in when they begin their studies. If you do this, you can reduce the cost of your child's accommodation while they are studying, and, if you decide to let other rooms in the property, you can make a decent income to pay for other aspects of your child's education.

However, as we have seen recently, the property market can be extremely volatile and it is possible to make significant losses as well as large gains. If you choose to invest in property to pay for your child's university education you must make wise decisions, understand the tax implications, know how to maximise your returns and avoid common pitfalls. These issues are discussed in this chapter.

Buying a second property

Some parents choose to buy a second property as soon as they can afford to do so. This may be at a time when you've paid off your existing mortgage, you have enough savings to lay down a large deposit, or the value of your house has risen so much that you are able to release equity in your home to buy another property (see Chapter 21 for more information about equity release plans).

If you choose to buy a second property there are issues that you need to consider before making your purchase:

- Think carefully before securing other debts against your home. Your home and your second property may be repossessed if you are unable to keep up repayments. This is of particular importance during times of economic uncertainty. Would you be able to pay for two mortgages if you and/or your partner were to lose your jobs through redundancy or illness?

- Make sure that your child is not saddled with your debts if you should die unexpectedly. Take out adequate life insurance, plan your estate carefully and consult a professional estate planner who is a member of the Society of Trust and Estate Planners (www.step.org).

- Decide what you intend to do with your second property. Empty properties attract vandals, burglars and squatters. It can be costly, time-consuming and stressful to repair damage, evict squatters, arrange insurance and maintain empty properties. However, letting your second property can also cause difficulty, especially if you live at a distance from it. You may find it prudent to employ a reliable letting agent to manage your property for you (see below).

- You must monitor the performance of the local and national housing market, and become familiar with the property market in the area in which you wish to buy. You can make a loss on your investment if you choose the wrong property or location, or pay too much when prices are falling. Failure to monitor the local and national housing market can lead to financial loss.

- Choose the right mortgage for the market conditions. For example, interest rates have fallen considerably over 2008/09. People on fixed-rate mortgages will not be able to take advantage of these lower rates, whereas those on tracker mortgages have seen considerable reductions in monthly repayments over this period.

- If you intend to sell your second property just before your child reaches university age, you could be at the mercy of short-term market fluctuations. If the market has slumped at this time you could make a loss on your property and not achieve the type of profit you require to help with your child's university costs. Also, you could be saddled with negative equity on the property. To avoid these problems you need to monitor the market carefully. If you feel the property may drop in value at the required disposal date, it may be prudent to sell early and invest your money in a safe account until your child starts university.

Buying a property for your student child

If you choose to buy a property for your children when they are still young, you need to view this as a long-term investment. Over the past 30 years, even with the recent fall in prices, property has represented a good long-term investment. However, if you decide to buy property in which your children can live while they are studying, this may be a short-term investment, especially if you intend to sell once they have completed their studies.

If you choose this option, there are additional issues of which you should be aware. These include the following:

● In general, the property market in well-known university towns tends to perform better than the property market in other areas. However, for this type of investment to work your child will need to study in an area where house prices are still rising, and this may not match their learning choices. Would you want to constrain their choices if you found that property prices are falling in the area in which they wish to study?

● If you buy a house for your children to live in while they are studying, they may grow attached to the house and location. They may not want to leave when their course finishes and this could cause friction if you want, or need, to sell. You can avoid this problem by making sure that you draw up a legally binding agreement in which you and your children are clear about what will happen to the property once their course has finished.

● If you buy your child's property in your name you will have to pay capital gains tax, depending on how much profit you make on the selling price.

● If you choose the wrong mortgage for your personal circumstances and make an unwise choice of property, you could lose out substantially on your investment. Taking out a buy-to-let mortgage in your name will influence your chance of obtaining another mortgage at a later date.

● If the buy-to-let market is saturated in the place in which your child decides to study, you may struggle to find tenants for your property. Also, you may struggle to find tenants during the long vacations when

students return to their parental home. Can you meet mortgage repayments in these cases?

- Your money will be tied up in the property and if you need to sell quickly to raise cash it will be very disruptive for your child's studies. If you have let other rooms in the house it will be difficult to sell the property while it is tenanted.
- You or your child will need to adopt the role of landlord if you intend to let any other rooms in the property. There are rules and regulations involved with this and the role does not suit everybody, especially if you are not willing to be on call 24 hours a day.
- It is hard to take your children's friends to court for rent arrears or damage to your property. You, or your children if they are acting as landlord, may find it hard to chase late payments. You can reduce problems by making sure that your tenants sign a legally binding tenancy agreement (see below).

Investing in buy-to-let

If you decide to invest in buy-to-let, you may find that it is less stressful and easier to hand over the letting of your property to a letting agent. Letting agents can provide a number of services, such as finding and choosing tenants, collecting rent and managing the property. You can find a letting agent in your area by consulting the Association of Residential Letting Agents website (www.arla.co.uk).

If you are thinking of using a letting agent, make sure that the agent is a member of the National Approved Letting Scheme as members have to work to certain standards and provide a certain level of service (details below). Check that it has the necessary insurance to protect your money if it should experience financial difficulties and find out whether it has suitable complaints procedures in place. Before you employ a letting agent you should receive a written statement of its services and prices. Compare prices and services between two or three letting agents in your area as these vary considerably.

Drawing up a tenancy agreement

A tenancy agreement is a contract between you and your tenants. Although it can be a verbal agreement in England and Wales, you should always produce a written contract which is signed by both parties and witnessed by a third party. This will protect you in cases of dispute. In most cases in Scotland you must produce a written agreement for your tenants. A tenancy agreement consists of 'express terms' that have been agreed between you and the tenant, and 'implied terms' that include the rights given by law and arrangements established by custom and practice.

In most cases, if you are letting your property privately and are not a 'resident' landlord, the tenancy is automatically an 'assured shorthold tenancy' ('assured tenancy' in Scotland). Contact the accommodation office or students' union at your child's university for information about their preferred tenancy agreement. Alternatively, the Residential Landlords Association has produced a tenancy agreement that is free to members or available from their website for a one-off fee of £5.00.

However, if your child lives in the property and wishes to let rooms to other students, there are different types of tenancy agreement, depending on the parts of the property that are let and used by the landlord and tenants. Again, if you and your child wish to follow this route you should seek advice from the university accommodation office and/or students' union. For comprehensive information and advice about completing an agreement, choosing tenants, conducting repairs and protecting your property see *The Complete Guide to Property Development for the Small Investor* (details below).

Producing an inventory

Many disputes with tenants involve the condition of the property at the end of the tenancy. Therefore, it is essential that you produce an inventory for your tenants. This should contain details of fixtures and fittings and describe their condition and that of the property in general. The inventory should be amended and updated with each new tenant. You and the tenant should check the inventory carefully at the beginning and at the end of the tenancy.

If you are a first-time landlord you may find it preferable to use an independent inventory agent. They will prepare the inventory accurately, including details of the contents and a description of their condition. You can find an inventory clerk in your area by visiting the Association of Independent Inventory Clerks website (www.theaiic.co.uk).

Letting rules and regulations

If you intend to let your accommodation you will need to take account of the following rules and regulations:

- You must find out whether your property is a 'house in multiple occupation' (HMO) as it will need to be licensed. An HMO is legally defined as any property that is occupied by persons who do not form a single household. Licensing criteria can vary between local authorities, but in general a licence will be needed if there are five or more people living in the property and the property has three or more stories. More information about obtaining a licence can be obtained from your local authority or from www.communities.gov.uk.
- It is your responsibility as landlord to maintain the property in good order, and to carry out any necessary repairs to the internal and external parts of the building and services. All structures, installations, services, sanitary fittings and heating systems must be maintained and kept in full working order.
- All gas appliances should be checked for safety every 12 months, and this must be done by a CORGI-registered installer. You should request a Landlord's Gas Safety Certificate, a copy of which should be provided to your tenants. More information about gas safety for landlords can be obtained from www.hse.gov.uk. Visit the CORGI website to find a registered installer in your area (www.trustcorgi.com).
- You are required to comply with the Portable Appliance Safety section of the Consumer Protection Act 1987 to ensure that all electrical items are safe. All portable electrical appliances must be inspected and tested regularly by an approved electrician. The Consumer Protection Act makes it an offence for a landlord to provide any portable electrical appliance that is either electrically or physically unsafe and that would be a danger to tenants or visitors to the property. More information can be obtained from National Inspection Council for Electrical Installation

Contracting (NICEIC) (www.niceic.com), Electrical Safety Council (ESC) (www.electricalsafetycouncil.org.uk) or National Association of Professional Inspectors and Testers (NAPIT) (www.napit.org.uk).

- You are required to comply with the Furniture and Furnishings Fire Safety section of the Consumer Protection Act 1987 to ensure that all items of furniture are safe. Furniture that does not meet the required safety standard must either be replaced or treated with a flame retardant substance.

- Your property must comply with the Housing Health and Safety Rating System (HHSRS). This is a risk assessment tool used to assess potential risks to the health and safety of occupants in residential properties in England and Wales. Separate housing legislation applies to Northern Ireland and Scotland. More information about the HHSRS can be obtained from www.communities.gov.uk.

- If you intend to take a deposit you should note that a new Tenancy Deposit Protection Scheme has been introduced by the government in an attempt to protect deposits from being withheld unfairly by landlords. The government has awarded the contract to three companies and you can find out about each scheme by visiting the relevant websites (www.thedisputeservice.co.uk, www.depositprotection.com, www.mydeposits.co.uk). Deposits should be paid before your tenants move in and you will need to provide them with details of the deposit scheme that is to be used within 14 days of the start of the tenancy agreement.

Choosing the right property

When looking for an investment property, you need to consider the following issues:

- Is the property market buoyant in the area and is it likely to remain that way for the duration of your investment, whether you intend to invest over the short or long term? Will you be able to sell the property for a profit? Is demand high for that type of property in that area? Will it remain so in the future? Although it is difficult to predict the future, you can reduce the risk through careful market analysis and through seeking professional advice if in doubt.

- Are there any plans, schemes or development issues that could have either a negative or positive influence on the price of the property? You can view the development plans held by the local authority to find out what schemes are taking place and proposed for the area. These plans can be viewed by entering your postcode on the Planning Portal website (www.planningportal.gov.uk). Remember that not all development is bad: some schemes, if handled carefully, could increase the value of your property.

- Are there any environmental factors that could affect your investment, such as flooding, pollution, airport extensions or proposed mobile mast installations? Visit www.environment-agency.gov.uk for information about flooding potential and www.sitefinder.ofcom.org.uk for information about mobile masts. Insurance companies have indicated recently that they may not insure new properties that have been built on flood plains, and this could make it hard to sell such properties in the future.

- Are there any highway development schemes that could affect the value of your property, or mean that part of your land will be subject to compulsory purchase in the future? Visit the Highways Agency website and click on the map to find out what is happening in your area (www.highways.gov.uk).

Maximising returns

You can maximise your returns by making sure that you conduct comprehensive research and choose the right property, at the right time, for the right price and in the right area. In a volatile property market you need to be aware of areas that are not performing well and make sure that you avoid these if you are to make a success of your investment. If your child chooses to study in such an area, you need to decide whether it is prudent to invest in property by working out how much you could save on accommodation costs for your child and how much you could make by letting other rooms in the house, and to assess what is likely to happen to the price of the property over the duration of your child's course.

Sources of information

There are various sources that you can use to help with your research. If your child is about to start university, the accommodation officer will be a very useful source of information. They understand how the student rental market is performing in the area and will be able to offer advice if you wish to let rooms to students. They will also be able to provide information about the level of rent that you can realistically charge and offer advice about the best areas in which to buy.

Also, contact local letting agents to find out more about the rent levels in the area and to find out more about the performance of the rental market. Are there plenty of opportunities available, or has saturation point been reached? What rents can you realistically charge for the type of accommodation you are offering?

Local estate agents will be able to offer advice about the performance of the housing market, and you can monitor the local and national press to see how house prices are changing. Another useful source for monitoring the housing market is the Land Registry (www.landregistry.gov.uk). It is possible to search the index at a national, regional, county or London borough level. If you live in Scotland a similar survey is produced by the Registers of Scotland Executive Agency (www.ros.gov.uk).

The Halifax produces the *Halifax House Price Index*, which is based on their mortgage lending in the United Kingdom and provides a useful indication of house prices and property market trends. On their website (www. hbosplc.com) you can access a regional house price map, a house price calculator and quarterly regional comments on the movement of the housing market. A similar survey is produced by the Nationwide, based on their lending data for properties at the post-survey approval stage (www.nationwide.co.uk).

Knowing about tax implications

If you intend to buy a property as a second home or buy a property for your child while they are studying at university, there are certain tax implications of which you should be aware. These are discussed below.

Stamp duty land tax

Stamp duty land tax (SDLT) must be paid on all land transactions of free-hold properties over certain amounts at the following rates (2009 figures):

- up to £175,000 (until December 2009, when this is due to be reviewed): zero;
- over £175,000 to £250,000: 1 per cent;
- over £250,000 to £500,000: 3 per cent;
- over £500,000: 4 per cent.

If the property that you buy is valued above the payment threshold, SDLT is charged at the appropriate rate on the whole of the amount paid for the property. For example, a house bought for £350,000 is charged at 3 per cent, so SDLT of £10,500 is payable.

If the property that you are buying is new leasehold or of mixed uses (such as residential and business use, for example a flat above a shop) different rates apply and you should consult the HM Revenue & Customs website for up-to-date rates (www.hmrc.gov.uk).

Capital gains tax

Capital gains tax (CGT) is paid on gains made from selling or disposing of assets, which includes residential property. When you sell your main home you do not have to pay CGT, as this qualifies for the private residence relief (PRR) exemption. However, it is payable on any other residential property that is not your main home, such as rental property or a second property. This tax is only payable where an asset has increased in value since you acquired it and you will not have to pay any CGT if your total gains are less than the annual exempt amount, which is £9,600 in 2009. Also, there are a number of allowances, reliefs and elections that can reduce the amount of CGT that you have to pay.

In April 2008 a flat rate of 18 per cent CGT was introduced. For up-to-date policy information, current figures and information about reporting gains or losses, visit the HMRC website (www.hmrc.gov.uk).

Council tax

If you let your investment property your tenants are responsible for paying the council tax. One council tax bill is sent to the property regardless of how many people live in it, unless you have divided your property into independent and separate living units. However, students will not have to pay the tax, provided that the house is solely occupied by students. This is important if you are thinking about buying an investment property for your children while they are studying, as, if you decide to let other rooms in the house to working people, your children may have to contribute towards the council tax bill, although they can apply for exemption (see Chapter 2 for more information about students and council tax).

Reducing your tax bill

In certain cases it is more tax efficient to buy the property in your child's name, especially if you hope to save on CGT and IHT. However, you can only do this if your child is aged 18 or over, as children under this age cannot legally own land or buildings.

If the property is in your children's name and they decide to let rooms in their home they could claim 'rent-a-room relief', which means that the first £4,250 of rent is exempt from income tax. This relief is available to individuals who let furnished rooms in their only or main home and therefore will be available to your child. More information about this relief can be obtained from www.direct.gov.uk.

If the property is in your name and you decide to let rooms to students, you will have to pay tax on any profit you make from letting your property if your total net income, including this profit, is more than your income tax allowance for the year (£6,475 in 2009/10). However, it is possible to offset any expenses such as fuel, insurance and maintenance costs against your rental income, if they are incurred when you are letting the property.

Avoiding pitfalls

If you are hoping to make money from property to pay for your child's university education, you must make sure that you make a profit on your

investment by avoiding common pitfalls. One of the positive outcomes from the present property market slump is that people have realised that investing in property does not automatically guarantee a large profit. Indeed, recently we have seen a massive increase in the number of homes and buy-to-let properties that have been repossessed.

The main reasons for this are that people have overstretched themselves financially and banks have been willing to loan large amounts of money that borrowers cannot afford to pay back. Also, people have bought unsuitable investment properties for too high a price. They have not conducted their market research, believing that tenants will come flocking to their door and pay the amount of rent that they require to cover the large mortgage. In certain areas, such as city centres dominated by apartment blocks, landlords have struggled to find tenants and apartments have remained empty, forcing a quick sale at a loss or leading to repossession.

Recent events illustrate the absolute importance of detailed market research if you hope to buy a second property to pay for your child's university education. You must have a thorough understanding of house prices in the area in which you wish to buy and you must understand how these prices might fluctuate over the term of your investment. Although it is not possible to know exactly what will happen in the future, you can make predictions based on careful and systematic market research.

You also need to become familiar with the area in which you wish to buy. If your child intends to study in a town or city about which you have no previous knowledge, your market research is all the more important. You must find out which are the most popular student areas, know how the market is performing in that area and know which areas to avoid. The students' union, accommodation office, local letting agents, estate agents, other landlords and housing staff at the local authority will be able to help you with this research.

Summary

Investing in property can be a lucrative source of finance to help to pay for your child's university education. However, comprehensive research has to be undertaken and wise decisions have to be made if you are going to make a successful investment and not lose out financially. This is of particular importance during times of market volatility. You also need to be

aware of the financial and tax implications, as an awareness of these can help to reduce your costs.

Another way that parents use property to pay for their child's university education is to raise cash from their family home. These issues are discussed in the following chapter.

Further information

More information about all aspects of property development, including maximising your returns from developing, letting and selling your property, can be obtained from another of my books: Dawson, C (2009) *The Complete Guide to Property Development for the Small Investor*, 3rd edn, Kogan Page, London.

If you are intending to invest in property for your children I have written a book that covers issues such as paying inheritance tax, estate planning, leaving property in trust and buying the right property: Dawson, C (2008) *Investing in Property for your Children*, Lawpack, London.

21 *Raising cash from your property*

In the previous chapter we saw how, with careful research and if you have the finances available, it is possible to invest in property to help to pay for your child's university education. However, this is not a viable option for some parents, perhaps because they are not working and are unable to secure a mortgage on another property, or perhaps because they don't have enough capital available to pay a deposit or stamp duty on a second property.

If you are unable or unwilling to purchase a second property, you may be thinking about raising money from your own home to help to pay for your child's university education. This may be a viable option for parents who have a considerable amount of equity tied up in their own home, but it is a decision that should not be taken lightly. Although there can be advantages, such as raising cash quickly for their education and helping to reduce your children's IHT liability when you die, there are disadvantages and pitfalls associated with this type of decision. These issues are discussed in this chapter.

Downsizing

If your children are about to go away to university you may feel that it is appropriate to sell your existing property and downsize to a smaller property. That way, you can use the sale of the larger property to raise cash to help to pay for your children's university education. However, you should find out whether they intend to come home during the vacations and perhaps after they have graduated. If you are happy with this arrangement you will need to make sure that you have space for them. If they live in university accommodation while they are studying, they may need to bring home all their possessions during vacations. Will you have room for this if you choose to downsize? (See quotation below.)

Mrs Peterson, Weymouth

Trevor was the last of our children to leave home so we decided we didn't need such a big place. The children come over on a Sunday, but they all have their own places so they don't stay over... So we sold up and bought a two bedroom bungalow... The extra money was so useful, especially as Alan had retired and we could give Trevor as much as he needed to see him through his studies. What we weren't quite expecting though was the amount of stuff he brought home every holiday. And it got more and more as his course went on. He only had the small room in the new place and all his stuff spilled out into the living room... But we didn't mind really. It was nice to have him home.

Some students return to the family home after they have finished their studies, deciding to find employment in their home town. Most of these students have to start to repay their student loan when they are earning over £15,000 a year and, because of the massive rise in house prices over recent years, they find it impossible to obtain a mortgage until they have worked and saved money for a number of years. Would you be happy for your children to return home after their studies, and would there be room for them to do so if you had downsized?

Before you choose to downsize, you also need to find out whether it is a financially viable option. You will have to pay stamp duty on any property you buy that is valued above the current threshold, and this could take a significant amount of the profit from your sale (see Chapter 20). Also, you will need to take into account moving and storage costs and mortgage arrangement fees (if relevant).

Valuing your home

To work out whether downsizing is financially viable, you need to obtain an accurate valuation for your own property. Invite estate agents to value your property; it is advisable to obtain quotations from at least three different agents as some will offer an enhanced valuation in the hope that you will do business with them. If you decide to use an estate agent, make

sure that they are registered with the National Association of Estate Agents or the Ombudsman for Estate Agents (details below), as they have to abide by a Code of Conduct and both organisations have a useful complaints procedure. Estate agents will charge anything from 1.5 to 4 per cent commission (VAT is added onto this price).

You should note, however, that estate agents are not fully trained surveyors and will not provide an accurate valuation. Therefore, it may be preferable to obtain the services of a professional surveyor. A surveyor experienced in this type of valuation in your area can be located by using the database available at www.ricsfirms.com.

You should also take into account aspects of the property that may increase the value: for example, what features do you have that are attractive to builders and developers such as location, a large garden and access to other land? If you have a large garden with access to the highway, it might be more profitable to sell the land separately. You can ask a much greater price for this land if you are able to obtain outline planning permission for a residential building on the plot. Advice about how to do this is offered in *The Complete Guide to Property Development for the Small Investor* (see Chapter 20).

Selling your home

If you have the time available, you can avoid paying commission to estate agents by selling the property yourself. If you use a property website, find out how much you need to pay, checking whether there is a one-off fee, commission and/or final charges when your property is sold.

You can erect a 'for sale' sign outside your home but you must comply with the Town and Country Planning (Control of Advertisements) Regulations 1992. In Scotland you must comply with the Town and Country Planning (Control of Advertisements) Regulations 1990. More information can be obtained from your local authority.

Releasing equity in your home

Releasing equity in your home can be a useful way of raising cash to help to pay for your child's university education. However, if you choose this option, make sure that you are in a secure financial position to release

equity safely, and check that you don't saddle your children with any unnecessary debt if you should die unexpectedly.

Recently there has been a great deal of media coverage about unsuitable and unethical equity release products. This has prompted the consumer group Which? to describe equity release products as 'expensive, inflexible and risky'. If you are thinking about following this route you must seek professional advice and make sure that you use a reputable organisation. Use the firm checker on the FSA website to check whether a firm is regulated and able to offer advice about equity release products (www.fsa.gov.uk/register).

There are four main types of equity release product that enable you to tap into the value of your home without having to sell, and these are described below. However, you should note that all equity release plans of this type should be approached with caution as you risk giving up a considerable amount of equity in return for what can be a small amount of money. Also, you must discuss all your plans with your children when they are old enough to understand the implications of your decisions. More information about equity release plans can be obtained from Safe Home Income Plans (SHIP) (www.ship-ltd.org). All SHIP plans carry a 'no negative equity' guarantee, which means that you will never owe more than the value of your home.

Home income plans

With this type of product a lender gives you a mortgage that you use to buy a lifetime income or annuity. Interest payments are taken from this income and the loan is paid off when your property is sold. You could use these payments to help to pay for your child's education, but if you should die unexpectedly your child may have to sell the family home to meet the obligations of the plan.

Home reversion plans

With this type of product a company buys a share of your home. When your property is sold the company takes its share from the proceeds of the sale. Over the last decade property prices have risen considerably. This has meant that the amount owed to the company has been substantial, which has led to problems with people who have inherited a property

being forced out of their home to repay the share of a plan taken out by their deceased parents or spouse. At this present time it is unclear how this situation could change as a result of the current slump in the property market. If you are elderly or suffering ill-health, you need to make sure that this decision would not leave your child without a family home, or their rightful inheritance, if you should die before your house is sold.

Interest-only mortgages

In this type of scheme a lump sum is loaned against the value of your property, which you could use to pay for up-front university costs such as tuition fees or accommodation. Interest on the mortgage is repaid monthly and the loan is repaid when the house is sold. With this type of agreement you must make sure that you have money invested elsewhere on which you can draw if the value of the property drops and you cannot pay off the loan. This is of particular importance during times of market uncertainty.

Lifetime mortgages

With this type of product a sum of money is borrowed, either as a lump sum or on a monthly basis (that is, an agreed monthly sum is released to you, as the borrower). You can use part of this sum to pay for your child's university costs, perhaps on a monthly basis if you choose this option. With this type of mortgage there are no monthly repayments to make as the interest is added to the loan and the whole amount is repaid when you die or move into long-term care, usually from the sale of the house. You should note that lifetime mortgages are a lifetime commitment and if you change your mind you may have to pay a substantial early repayment charge.

Remortgaging your home

Another way that you can raise money from your home to pay for your child's university education is to remortgage. In this present volatile market however, banks are much less willing to loan money, so you will need to prove that you are in a stable financial position and that your home is worth much more than the amount you hope to borrow. This may be a

viable option for you if you only have a small mortgage on your property, if you have already paid off your mortgage or if the value of your house is considerably more than the amount you initially borrowed.

If you think that remortgaging is a viable financial option, there are a variety of mortgage comparison websites that enable you to compare and contrast the best mortgage deals. These include www.moneymadeclear. fsa.gov.uk, www.moneysupermarket.com, www.fool.co.uk/mortgages and www.moneynet.co.uk. Shop around for the best deals and make sure that any lender you choose is an FSA-regulated firm (details above).

Understanding tax implications

If you are selling a home in which you have lived you will not have to pay any capital gains tax (CGT) on the profit that you make (see Chapter 20). However, you will have to pay stamp duty land tax (SDLT) on the new home that you buy, if it is above the SDLT threshold. Up-to-date SDLT figures are provided in Chapter 20.

One of the possible benefits to be gained by downsizing is that your child may have less of an inheritance tax (IHT) liability when you die. As we have seen in Chapter 17, IHT is paid on the estate of a person who has died if the taxable value of their estate is above £325,000 (2009/10 levels). This figure is known as the 'threshold' or 'nil rate band'. The tax is only paid on the part of the estate that is above this limit, and if your estate is worth less than the nil rate band there is no IHT to pay. This can be a large amount of money for your children to pay on your death, and in some cases it means that children have to sell the family home to be able to pay the tax bill. You can reduce this liability for your children if you reduce the value of your estate before you die, and one useful way to do this is to help to pay for their university education.

However, you should note that all gifts of money must be made within the IHT rules, which are discussed in Chapter 17. It is possible to help your child financially by arranging appropriate life insurance to cover your children's IHT liability. Comprehensive information and advice about all these issues can be found in *Investing in Property for your Children* (details in Chapter 20).

Avoiding pitfalls

The most common pitfalls associated with equity release and mortgage products are:

- failing to conduct adequate research to find the most suitable product for your needs;
- going ahead with the first product offered;
- failing to recognise market conditions, trends and prospects, and taking a product that is not suitable for these conditions;
- failing to read the small print;
- acting on unsuitable advice from a 'tied' adviser who can only offer advice about products from one company, whether or not this product is the most suitable for your needs;
- being persuaded by an unscrupulous, yet extremely persuasive, salesperson;
- failing to take out adequate insurance to cover you if you should lose your job, fall ill or get a divorce.

If you are thinking about releasing equity in your home or remortgaging, you must carry out comprehensive market research and/or seek independent professional advice (see useful organisations and websites below).

Summary

It is possible to raise money for your child's university education from your property. Ways of doing this include selling and downsizing to a smaller property, releasing equity in your home or remortgaging. However, all these courses of action should be approached with caution as there are many unsuitable products on the market. Also, you need to be aware of the financial implications for your child if you should die unexpectedly, and you need to check that market conditions are favourable for your plans. An awareness of tax implications is important, especially in terms of how your decisions could affect your child's IHT liability. If you are in any doubt you should seek appropriate professional advice.

This part of the book has discussed the ways that you, as parents, can invest, save and raise money to help to pay for your child's university education. Part Four goes on to consider ways that students themselves can help to pay for their education, beginning with earning money during a gap year.

Useful organisations

National Association of Estate Agents

The National Association of Estate Agents is the largest professional estate agency organisation in the United Kingdom. All members must operate to a professional code of practice. A list of members is available on the website.

National Association of Estate Agents
Arbon House
6 Tournament Court
Edgehill Drive
Warwick CV34 6LG
Tel: (01926) 496 800
Fax: (01926) 417 788
e-mail: info@naea.co.uk
www.naea.co.uk

The Ombudsman for Estate Agents

The Ombudsman for Estate Agents has been established to provide a free, fair and independent service to buyers and sellers of residential property in the United Kingdom. You can find contact details of members in your area from the website, access housing survey information and find out about its code of practice.

Ombudsman for Estate Agents
Beckett House
4 Bridge Street
Salisbury
Wilts SP1 2LX

Tel: (01722) 333 306
Fax: (01722) 332 296
e-mail: admin@oea.co.uk
www.oea.co.uk

The Council of Mortgage Lenders

The Council of Mortgage Lenders (CML) is the trade association for the mortgage-lending industry in the United Kingdom. The organisation provides a range of general information for the consumer, including guides about home buying and selling, equity release products, buy-to-let products and mortgage information.

Council of Mortgage Lenders
Bush House
North West Wing
Aldwych
London WC2B 4PJ
Tel: (0845) 373 6771
e-mail: info@cml.org.uk
www.cml.org.uk

The Society of Will Writers and Estate Planning Practitioners

The Society of Will Writers and Estate Planning Practitioners is a non-profit-making, self-regulatory organisation that seeks to protect the public and serve the interests of its members. You can use the members' directory on the website to search for a will writer or estate planner in your area.

The Society of Will Writers
Eagle House
Exchange Road
Lincoln LN6 3JZ
Tel: (01522) 68 78 88
e-mail: info@willwriters.com
www.thesocietyofwillwriters.co.uk

Useful websites

www.tax.org.uk

This is the website of the Chartered Institute of Taxation, the professional body for chartered tax advisers. You can search for a tax adviser by specialism in your area on this website.

Part Four

How can I pay, as a student?

22 Earning during a gap year

One of the ways that you can help to pay for your university education is to earn money during a gap year. In the traditional meaning of the phrase, a gap year is taken to be a year away from full-time study between the completion of full-time further education (usually A-levels, at school or at college) and before the start of full-time higher education. However, adult students are also beginning to take advantage of this type of earning potential, perhaps taking a break between different types of further or higher education course, sometimes dipping in and out of education while they earn enough money to pay for the next part of their course. In this chapter, therefore, 'gap year' is taken to mean any year taken out of full-time education for the purpose of earning money to pay for the next level of education.

This chapter offers advice for all types of student who are thinking about taking time away from their education, at whatever stage, to earn money to help them to pay for the next part of their course. It discusses the opportunities that are available, the levels of pay, national insurance and tax issues, and efficient savings strategies to make the most of wages earned during the gap year.

Knowing about types of work

There are many different gap-year working opportunities available. However, if you are hoping to save money to help you to pay for your university education, it is less likely that you will be able to consider the voluntary or low-paid opportunities that exist, however exciting these might be. You will also have to avoid programmes that require you to pay a fee to take part or require you to raise your own funds from sponsorship.

This type of project tends to include work with vulnerable groups, either in the United Kingdom or overseas.

Instead, you will need to consider gap-year opportunities that enable you to earn a higher salary that can be sensibly invested for your education. Also, you could choose to take advantage of work opportunities in areas that you may be thinking about considering for a future career. Indeed, it might be possible to persuade a gap-year employer to sponsor you through your studies if you would both be happy to continue your contract after you have graduated (see Chapter 24).

The type of work that you do depends on a number of factors, including the opportunities available in the area that you live or wish to work, your existing skills, talents, likes and dislikes, your personal motivation, current vacancies, current salary levels and perhaps a little bit of luck. Examples of the type of work that you could consider include:

- administration;
- secretarial;
- IT;
- trainee management/supervisory;
- retail;
- sales (in shops, offices or call centres);
- bar work;
- waiting and service;
- manufacturing (production lines, machine operating);
- fund-raising;
- any trainee role for a profession, such as accountancy or law, especially in cases where a company may be willing to sponsor you through your studies and/or offer you a job after you graduate.

> ## Dave, 21, Northamptonshire
>
> I knew I needed to earn as much as possible but there wasn't a lot going on in our village because it's fairly small. But I wanted to live with mum and dad because I knew they wouldn't ask for rent... When I did my A-levels I worked in the local chip shop and my boss said I could carry on if I wanted. Mum and dad thought that was rubbish. They said it wouldn't give me any proper work experience. But my boss trained me up... I worked as a fryer, a manager, I ordered stuff in, I did stock taking, I opened up and locked up. It was a lot of responsibility... I got a lot out of that job and had almost five grand in the bank when I started uni... My boss gave me a brilliant reference and now I'm a trainee manager in a posh restaurant.

Knowing about salary levels

Salary levels vary enormously, depending on the type of work that you undertake. The best-paid jobs tend to be those that require high-level qualifications, lengthy training and/or considerable talent. Obviously, if you are a school leaver, you will not have the qualifications or training required to obtain this kind of job. However, it may be possible to convince an employer that you have the required talent (or potential), even if you don't have the required experience and qualifications.

Some employers are willing to look favourably on applications from gap-year students, firstly because they can pay less than they would need to for a fully qualified employee, and secondly because they are employing you on a temporary basis and therefore do not need to assign you the same employment rights as someone on a permanent contract. You can use these points to your advantage when looking for suitable opportunities. Although you will be paid less then a fully qualified, permanent worker, you can still negotiate a decent salary that to you, if you are a school leaver, represents a considerably amount of money.

Table 22.1 illustrates the type of opportunities that may be available, taken from eight large employers based in Dorset. The employers were asked to think about the type of position within their company that could

realistically be offered to a gap-year student. They were then asked to provide information about how much they would pay a fully qualified, permanent member of staff, how much they would pay a gap-year student, whether they would be willing to sponsor such students through their studies, and whether they would be willing to take the students on as full-time employees once their studies were completed.

Table 22.1 Employment opportunities for gap-year students

Type of organisation	Position	Average salary for qualified employee	Average salary for gap-year employee	Would they offer sponsorship?	Would they employ after graduation?
Media group	Administration	£14,000	£10,000	No	Maybe
Local charity	Fund-raising	£15,500	£9,000	No	Yes (if good)
Retail group	Trainee manager	£20,295	£20,295	No	Yes
Law firm	Reception	£13,000	£10,000	No	Yes (if law)
IT company	Programmer	£18,000	£11,000	Maybe	Yes
PR company	Secretary	£18,000	£12,000	Yes	Yes
Travel firm	Representative	£15,500	£15,500	No	No
Manufacturer	Operator	£21,000	£12,000	No	Maybe

Paying tax

If you decide to take a gap year to earn money to pay for your university education, there are two types of tax that you will be liable to pay. The first is income tax, although your liability to pay will depend on how much you earn. The second is council tax, and this will have to be paid if you are not in full-time education and are living in England, Wales or Scotland.

Paying income tax

Income tax is paid by everyone who earns over a certain amount of money in the tax year. A tax year starts on 6 April and finishes on the following 5 April. People also pay income tax on interest earned from savings and

share dividends. Generally, the more you earn the more tax you pay. The money is used as a contribution towards government spending and is collected from employees through the Pay as You Earn (PAYE) system.

You will have to pay income tax if you earn over a certain amount of money even if your work is part time. In the tax year 2009/10 your personal allowance is £6,475. If you earn over this amount you will have to pay income tax. If you decide to take a gap year, you are treated like any other person and are liable to pay tax on any earnings above your personal allowance. However, your gap year is likely to straddle two tax years so you are entitled to a personal allowance for both years.

If you decide to work abroad during your gap year, you need to obtain information relevant to your specific circumstances. You can do this by telephoning the Centre for Non-Residents: (0845) 070 00 40.

Paying council tax

Although full-time students are exempt from council tax, if you take a gap year you will have to pay it. Some students, however, live in the parental home during their gap year and often parents are willing to pay all the tax themselves (see below). More information about council tax is provided in Chapter 2.

Paying National Insurance

National Insurance Contributions (NICs) are paid by most people who work, so if you work during your gap year you will have to pay NI. The contributions are used to help build up your entitlement to benefits such as Jobseeker's Allowance, Incapacity Benefit and State Pension. You only pay NICs on the income that you earn and this contribution is taken from your wages by your employer, before you receive your wages.

However, there is a 'primary threshold' of £110 per week (2009/10 figures). If you earn below this amount you will not have to pay NICs. There is also a lower earnings limit of £95 a week (2009/10 figures). If you earn between this limit and the 'primary threshold' you will be treated as having actually paid contributions on your weekly earnings. This means that even though you are not paying NICs you are building up your entitlement to benefits.

Saving your wages

If the goal is to earn as much money as you can during your gap year, you need to make sure that you save your money in the most efficient way – that is, the way that earns you the most interest – and that you spend as little as possible.

Many students who take a year off to earn money find that the cheapest way to do this is to obtain a job in their home town and live with their parents, who may be willing to charge a reduced rent or no rent at all. They may also be willing to provide food and pay for other living costs while you are working. Although you are liable to pay council tax, your parents have to pay this tax for their property anyway, and may be willing to pay for you while you are living at home and saving money for your university education.

However, this option may not be viable if there are no decent employment opportunities in your home town, if your parents are unable or unwilling to help you financially, or if you are too old to rely on your parents for help. In these cases you will have to make careful decisions about the jobs that are available, the salary that you will be paid and how much you will have to pay for living costs and on tax. Some people, especially mature students, choose to obtain employment in the town or city in which they intend to study. This means that they set up home only once, thus reducing costs, and are able to become familiar with the place in which they intend to study. Some are also able to continue working part time for their gap-year employer while they are studying.

Opening a bank account

If you intend to save as much money as possible while you are working, you will need to open a current account and a savings account. These do not have to be at the same bank so you should shop around for the best interest rates, which will be minimal on current accounts but higher on savings accounts. There are a number of websites that enable you to compare banks accounts, including www.yourbankingguide.co.uk, www.moneysupermarket.com and www.fool.co.uk. You may also find it useful to read the *Which?* review of student bank accounts, which can be found at www.which.co.uk.

There are other savings plans that may help you to save your earnings, such as cash or equity ISAs, or bonds (see Chapters 18 and 19). However, most of these perform better over the long term, and with the current economic crisis, many are not performing well at all. Therefore, you may find it preferable to place your wages in the savings account with the best interest rate that you can find at this time. If you are the type of person who can be a little reckless with their money, you should think about opening a savings account that needs notice before you withdraw your money. Interest rates tend to be higher on this type of account and it will give you chance to think about whether you really do need to withdraw the cash. However, you will need to make sure that you have enough cash readily available for day-to-day living costs and unexpected emergencies.

Summary

Many students decide to take a year from their studies so that they can earn and save money to pay for the next part of their education. There are many gap-year opportunities available, but it is important to choose those that are well paid and don't require a deposit or personal fund-raising to take part. In effect this means that you are treating your gap year as work placement or work experience, which will be useful information to include on your CV when you graduate. Salary levels vary considerably, depending on the type of job, type of employer, your skills and talents, and the location in which you live or decide to work.

Other students decide to work while they are studying to help fund their university education. This can include vacation work and part-time work during term. The opportunities that are available for this type of employment are discussed in the following chapter.

Useful websites

www.prospects.ac.uk

Prospects is an organisation that provides careers advice for graduate students. On this website you can find information about a variety of

organisations that offer year-long work placements, vacation placements, summer internships and trainee opportunities. Each listing provides information about the salary level, the skills required, the minimum number of UCAS points and degree expectations.

www.targetjobs.co.uk

This website has a useful database that you can search for all kinds of jobs, including short-term jobs for work experience. You can search the database by sector, keyword and region.

www.itraineeship.com

This website seeks to match graduates with international employers. It provides detailed listings of a variety of international employers, work and placement opportunities, including short and long-term contracts before, during and after your course.

www.topinternships.com

This website provides information on internships and placements for UK undergraduates. You can search the database by sector, discipline, date, location and keyword. You will need to register to view the results of your search.

23 *Undertaking part-time and vacation work*

As we have seen in the previous chapter, some students find that it is preferable to take a year out of studies to earn money for their university education. Others find that they prefer to work through the vacations and/ or while they are studying during term-time to help to see them financially through their studies.

If you choose to work while you are studying there are various positions available, some on campus and a wide variety off campus, and many of these will be advertised by university employment services. You also need to know about salary levels, understand working conditions and be aware of tax and national insurance issues. This information is provided in this chapter.

Knowing about student employment services

Research by the National Union of Students suggests that over 90 per cent of UK-based students work in paid employment during the vacations, with between 40 and 70 per cent working in paid employment at some point during the term-time. For some students this need to work is due to financial necessity, whereas for others the aim is to gain valuable work experience (see quotation below).

Angie, 24, Weymouth

Yes, I had to work... I just couldn't have afforded to do the course otherwise. I worked in a call centre, which suits me because I've the gift of the gab as you can probably tell. I got a basic wage and the commission on top... I worked for my first two years and then in the holidays... I didn't do any work in the final year but I'd saved enough money.

To meet the demand for student employment, universities have set up their own employment services. It is estimated that these employment services now provide access to working opportunities for over 120,000 students a year. Contact details of all these employment services can be obtained from the National Association of Student Employment Services (NASES) website (see below). Advisers in the employment services liaise with employers in the local area and advertise opportunities in their offices, via a newsletter and/or e-mail to individual registered students. However, the employment services are not agencies, so you will have to liaise with each prospective employer, apply for the job and be paid by the employer.

Many employment services have made an agreement to enable you, as a student, to access the services of another college or university to find employment. This is useful if you go home for the vacation and want to find part-time work.

Knowing about types of work

Over half of all employed students obtain jobs on campus. The following jobs are commonly available on university campuses throughout the United Kingdom:

- bar work, in students' union and university bars;
- glass collectors for students' union events, university events and outside events;

- waitresses/waiters for students' union or university restaurants, canteens and cafés;
- cooks/chefs;
- dish washers/loaders;
- cleaners for halls of residence, offices and teaching rooms;
- administrators for student finance or student accommodation;
- tour guides for new students, school parties, prospective students and parents;
- note-takers for students with hearing impairment or other relevant disability;
- mentors for new students or those experiencing learning difficulties;
- demonstrators for science subjects;
- lab assistants;
- research assistants;
- research participants;
- receptionists;
- security personnel, usually at entertainment events.

Popular jobs for students off campus tend to be in offices, pubs, cafés or restaurants. However, a major growth area in many parts of the country is in telesales and working for call centres. Many students are finding work in this sector as the working hours are flexible, with plenty of evening and weekend work available. Also, for those who are good at what they do, incentives and bonus schemes can mean that wages are increased considerably (see quotation above).

Working hours

The number of hours you decide to work is usually your own decision and will depend on how much time you can spare and how much money you need to earn. However, some universities have regulations about the number of hours a week you are able to spend in paid employment during term-time if you are a full-time student. These limits are imposed in an attempt to make sure that your employment does not have a detrimental impact on your studies. If you are thinking about obtaining a job you must find out whether your university has such regulations. Visit your students' union, student finance office or university employment service for more information.

Knowing about salary levels

On 1 October, 2008 the national minimum wage was set at £5.73 for adult workers aged 22 and over. The development rate for workers aged 18–21 inclusive was set at £4.77 an hour. If you are aged 16 or 17 years old (above the compulsory school leaving age) the rate has been set at £3.53. Decisions on whether this minimum wage is to be raised in October 2009 are yet to be made, but the British Chambers of Commerce (BCC) believes that it should be left at current levels in 2009 due to the economic downturn. This is a decision that would be extremely unpopular with relevant campaign groups and low-paid workers.

It is estimated that up to a quarter of all students in employment earn below the national minimum wage, so you should make sure you are not one of these people. If you obtain employment in which you are paid less than this amount, you can make a confidential complaint by ringing the National Minimum Wage Helpline (0845 6000 678). In April 2009 the Employment Act 2008 came into force and introduced a penalty payment for employers who don't pay a fair wage, and making it easier for compliance officers to make inspections.

Part-time wages vary considerably depending on the type of work that you do. Table 23.1 provides an example of student jobs and gives you an idea of the type of wages you can expect for working in different jobs within a variety of sectors. The table has been created from actual student jobs advertised by university employment services from around the United Kingdom (January, 2009).

Table 23.1 Student employment and salary levels

Employer	Type of job	Working hours	Wage (per hour)
FE college	Canteen staff	Part-time, flexible	£5.73
University	Bar staff	20 hours a week	£6.00
Students' union	Security staff	Events	£25.00 per event
Call centre	Sales	Part-time, flexible	£5.73 + bonuses
Town-centre shop	Sales staff	14 hours a week	£6.00
Fish-and-chip shop	Counter staff	Weekends	£5.73
Public house	Bar staff	Flexible	£6.00
Burger bar	Supervisor	25 hours a week	£7.50
Football ground	Hospitality	As required	£8.75
University	Note-taker	As required	£8.50 per lecture
Local charity	Fund-raiser	Flexible	Commission only
Valet firm	Car-washer	Weekends	£5.73

Knowing about working conditions

Nearly all workers, regardless of the hours they work and their age, have certain legal rights. The rights that are most relevant to you as a student employee include the following:

- The right to know the terms of your employment. If you have worked for an employer for less than two months these terms only have to be verbal. However, if you have worked for an employer for more than two months you should receive a written statement or contract of employment.
- The right to a payslip that shows what you have been paid and the deductions that have been made. This applies from the day that you start work.
- The right to be paid at least the minimum wage, which again applies from the day that you start work.
- The right to paid holiday. Full-time employees are entitled to at least 24 days a year, whereas part-time employees are entitled to a pro-rata amount, depending on the amount of hours that you work.
- The right under Health and Safety law to weekly and daily rest breaks. Adult workers (over the age of 18) are entitled to 11 hours' consecutive rest per day, and a minimum 20-minute rest break if their working day is longer than six hours. Adolescent workers (16–18 years old) are entitled to 12 hours' consecutive rest per day, and a minimum 30-minute rest break if they work for longer than four and a half hours. More information about health and safety at work can be obtained from www.hse.gov.uk/workers (England and Wales) and www.safeandhealthyworking.com (Scotland).

Paying income tax

As we saw in the previous chapter you will have to pay income tax if you earn over £6,475 a year, even if your work is part time (2009/10 figures). However, some sources of finance are not taxable and do not count towards this personal allowance.

For most students the following types of income are not taxable:

- student loans;
- maintenance grants;
- university bursaries;
- parental contributions;
- most educational grants from charities or trusts;
- Access to Learning Funds (England);
- Hardship Funds (Scotland);
- Support Funds (Northern Ireland);
- Financial Contingency Funds (Wales);
- prizes won by students for academic excellence;
- most scholarships;
- most research awards;
- most gifts and loans from relatives;
- income from Individual Savings Accounts (ISAs).

Taxable income

The most common types of taxable income for students are:

- earnings from full or part-time work, including tips and bonuses;
- income from self-employment;
- dividends from shares in a company;
- interest from some National Savings Accounts;
- interest from savings with a bank or building society.

However, if you earn below your personal allowance you do not have to pay income tax on the above and will be able to claim a refund if you are taxed at source. If you are working in the vacations and think your total taxable income in the whole tax year is going to be less than your personal allowance of £6,475, you need to ask your employer for a form P38(S). Once you have filled in this form and returned it to your employer, you should be paid without the deduction of tax. However, this form applies only to vacation work. If you are employed regularly in part-time work throughout the year, you will have to claim back any tax you have over-paid at the end of the tax year.

Claiming a refund

When you start to pay income tax it is important to keep all records of every transaction. You will need these to prove that you have overpaid and are due a refund. You should file the following items in a safe place:

- all payslips;
- any P60 or P45 forms you are given;
- bank statements detailing income received and tax paid;
- share dividend statements (if relevant).

If you think you have overpaid, ask you tax office for a repayment claim form P50 or download a form from www.hmrc.gov.uk. Alternatively, you can ask your tax office to review your case at the end of the tax year. This is often a good idea if you think you might get another short, part-time or Christmas job before the end of the tax year. Remember to keep any P45 you receive from an employer once you have finished a job.

Tax is taken off any savings you might have, so remember to claim a refund on this tax if you have overpaid. However, if you know you are going to earn below your personal allowance in a tax year, you can request from R85 from your bank or building society. Once you have completed this form you will be paid interest without the deduction of tax. When you open a student bank account, most good advisers will give you this form. If you start earning more than your personal allowance you must inform your bank or building society so that tax can be deducted from your account.

Reducing income tax

There are a number of ways that you can reduce the amount of income tax you pay as a student:

- Try to obtain money from the non-taxable sources listed above.
- Boost income from non-taxable sources by earning just below your personal allowance of £6,475.
- Keep track of your income tax expenditure and make sure that you claim any refund due to you, including tax you have paid on savings and earnings.

● Make the most of the tax-free Individual Savings Accounts if you have money to invest. If you choose to do this, seek the advice of a professional as there are a variety of different ISA products on the market and you need to make sure that you invest your money in the most appropriate product for your needs.

Paying National Insurance

National Insurance is a tax levied on wages and salaries in the United Kingdom that is used to finance state benefits. As you approach the age of 16 you are issued with a National Insurance card by HM Revenue & Customs. This contains your unique NI number. This is an important number and will be needed should you obtain a part-time job or wish to contact HM Revenue & Customs. When you begin working your employer will ask you to supply your NI number. Your employer is responsible for collecting your contributions and will deduct them from your pay, usually at the same time as Income tax is deducted. Different rules apply if you are self-employed, and these are discussed in Chapter 26.

People only pay National Insurance Contributions on the income that they earn. As a student this will be from vacation work, part time work or self-employment. Income from other sources such as grants, loans and hardship funds does not count as earned income. If you do not undertake any paid employment, you will not have to make NICs while you are a full-time student. For information about the primary threshold and lower earnings limit, see Chapter 22.

Summary

Many students find that they have to obtain part-time and/or vacation work to help them to pay for their university education. Some also find this valuable work experience that helps them to obtain a job after graduation. Jobs can be obtained in a variety of sectors, with many opportunities available on university campus or within the local town or city centre. Wages vary considerably, but you should make sure that you are paid at least the amount specified as the minimum wage. If you earn over your

personal income tax allowance you will have to pay income tax. NI contributions will have to be paid if you earn over £110 a week.

In addition to earning money to fund your studies, you may be able to obtain additional funds from sponsors. These issues are discussed in the following chapter.

Further information

Further information about all aspects of income tax can be obtained from www.hmrc.gov.uk/students. A student tax checker is available on this site and all the forms that you may require are available for download.

Useful websites

www.nases.org.uk

The National Association of Student Employment Services (NASES) is the national representative body for practitioners from all styles of student employment services. On the NASES website you can find an alphabetical list of student employment services in universities throughout the country. The website contains information leaflets covering issues such as applying for jobs, income tax and national insurance.

www.direct.gov.uk

More information about your employment rights and the national minimum wage can be obtained from this website.

24 *Obtaining sponsorship*

Obtaining sponsorship can be a useful way to pay for your university studies. There are various opportunities available, including sponsorship for sports and sponsorship by a potential employer. The opportunities vary considerably and depend, in part, on the course that you wish to study at university and what you hope to do after you graduate. These funding opportunities are discussed in this chapter.

Sponsorship for sports

Individual scholarships and bursaries are available for students who display exceptional talent for their chosen sport. Some of these bursaries are offered as part of the university bursary scheme (see Chapter 12), while others are special scholarships that are funded by universities, private organisations and/or alumni (previous students of the university).

Eligibility criteria, application procedures and amounts of funding vary according to the type of bursary or scholarship, with amounts usually ranging between £500 and £4,000 per annum. Most bursaries will be offered on the basis of financial need, performance, actual skill or expected potential. Individual bursaries and scholarships are designed to help with some or all of the following:

- to enable access to training and coaching facilities;
- to help with travel costs and other costs associated with competition;
- to ensure that the required academic support is available;
- to ensure that students are able to concentrate on their sports and studies, and not worry about lack of finance.

A **Balfour Beatty** Company

Balfour Beatty
Construction

Want a degree – but don't want the debt?

Then choose a part time degree and earn while you learn.

Commercial/Engineering Trainees

Trainees have the opportunity to:

- graduate with money in the bank, not in debt
- gain excellent experience
- obtain a professional qualification
- move upwards into management

Balfour Beatty Construction Ltd. is a leading player in one of the UK's largest and most dynamic industries – Construction. We build major projects for both the public sector – such as hospitals and schools – and the private sector – such as offices and retail developments.

There are exciting opportunities for suitably qualified individuals to work on a wide range of building projects in their local area with an innovative and growing company and be able to study for a degree on a day release basis.

Trainee Engineers

You would work on site and play a key role in ensuring that our projects are built to the correct dimensional accuracy and planning and supervising the work of sub-contractors.

Commercial Management Trainees

You would work as a Quantity Surveyor, managing the commercial and legal aspects of a construction site, making sure costs are controlled and that our clients are getting value for money.

Both these positions include full structured and accredited on-the-job training and the opportunity to study for a part-time Degree in Civil Engineering, Construction Management or Quantity Surveying. After your degree, you will be supported all the way to Chartered Surveyor, Engineer or Builder status.

To join us you will need good A levels/ Highers/ Construction AVCE (230+ UCAS points), or ONC/ HNC in a Construction-related subject.

We offer a competitive salary, funding for college study and an interesting and diverse career path leading to managerial responsibility.

Please send a CV and covering letter by e-mail to student.recruitment@bbcl.co.uk quoting ref: TJE/WN/07.

For more information visit www.bbcl.co.uk

INVESTOR IN PEOPLE

Balfour Beatty is an equal opportunity employer

WANT A DEGREE, BUT DON'T WANT THE DEBT?

Rather than graduating after a degree owing thousands of pounds, there is now an exciting alternative. After your A-levels or Highers, you could join a prestigious company in full-time employment and study for a degree on a part-time basis.

The construction industry is the UK's biggest single industry, responsible for 10% of GDP and employing 1 in 9 of the working population.

By joining Balfour Beatty Construction you could work on a construction site in a management training scheme for four days a week and attend university the other day. It takes 5 years to get a degree – only one year longer than a full-time sandwich degree – and you would gain an enormous amount of work experience. Your tuition fees are paid and you receive a competitive and rising salary

Trainees will develop their career during their training and will continue into management after qualifying as a Chartered Builder, Engineer or Surveyor. The final goal is Project Management – being responsible for turning an empty field into a new hospital, school or office!

The scheme gives young people the opportunity to both gain a degree and lots of work experience without having to suffer the financial hardships associated with full-time study today. The construction industry is booming and there are lots of long term opportunities to join a dynamic and interesting industry in which you can move up the management ladder quickly.

Balfour Beatty Construction manages the construction of building for both the public and private sectors throughout the UK. Annual turnover is over £600 million and we are part of the Balfour Beatty Group – a £7 billion turnover international construction, engineering and services company.

Opportunities are available across the North of England and Midlands.

Consult the websites or prospectuses of universities in which you are interested for more information. Most universities will not accept an application until you have been offered a firm place at the university. However, you should apply before the start of the academic term to make sure that payments are made as soon as possible.

Company sponsorship

Some companies are willing to sponsor students through their studies by providing an agreed sum of money for one, two, three or four years of study. Contracts will vary considerably. If a company offers a significant amount of money, you will be expected to work for it for a certain number of years after completing your studies.

However, this type of sponsorship is now quite rare. Instead, companies tend to offer smaller sums, providing working opportunities through vacations and during sandwich years or placements. This type of sponsorship tends not to tie you into working for the company once you have graduated, although many students find that they are offered a job on successful completion of their course. Indeed, the 'Everything you Wanted to Know' website points out that many companies take 60 per cent or more of their graduate intake each year from students who have been on sponsorship or placement programmes (details below).

In general, companies are interested in vocational courses or those that provide the opportunity for work placement. The following subject areas tend to receive the most sponsorship:

- engineering;
- sciences (particularly physics);
- information technology and computing;
- financial management;
- business management;
- banking;
- economics;
- medicine;
- dentistry.

Many of the big companies, especially in construction, banking and accountancy, offer sponsorship; consult their websites, or contact them direct for more information. Professional bodies, such as the Institution of Civil Engineers (details below), will offer sponsorship deals, as will some government departments. Details of this type of scheme can be found on the Hot Courses 'Scholarship Search' website (details below). Armed Services sponsorship is available with the Army, Royal Air Force, Royal Navy and Royal Marines (see below).

Amount of funding

The amount of money offered varies enormously, and will depend on what you and the company want to get out of the agreement. Some students may receive a large sum that is enough to cover tuition fees and living expenses for three or four years; in some cases this may be up to £9,000 a year. If you receive this type of sponsorship, the company will need to make sure that you pay back what you have been given in terms of how long you work for it after graduation. You will need to sign a contract in which you agree to their terms and conditions, so you must check that you are happy with these before you sign.

Other companies will give small amounts of money, maybe for specific projects, or for only one year of study. This could be any amount up to £3,000. In these circumstances you may not be tied into a long-term contract with the company.

Making an application

Most companies will want to know that you have been offered a university place before they will consider sponsoring you. However, some companies work closely with specific universities so, if you know that you want to follow this route, contact the company in which you are interested prior to making your UCAS application. That way you can make sure that your choice of university and course is suitable for the company.

Applying for sponsorship is similar to applying for a job, especially if you will be working for that company during the vacations or when you have completed your studies. You will need to show that you are keen to work for the company, are committed to your studies and will not break

any contract that you have signed. Application procedures vary from company to company, but in general you will need to complete an application form and attend a selection interview (see quotation below).

> ## Rory, 20, third-year student, Bournemouth
>
> There was me and nine other people. We had to go for a whole day and do all sorts of things... we had a tour then we split into pairs [to] do some weird tasks, you know, like build a bridge with match sticks. There were four people watching us all the time... Then we had a meal and met people on the graduate programme and talked to them. Then we had a test and then we had individual interviews... I got offered a place so I had to work for them in the summer and then they gave me £3,500 for my final year... I will work for them when I finish.

Armed Services sponsorship

If you are sponsored by the Armed Services you will be expected to serve for a set period of time after graduation. Also, you may be expected to attend weekend training sessions and summer camps while you are studying at university. If you leave any one of the Armed Services before the service commitment is concluded, you can be asked to repay the whole of the cash advance. There are several types of sponsorship available, as described below.

The Defence Technical Undergraduate Scheme

The Defence Technical Undergraduate Scheme (DTUS) is run jointly by the Royal Air Force, the Royal Navy, the Army and the MOD Civil Service. The scheme is available to undergraduates studying an accredited engineering or scientific degree course at one of the following universities:

- University of Southampton;
- University of Newcastle-upon-Tyne;
- Aston University;
- Northumbria University;

- Loughborough University;
- University College London;
- University of Oxford;
- University of Cambridge.

As an undergraduate on the scheme, you are offered a bursary of £4,000 for each year of your studies, an additional grant of £33 to pay for you to attend the Support Unit within the university and a salary of £14,025 per year (pro rata) for work placement during the summer vacations (2009 figures). You (or your parents or guardians if you are under 18) must agree to pay back the money if you fail to complete your studies or leave your chosen Armed Service before serving three years (unless you leave due to medical reasons).

For more information about the scheme, including eligibility criteria, visit www.desg.mod.uk. Application forms and tutor reference forms can be downloaded from this site.

Royal Air Force sponsorship

The Royal Air Force offers five types of funding, in addition to the DTUS described above, for students who want to continue their studies and are interested in a career with the RAF:

- A sixth-form scholarship of up to £2,000 is available for upper sixth-form students who wish to become RAF officers.
- Free tuition and a maintenance grant are available for students from low-income families who decide to study for their A-levels at the Defence Sixth Form College at Welbeck. Visit www.welbeck.mod.uk for more information about the college and the funding that is available.
- University sponsorship of up to £4,000 is available to university undergraduates who are preparing for a career in the RAF.
- Medical sponsorship of up to £50,000 for the whole course is offered to students who are studying to be doctors before joining the RAF.
- Dental sponsorship of up to £30,000 for the whole course is available for students who are studying to be dentists before joining the RAF.

For more information about careers in the RAF and sponsorship deals, visit www.rafcareers.com. If you wish to speak to a careers adviser you can telephone (0845) 605 5555. Alternatively, contact the Armed Forces Careers Liaison Officer via careers staff at your school or your local Connexions office.

Royal Navy sponsorship

There are five types of sponsorship, in addition to the DTUS described above, available for students who want to continue with their studies and are intending to join the Navy:

- A scholarship of £1,050 per year is available for A-level students who intend to serve as officers in the Navy once they have completed their studies. If you are in receipt of this sponsorship you can go on to apply for a bursary during your studies at university.
- A standard bursary of £1,500 per year is available for university students in the arts who wish to join the Royal Navy once they have completed their studies. The bursary is available for each year of study and does not limit you to a particular area of study.
- Technical bursaries of £4,000 per year are offered to students who wish to study an engineering subject at university and then join the Navy once they have completed their studies.
- A university cadetship is available for people who really want to join the Navy and who decide to become officers before studying for their degree. You have to complete one full year of naval training before beginning your degree course and you are paid an annual salary during your studies.
- Medical and dental cadetships are available for medical and dental students on accredited degree courses. This scheme pays a 'substantial' salary for the last three years of study.

More information about sponsorship by the Royal Navy can be obtained from www.careers.royalnavy.mod.uk. Alternatively, you can request specific information and advice by ringing the Recruitment Line on (08456) 07 55 55.

Army sponsorship

There are five types of funding available to students who want to continue with their studies and intend to enter the Army:

- The Army FE Bursary Scheme offers £4,000 (£1,000 each year for up to three years and £1,000 on completion of the first stage of Army training) to students aged 16–32 who are thinking about going into further education. You will be prepared for work in the Army while you study and will be required to commit to serving for four years in the Army when you have finished your course.
- The Army sixth-form scholarship provides your parents with £1,500 per year while you complete your last two years of schooling. You are guaranteed acceptance at the Royal Military Academy Sandhurst (RMAS) and must complete three years in commissioned service.
- The Army Undergraduate Bursary of £6,000 for a three-year course, £7,000 for a four-year course or £8,000 for a five-year course is offered to students who wish to study for a degree and who are willing to commit themselves to a minimum of three years in service after they have graduated. In addition to this you will need to attend the 44-week officer-training course at the RMAS.
- Welbeck College is the Army's sixth-form college. It offers a two-year residential A-level course for students who wish to enter one of the technical branches of the Army. Tuition is free, although a means-tested parental contribution will be required. Membership of the Combined Cadet Force is compulsory, but you will remain a civilian while you are studying at the college. For more information visit www.welbeck.mod.uk.
- The Army Undergraduate Cadetship Scheme offers an annual salary of around £14,000 for the last three years of study and a book allowance of £150 for applicants interested in joining the Army as doctors, dentists, nurses or veterinary surgeons.

For general information about the range of opportunities in the Army, you can telephone (08457) 300 111. For information about joining the Army as an officer and for sponsorship opportunities, visit your local Army Careers Office or consult www.armyjobs.mod.uk.

Summary

There are a variety of organisations that offer sponsorship for your university studies. These include private companies, professional bodies and the armed services. Eligibility criteria and application procedures vary, so contact the organisation in which you are interested for more information specific to your circumstances. If you are a talented sportsperson, contact individual universities to find out what sponsorship is available for your chosen sport.

It is possible to obtain additional funds for university study from a variety of local and national educational trusts and charities. These issues are discussed in the following chapter.

Further information

The *Sponsorship and Funding Directory* (published by Hobsons) lists scholarships and sponsorship available for students. It should be available in your public library or from your school careers office.

Useful websites

www.connexions-direct.com

More information about sponsorship and the opportunities on offer to school leavers wishing to continue their education is available on this site. Alternatively, visit your local connexions adviser for more information.

www.scholarship-search.org.uk

Visit the 'sponsorship' section of the Hot Courses website to find out what opportunities are available. The listings provide details of the amount of sponsorship, duration, application opening and closing dates, number of awards and subject area. There is also a link to the relevant sponsor's website.

www.everythingyouwantedtoknow.com

Visit the 'job/placement' section of this site to find out about sponsorship, placement and graduate opportunities.

www.ice.org.uk

This is the website of the Institution of Civil Engineers. Here you can find more information about their undergraduate scholarship scheme, which currently offers £3,000 per year and work placements during the summer vacation.

25 *Obtaining trust or charity funding*

Throughout the United Kingdom there are a number of local and national educational trusts and charities that offer bursaries and grants for study at university. The funds have been set aside by individuals or corporations to help specific kinds of people, and may be available to help with costs such as maintenance, fees, books, equipment, childcare, travel and field trips. This chapter offers advice about applying for trust and charity funding, and includes information about three national trusts: The Helena Kennedy Foundation, the Leverhulme Trade Charities Trust and the Gilchrist Education Trust.

Obtaining money from trusts and charities

The amount of money offered by trusts varies considerably. For example, some might agree to help you with your travel expenses, perhaps up to £300 per year, while others may agree to pay your tuition fees throughout your course. You will need to contact each trust individually to find out how much money it can provide. To find out about local trusts and charities that may be able to provide funds in your area, contact your LA, ELB, local clergy or parish council. To find out about national trusts, consult the publications and databases listed at the end of this chapter.

If you decide to apply to an educational trust or charity, you should first of all make sure that you have exhausted all sources of statutory funding (see Chapters 8, 9, 10 and 11). Trusts and charities will want to know that you have done this and will ask for details of any refusals. Most have quite specific eligibility criteria so check that you meet these criteria before making your application (see quotation below).

> ### Beverley, 32, Norwich
>
> I found a charity in a whacking great book in the library. It said they funded women writers and I was doing a writing course at the time. I really was skint so I contacted them, got an application form and filled it in. Five months later I found out I'd been unsuccessful... Turns out they didn't give money for studies, only for people who were working as writers. I should've found that out before I wasted time filling in the form.

Most trusts and charities will provide an application form. When you fill in this form, tailor your application to suit the charity and make sure that you provide all the details requested. You should note, however, that funds are limited and competition for these funds can be fierce. Don't get too disheartened if you are unsuccessful, but move on to another trust or charity. Remember that you can also apply for university hardship funds once you have started your course, if you are facing serious financial hardship (see Chapters 8, 9, 10 and 11).

The Helena Kennedy Foundation

The Helena Kennedy Foundation was launched in 1998. It is a registered educational charity established to encourage social inclusion and wider participation in further and higher education. It supports disadvantaged students who have overcome significant barriers to continue with their education. These may be students who are 'in transition', emotionally and/or geographically, and those who are facing severe financial hardship and cultural disadvantage.

The Foundation awards single bursaries of £1,500 (2009 figures), which are paid in two instalments, to successful students. It also provides person-alised student support to the recipients of the bursary. This includes maintaining regular support with students, helping to find accommodation, providing references and finding work and voluntary opportunities for students.

Eligibility criteria and application procedures

To be eligible for a bursary you must be in the final year of study at a publicly funded further education college and aim to move on to higher education. This must be your first time in higher education and you must be anticipating financial difficulty. There is no age or nationality restriction. Bursaries are not available for postgraduate courses, international study or courses at private institutions.

The Foundation receives at least 1,500 applications each year, so competition is strong. You should familiarise yourself with the eligibility criteria and make sure that you provide all the required information to increase your chances of success.

Application forms can be obtained from the Foundation (details below) or downloaded from their website. Only official application forms will be accepted and the Foundation asks that you don't send speculative application letters. Applications are accepted from January, with the closing date usually at the end of March. Specific dates are clearly displayed on the website.

The Leverhulme Trade Charities Trust

A limited number of bursaries are offered through the Leverhulme Trade Charities Trust to undergraduates who are the son, daughter, spouse, widow or widower of someone engaged in one of the three trades listed below:

- *Commercial travellers*: this includes sales representatives or agents of companies who sell to industry or commerce, but not to the general public. They will need to have travelled for five consecutive years for at least six months in each of those years for the purpose of securing orders and/or promoting business.
- *Chemists*: this includes any member of the Royal Pharmaceutical Society engaged in selling or dispensing medicines direct to the public.
- *Grocers*: this includes people who are engaged or employed in the retail sale of groceries and related provisions. It excludes people who own or are employed by a business having more than 50 employees.

Funds are intended for those in financial hardship and can be used for maintenance, tuition and examination fees, travel, study materials, accommodation or childcare. The maximum amount you can be awarded is £3,000 per year (2009 figures). This sum will be adjusted according to your individual circumstances and needs, and the funds available. The annual bursary is available for the duration of the course although payments will not be backdated. Funds are distributed to the university and not to individual students.

Eligibility criteria and application procedures

To be eligible for an award, you must be the son, daughter, spouse, widow or widower of a commercial traveller, chemist or grocer. Bursaries will not be awarded to individuals outside these three categories. You must register for a full-time degree course at a recognised UK institution.

Application forms may be available from your university or can be downloaded from the Trust website (details below). You must complete the application form and return it to your university so that it can be countersigned and returned to the Trust. Applications must reach the Leverhulme Trust by 1 November or 1 March. Universities will be notified of the result of applications by the end of November or the end of March, depending on when the form is sent.

The Gilchrist Education Trust

This trust was set up in the 19th century 'for the benefit, advancement and propagation of education and learning in every part of the world as far as circumstances will permit'. Through this trust, individual grants of various amounts are offered to higher education students who are facing serious financial difficulty (in 2008 the average grant was £873). Grants are also paid to students who are required to spend a short period of study in another country (in 2008 the average grant was £465).

Eligibility criteria and application procedures

Students must be studying full time and funds will not be available for students seeking funds to help pay for dependants. Application forms will

be sent to eligible students who make enquires to the Trust and can be submitted at any time of the year. All forms must be submitted by post: e-mail applications will not be accepted. Contact the Trust for more information and to receive an application form (details below).

Summary

Funds may be available through educational trusts and charities to help with the cost of university. However, funds tend to be limited, so you need to make sure that you apply only to relevant organisations and that you meet the eligibility criteria. In most cases you will need to make sure that you have applied for all types of government support before applying to the trust or charity.

Another way that students can help to pay for their university education is to set up their own business and become student entrepreneurs while they are studying. These issues are discussed in the following chapter.

Further information

Visit your local public library or university library to find out whether they subscribe to FunderFinder. This is a UK charity producing software and other resources, mainly for grant-seekers. More information about this database can be obtained from www.funderfinder.org.uk, although you will not be able to access the search facility. This website contains useful information and advice about searching for funding from charities and trusts.

Your public library or university library should hold copies of publications such as the *Charities Digest*, the *Grants Register*, the *Directory of Grant Making Trusts* and the *Educational Grants Directory*. These all contain listings of local and national trusts that may be able to provide funds to help with your studies.

Further information about educational trusts and charities can be obtained from the National Union of Students: www.nus.org.uk.

Useful organisations

Educational Grants Advisory Service

The Educational Grants Advisory Service is an independent advice agency for people who want to obtain funding for post-16 education. More information can be obtained from:

Educational Grants Advisory Service (EGAS)
501–505 Kingsland Road
Dalston
London E8 4AU
Student advice line: (020) 7254 6251 (open Tuesday, Wednesday and Thursday, 2 pm to 4 pm)
www.family-action.org.uk

The Helena Kennedy Foundation

More information about the bursaries and personal support offered by this trust can be obtained from the following address and website:

Helena Kennedy Foundation
The Mansion
Bletchley Park
Bletchley
Milton Keynes MK3 6EB
Tel: (01908) 363452
e-mail: admin@hkf.org.uk
www.hkf.org.uk

The Leverhulme Trade Charities Trust

Although the Leverhulme Trade Charities Trust operates separately from the Leverhulme Trust, it shares the same offices. Information about other grants, awards and bursaries available from the Trust can be obtained from these offices and websites:

The Leverhulme Trust
1 Pemberton Row
London EC4A 3BG
Tel: (020) 7822 5227
Fax: (020) 7882 5084
e-mail: enquiries@leverhulme.org.uk
www.leverhulme-trade.org.uk
www.leverhulme.ac.uk

The Gilchrist Education Trust

More information about grants for individual students can be obtained from the following address:

The Gilchrist Education Trust
13 Brookfield Avenue,
Larkfield,
Aylesford ME20 6RU
e-mail: gilchrist.et@blueyonder.co.uk
www.gilchristgrants.org.uk

Useful websites

www.studentcashpoint.co.uk

This site claims to be the United Kingdom's most comprehensive source of information on student grants, loans, bursaries, scholarships and awards. On this site you can find out about trusts and grants that provide money for individual students. You will need to register to use the service.

26 *Becoming a student entrepreneur*

One way that enterprising students raise money to pay for their university education is to become student entrepreneurs, which can be done before their studies begin or while they are studying at university. Many students find this a rewarding activity that can help them in their future working life.

Today, student entrepreneurship is becoming increasingly popular, with more organisations being set up both within and outside universities to help students with their endeavours. If you are interested in becoming a student entrepreneur you need to assess the feasibility and develop your idea, work out your finances, consider tax issues, build your business effectively, and successfully manage your business and studies. These issues are discussed in this chapter.

Assessing the feasibility

A useful way to assess the feasibility of your idea is to ask the five 'W' questions:

- *What* is your idea? *What* kind of business do you need to set up to develop your idea?
- *Why* is your idea a good one? *Why* would people pay for your product/ service?
- *When* is the best time to start your business? *When* will your customers be available and will this fit in with your university plans? *When* will be the best time to generate sales?
- *Where* is the best place to establish your business? Does this fit in with where you intend to study? Will your customers be available in this location?

● *Who* are your customers? Will these people be willing and able to pay for your product/services?

Conducting a risk assessment

Once you have assessed the feasibility of your idea, you should carry out a risk assessment. This is a careful examination of what could go wrong and cause harm, whether this is physical, such as injuries and damage, or emotional, such as stress and anxiety. This will help you to make sure that your student entrepreneurship does not have an adverse influence on your studies. An example risk assessment is produced in Table 26.1.

Table 26.1 Conducting a risk assessment

Risk	Action
Problems with too much work	Plan business carefully
	Assess course needs
	Find out if the university has regulations about working hours
	Choose a business that will complement/add to coursework
	Find out if you can obtain credits for your business that contribute to your course credits
Lack of knowledge/skills	Utilise expertise at university
	Visit the student entrepreneur office for advice
	Join the entrepreneur society and network
	Take advantage of free courses
	Use professionals where appropriate and if financially viable
Administrative problems	Install good IT equipment with anti-virus software
	Use the services of a reliable, competent IT company or individual
	Develop appropriate skills or employ skilled administrator
	Back-up records and store safely
	Keep administration neat and orderly

Risk	Action
Financial loss	Conduct thorough market research
	Produce comprehensive profit/loss plan and cash flow forecast
	Don't go over budget
	Make sure appropriate finance is available
	Develop appropriate financial skills
Misunderstandings/ arguments	Plan and discuss everything thoroughly
	Involve significant others/partners in all discussions
	Negotiate/delegate appropriately
	Obtain agreements in writing
	Ensure all contracts are clear and legally binding
Personal injury	Carry out health and safety risk assessment (employ a professional if in doubt)
	Learn and adhere to rules and regulations
	Obtain appropriate insurance
	Employ qualified, competent, insured workers
Theft/burglary	Obtain insurance
	Install appropriate security devices
	Don't leave stock/equipment where it can be taken

Through careful planning at the outset you will more aware of what could go wrong with your project and you will be better able to tackle the problems when they arise. Some problems cannot be avoided, but if you are aware that these problems may occur, and you have appropriate insurance to cover yourself (and others, if relevant), you and/or your business will not suffer financially.

Developing your idea

Once you have addressed the five 'W' questions and carried out a risk assessment, you can go on to think about how you intend to develop your idea. The first thing you need to do is to produce a business plan that can be taken to possible funders. This should contain the following sections:

- *Summary*: this should include an introduction to your business and a financial overview.
- *Management*: who is to manage your business and what are their/your qualifications and experience? If you are setting up the business on your own, you will be the manager. If you intend to set up the business with someone else you need to discuss this issue carefully and make sure that you and your partner agree, and are happy, with the allocation of roles.
- *Product/service*: this will include a description of the product/service you intend to offer and some information about numbers/volume.
- *Marketing*: how do you intend to market your business? Who are your competitors? What is your customer profile?
- *Sales*: what is the unique selling point? What advertising and promotion work do you expect to undertake? What are the costs of this work?
- *Operational*: what equipment will be required? Who is going to undertake the day-to-day running of the business? What are the costs involved?
- *Short-term trading*: what are your short-term objectives? What contingency plans do you have in place in case of problems?
- *Financial documents*: these will include your profit/loss plan and cash flow forecast (see below).

Deciding how to trade

All student entrepreneurs need to think about how they are going to trade. There are three main ways of trading: as a sole trader, in a partnership or as a limited company. Different rules and regulations apply to each method of trading, and you should seek advice about the method most appropriate to your personal circumstances. Comprehensive information and advice about all aspects of setting up a business, including personal advice, can be obtained from your local Business Link. To obtain contact details and more information, visit www.businesslink.gov.uk.

A sole trader

Setting up as a sole trader is the simplest and most common way of running a business as there are fewer legal requirements involved. However, as a sole trader you are personally liable for any losses your business makes and creditors can pursue you for both business and personal assets.

A partnership

If you intend to set up your company with someone else, you could think about setting up a partnership. With this type of agreement, you and your partner share the risks, costs and responsibilities of being in business. You are both self-employed and take a share of the profits. However, you are both also personally responsible for any debts that the business runs up. If you do decide to work with a partner, choose someone who is able to bring something useful to the partnership. This could be financial backing or knowledge and skills that you don't possess. However, you need to think carefully about going into business with friends and family: what would happen to your relationship if things go wrong?

A limited company

There are two types of limited company. A private limited company is the most typical set-up for small businesses in the United Kingdom. It cannot offer shares to the public, but can have private shareholders. A public limited company, on the other hand, is permitted to sell shares to the public and raise funds in this way. Although legal requirements, rules, regulations and paperwork are more complex when setting up a limited company, your personal assets are safe in most cases. To set up a limited company, contact Companies House (see below).

Sorting out your finances

Part of your business plan will involve a careful assessment of your finances. If you are setting up a business to help pay your way through university, you need to make sure that you make enough money to cover university costs without adversely affecting your studies. To do this you

should produce a profit/loss plan and a cash flow forecast. A profit/loss plan is a careful assessment of what you expect to happen with the income and expenditure of your business and will help you to determine whether your project is feasible. A cash flow forecast will show you how much money you need to set up and run your business.

To produce a profit/loss plan you will have to familiarise yourself with the relevant market and work out all the costs involved before you start your business. This could include the set-up costs, professional fees, office/manufacture space, materials and equipment, sub-contracted work and labour. Then you need to work out how much you intend to make from sales. The difference between the income from sales and your direct costs is your gross profit (or loss).

You then need to think about how much it will cost to run your business. This could include materials, equipment, transport, administration, insurance, promotion, professional expenses and interest on loans. These are your overheads and are deducted from your gross profit. The figure you have left is your net profit (or loss).

From this profit/loss plan you can produce a cash flow forecast, which will show you the areas of peak cash requirement through the year. A profit/loss plan and cash flow forecast may show that there are periods of loss during the year, but also periods of gain.

It is important to note that businesses fail because they are under-capitalised: starting a business costs money, but experiencing losses also costs money, so you need to plan ahead to minimise potential loss. You also need to think about how you will cover running costs if you are unable to make enough sales at certain times through the year. This could be when you are revising for and taking examinations. Will you be able to continue your business at this time? Will you be able to employ someone to work for you? Is it prudent to do so? How much will it cost? All these issues will need to be considered when you produce your profit/loss plan and cash flow forecast (see quotation below).

> ## Michael, 29, Northampton
>
> I had this idea to set up a gardening company. I was going to be the boss and I'd get other mates to do the work, like any student who needed some extra cash... When I looked into it, it got really complicated. There were insurances issues, wages issues, equipment and all... I just hadn't got enough money to set it all up and I wasn't sure I'd be able to manage the business and do my uni work... I chickened out and got a part-time job... When I left university I set up the business with my brother and we've got three full-time employees and quite a decent turnover.

Understanding tax implications

If you are intending to become a student entrepreneur you need to think about the tax implications, which will depend on the method of trading. If you decide to trade as a sole trader you will need to register with HM Revenue & Customs as self-employed. You will need to keep up-to-date books and records for tax purposes and submit an annual self-assessment tax return. More information and contact details of your local Inland Revenue Enquiry Centre can be obtained from www.hmrc.gov.uk.

Tax implications for a partnership are similar to becoming a sole trader: each partner will need to inform HM Revenue & Customs of their intention to become self-employed. Up-to-date accounts will need to be kept and both individuals and the partnership will need to submit an annual self-assessment tax return.

Limited companies will need to file annual accounts at Companies House and produce corporate tax returns each year. Tax issues for limited companies are much more complex, so if you are thinking of following this route you may need to obtain the services of an accountant (or an accountancy student, who may agree to help you as practical experience for their course). This person would be able to offer advice about discounts, savings and incentives that can help you to reduce your tax bill considerably, thus recuperating the fee for their services. To find an accountant in your area visit the relevant Institute of Chartered Accountants website

(details below) or contact the accountancy department at your university, if relevant.

Paying National Insurance

All self-employed people are responsible for paying National Insurance Contributions themselves. There are two types of contribution and these depend on how much you earn and the amount of profit you receive:

- Class 2 contributions are flat-rate payments collected by the HM Revenue & Customs National Insurance Contributions Office. If your earnings are low (below £5,075 in 2009/10) you can apply for exception from these payments, but you have to apply early. In 2009/10 the weekly Class 2 contribution is £2.40. For further information about Class 2 contributions ring the Self-Employment Services Call Centre on (0845) 9154 655.
- Class 4 contributions are profit-related and collected by HM Revenue & Customs on the basis of your personal self-assessment.

More information can be found in leaflet SE1 *Thinking of Working for Yourself?* If you are thinking about self-employment while you are a student, read this leaflet as you could be liable to pay both National Insurance Contributions and income tax, both of which could significantly reduce your income. The leaflet can be downloaded from www.hmrc.gov.uk.

Building your business

As your business grows you may find that you are lacking in certain skills and knowledge to take your business forward. One option is to find out whether there are relevant courses or training sessions available at your university. Most of these will be free to students and, depending on your course, you may be able to take a relevant business module as part of your course.

Entrepreneur office

Many universities now have a student entrepreneur office, and staff within this office will be able to offer advice and guidance about what is avail-

able. Through working closely with staff you will be able to obtain free professional advice, network with other student entrepreneurs and find out about free training courses, conferences and entrepreneurial competitions, all of which will help you to build your business.

Entrepreneur societies

Many universities have an Entrepreneur Society that enables you to meet with like-minded students to discuss inspirational ideas, meet possible partners and obtain support and advice. Contact your university students' union to find out whether such a society exists. If it does not, you could think about setting one up. Advice and guidance about doing so can be obtained from your students' union. Two examples of these societies can be viewed at www.oxfordentrepreneurs.co.uk and www.fishontoast.com.

Using professionals

If you don't have the required expertise to build your business and it is not available at your university, you can think about employing professionals. However you will need to undertake a careful financial assessment to work out whether this is financially viable. Professionals charge high fees, so make sure that you obtain a breakdown of these fees prior to signing a contract. Make sure that any professional you employ is a member of a respected professional body and don't be tempted to use those who cold call. Relevant professionals can be contacted from the following organisations:

- solicitor: www.lawsociety.org.uk;
- chartered accountant: www.icaew.com for England and Wales, www.icas.org.uk for Scotland and www.icai.ie for Ireland;
- financial adviser: www.aifa.net;
- investment manager or stockbroker: www.apcims.co.uk;
- advertising agents: www.ipa.co.uk;
- insurers: www.abi.org.uk.

Managing work and study

If you hope to run a successful business and obtain a good degree, you must be able to manage your time efficiently and effectively. Time management is all about taking control of your own time. You need to be able to make things happen in a way that will benefit you, your studies and your business, and you need to stop other people controlling your time. The following points should help you to do this:

- Draw up a list or create a chart of non-negotiable activities that you must carry out each week, for your studies and for your business. This will include attending lectures, seminars and tutorials, and essential activities for your business such as sending out goods, invoicing and updating databases. Make sure that friends, family and partners know that these cannot be altered and that you are unavailable at these times.
- Spread your time evenly between all subjects or modules on your course. Don't let your business take up so much time that you begin to neglect certain modules, especially those that you may not particularly like.
- Don't neglect your private studies. Keep some time free for this, even if business interests seem urgent. Find out what part of the day is most productive for your personal study and try to keep this time available.
- You should avoid marathon study sessions: shorter sessions tend to be more productive, especially in terms of committing material to memory. Set a clear start and stop time for your study. Work out how much you would like to complete in the time and concentrate only on your studies. Don't let your mind wander towards your business needs.
- Fill your least productive or least creative time of the day with mundane business tasks that need little thought, but must be completed, such as addressing and mailing parcels.
- Think of the most efficient way to carry out a task or cope with a problem. Many student hours are wasted trying to sort out a computer problem or find a particular reference in the library. Contact the computer help desk, ask a knowledgeable friend or speak to a librarian rather than waste time searching by yourself.
- Recreation and socialising are important for your frame of mind and well-being. Set aside enough time for these activities, even if you feel your business and studies need your constant attention.

● Don't work at a time when you should be sleeping; sleep is essential for your intellectual, emotional and physical health.

Summary

Becoming a student entrepreneur can be a useful way to raise money to pay for your university studies. However, you have to make sure that your plans are viable, both in terms of the amount of work you will have to do and the financial returns. If you choose to follow this route it is important that you produce a comprehensive business plan, a profit/loss plan and a cash flow forecast, and understand how you are going to trade. It is also important to carry out a risk assessment, both in terms of physical health and safety issues, and in terms of problems that could be caused by overwork and stress. Careful time management is of particular importance if you are to successfully juggle your business and studies.

This section of the book has looked at how you, as a student, can pay for your university education. To conclude the book the final chapter considers ways that you can reduce your university costs, so that any income that you have generated can go that little bit further. These issues are discussed in the following chapter.

Further information

You can register as self-employed by ringing the helpline for newly self-employed people on (08459) 15 45 15, or online at www.hmrc.gov.uk/startingup. Once you have registered you will be given a guide called *Starting up in Business*, along with details about paying income tax and National Insurance Contributions. As a self-employed person you will need to complete a self-assessment tax return, and leaflet SA/BK8 *Self Assessment: Your guide* will explain this in more detail.

Useful organisations

Companies House

The main functions of Companies House are to incorporate and dissolve limited companies, examine and store company information delivered

under the Companies Act and make this information available to the public. More information can be obtained from the following address.

Companies House
Crown Way
Maindy
Cardiff CF14 3Uz
Tel: (0303) 1234 500
e-mail: enquiries@companies-house.gov.uk
www.companieshouse.gov.uk

Useful websites

www.speedproject.ac.uk

Student Placements for Entrepreneurs in Education (SPEED) is a new, funded project led by Wolverhampton University, with many other universities taking part. The aim of the project is to provide students with the skills and knowledge they need to start up their own businesses. Visit the site for more information about the project.

http://royalsociety.org/enterprisefund

On this site you can find out more information about Royal Society funding to help entrepreneurs to commercialise their ideas. It is available to help UK scientists and engineers (including students) to turn their inventions into businesses.

www.icaew.com

This is the website of the Institute of Chartered Accountants (England and Wales). You can use the database on this website to search for a fully qualified accountant in your area. Useful information about setting up a small business is also provided on the website. Scottish students should visit www.icas.org.uk and students from Northern Ireland should visit www.icai.ie.

27 Reducing the cost of university

As we saw in Part One of this book, studying at university can be expensive, especially when tuition fees, accommodation costs and other living expenses are taken into account. However, there is financial help available to help you to meet these costs, and this was discussed in Part Two. Sources of finances that may be available to parents were discussed in Part Three, and other sources of finances that may be available to students in Part Four.

To conclude, this chapter goes on to illustrate how it is possible to reduce your expenditure, both before and during your course, with careful planning and increased knowledge about what is available. Advice is offered about how you can reduce your costs on accommodation, utilities, IT equipment, travel, course materials, entertainment, sports and leisure. The chapter goes on to offer advice about managing your money, knowing how to budget and avoiding problems with credit cards and loans.

Reducing expenditure on accommodation

As we have seen in Chapter 2, perhaps the best way to reduce accommodation costs is to live with your parents while you study at university. However, this option is not possible for mature students and people who do not have a university in their home town or who wish to study on a course that is not offered locally. Also, some students and parents feel that it is preferable to study away from the parental home, as learning how to live independently is such an important part of university life.

If you decide to live away from the parental home, there are various ways that you can reduce the costs of accommodation, as the following points illustrate.

University accommodation

As we saw in Chapter 2, many universities offer discounts on hall fees to students who agree to pay the fees in full at the start of the academic year. Others will offer a discount to students who agree to set up a direct debit to pay their fees. In some cases this can be as much as 8 per cent of the annual fee. Check with your chosen university to find out what discounts are available.

All universities will refund your deposit at the end of the year, if you have not caused any damage or breached the regulations. Make sure you look after your room and adhere to regulations so that you don't lose out financially by forfeiting your deposit. Also, don't lose your key. Universities will charge for a replacement, usually around £20.

Think carefully about what facilities you need. Do you need internet access in your room? All universities have open-access computers on campus and many halls have computer rooms available to all residents. Do you need en-suite facilities or can you share with up to five other students? Some of the cheaper halls can have other advantages, such as proximity to the university. A shorter walk in the morning might outweigh the advantages provided by a launderette, for example. Don't get caught up in the idea that more money means everything will be better.

If you are in a self-catering hall, share the cost of food with other students and cook meals together, as this works out cheaper. If you are in catered halls, make sure you eat every meal for which you have paid.

If you have a car, check that you are not expected to pay for parking in your hall of residence car-park. More and more universities are charging for car-parking, sometimes as much as £150 per annum. Some universities will also charge for the use of a bike shed.

Private rented accommodation

Shop around for the cheapest deals and begin looking as early as possible. Find out which are the best student areas and obtain some sample rents. However, you must make sure that you move to a safe area. Your students'

union or accommodation office will be able to offer advice on which areas to avoid.

Try to find like-minded people to live with. It is not sensible to move in with people from wealthy backgrounds as they will not understand the need to budget, which could lead to problems when you have to split bills equally.

If you have a car make sure that you can park near to your house and that there is not a charge for this parking. Some areas have a residents' parking scheme that could cost you around £50 a year. Parking fines are expensive so don't live in an area where you might be tempted to park illegally.

Reducing expenditure on utilities

There are a number of ways to save money on your gas, electricity and water:

- In private rented accommodation, make sure you pay only for what you have used. As soon as you move into a property, take a meter reading. Contact the relevant companies, giving the exact date you moved in and give them your meter reading. This might be different from that supplied by the landlord or the previous tenants, so make sure that you do not pay for fuel you have not used. When you leave the property do the same: take a meter reading and inform the company of the exact date of moving out.
- Save energy:
  - don't leave on lights;
  - only boil as much water as you need in the kettle;
  - don't leave videos, televisions and computers on stand-by for too long;
  - don't use the heating unnecessarily: put on an extra jumper instead;
  - cook together and/or adopt one-pot cooking strategies;
  - take a shower instead of a bath and persuade your housemates to do the same;
  - if you have a water meter, don't use a hosepipe for the garden or for your car and don't take baths too often.
- Take advantage of prompt payment discounts on utility bills as you could save up to 5 per cent of your bill.

Reducing the cost of IT equipment

There are several ways to reduce your spending on IT, as the following list illustrates:

- Take advantage of all the free services and equipment offered by the university. Most IT departments will produce information sheets and web pages that will help you to diagnose problems.
- Contact the university computer services for details about software available directly from the university network.
- Take advantage of free software advertised by manufacturers but, if downloading at university, make sure that you are not doing anything illegal or breaching university regulations. When downloading software consult with computer services about the latest virus detection and avoidance methods.
- Take advantage of educational discounts offered by software manufacturers. Some of these discounts are substantial and you could save up to 80 per cent on retail prices. You will need to prove that you are a full-time student. Some products available through this scheme will be offered under a limited licence or will time-out after a specified amount of time.
- Some universities are giving away free laptops as part of their bursary agreements. These are usually yours to keep if you complete your course. Consult the relevant university website for more information.

Reducing the cost of travel

There are a variety of ways to reduce your travel expenses:

- Running a car is usually the most expensive option so think twice about owning a car while you are a student. Is it really necessary? Can you afford to run a car?
- If you intend to travel by train more than three times a year, invest in a Young Person's Railcard as this enables you to receive a third off most rail journeys. This is available for anyone between the ages of 16 and 25 and for mature students. For more information visit your local train station or consult www.16–25railcard.co.uk. When travelling by train

book your tickets well in advance and travel off-peak as it is much cheaper.

● If you prefer to travel by coach purchase a National Express Student Discount Coachcard. This is available to any full-time student and enables you to save up to 30 per cent on the normal adult fare. Many universities have their own coach stop on campus, and National Express serves over 1,200 destinations. To obtain a Student Discount Coachcard, visit your local National Express agent or consult www.nationalexpress.com.

● Very cheap intercity travel in the United Kingdom by bus or train can be obtained from www.megatrain.com/uk.

If you are really struggling with your travel expenses, some educational grants, charities and hardship funds are available to help specifically with travel costs (see Chapter 25). If you find yourself in trouble once at university, visit your students' union or the university welfare officer for advice about funds that may be available.

Reducing the cost of course materials, books and stationery

There are several ways to reduce your spending on course materials, books and stationery:

● Purchase stationery and course materials from your students' union shop as most items are offered at a cheaper price than they are in high-street shops.

● Whenever you buy anything needed for your course from high-street shops, check whether they offer a student discount. Always take your library card or NUS card with you so that you can prove that you are a student. Some bookshops, especially those situated near to a university, will offer student discounts of up to 10 per cent.

● Don't buy all the books on the reading list. Find out which are the key texts and see how many copies are available in the university library. If you feel you cannot do without a key text, consider buying a second-hand copy. Some students' union shops or university bookshops buy

and sell second-hand books. Also, consult student noticeboards and auction websites.

- Find out whether it might be worth purchasing an NUS discount card. These provide access to a range of specially negotiated discounts in a wide variety of shops, restaurants and bars. More information can be obtained from www.nus.org.uk.

Reducing your spending on entertainment and social activities

There are a number of ways to reduce your spending on entertainment and social activities, as the following list illustrates:

- Do your research: locate all the facilities that are free to students and make sure you take advantage of them.
- If your university has a number of bars and entertainment outlets, do your research, as you may find that some are cheaper than others.
- Make sure you join the students' union and receive all the free gifts and discounts to which you are entitled. Always carry your NUS card as proof of your student identity so that you can take advantage of cheaper entrance fees for entertainment venues.
- Some students recommend only taking a certain amount of money with you if you decide to go for a night out and leaving your cash cards at home. However, you must make sure that you have enough money to get home safely. Some universities have special arrange-ments with local taxi firms that enable students who have run out of money to get a taxi home and pay at a later date. Contact your students' union for more information.
- Join the entertainment committee of the students' union. Although you will have to work before or during gigs, you are entitled to attend all or most events free of charge.
- Some universities are offering free entertainment and social activities as part of their bursary schemes. Contact your chosen university for more information.

Reducing the cost of sports and leisure

If you want to reduce spending on sports and leisure facilities the following points may help:

- Do your research: take note of all the sports and leisure facilities that are free to students and make sure that you take advantage of them.
- Become a member of a club if you have an interest in a specific sport. You will have to pay a membership fee but will gain access to university facilities at a greatly reduced rate and could take advantage of similar facilities at other universities.
- In general it is cheaper to use university sports and leisure facilities than those available in the local town. If you intend to use the facilities on a regular basis, purchase a sports card as there will be discounts available (see Chapter 4). However, shop around as you may find that some facilities in town are cheaper, especially during the winter months and once student discounts are taken into account.
- If you excel at a particular sport, find out whether your university offers a sports bursary. These are available at some institutions for talented sportspeople and can pay up to £4,000 a year to help with sports-related costs (see Chapter 24).

Knowing how to budget

A recent survey by the Financial Services Authority (FSA) has shown that 34.4 per cent of students who considered dropping out of university did so because of financial difficulties. If you start thinking about your budget before you go away to university, and get into the habit of keeping careful records, you will be better prepared to deal with the financial cost of student life and avoid getting into debt.

Keeping records

You cannot plan your budget efficiently if you do not keep records of your income and expenditure. You need to know what income you are going to receive on what date and keep records of all expenditure so that you know exactly where your money has gone. Get into the habit of keeping

a record every time you write a cheque or use your switch/debit card. Remember also to take note of any money you take from a cash machine.

When you receive bank statements file them carefully as you may need them later to check your income and expenditure. Some banks will charge you for extra copies so you can save money by being organised from the outset. Other banks encourage you to opt out of receiving paper statements and enable you to manage your account online, which is useful as you can search your statements electronically when organising your finances.

If you have applied for government funding and a student loan, find out when you can expect to receive payments and make sure they come on time. If you know when they should arrive you can chase up any late payment promptly. You should do this if you are receiving money from other sources such as sponsorship, grants or scholarships. If you obtain part-time or vacation work, find out how much you will be paid (after deductions) and when you will receive this income. Again, this will help you to plan your budget efficiently.

Planning your budget

There are four simple stages to planning your budget:

1. Keep all records of your income and expenditure.
2. Calculate your income.
3. Calculate your expenditure.
4. Work out the difference between the two.

If the difference between the two is positive, you need to try to keep it that way. If the difference between the two is negative however, you need to reduce your expenditure and/or increase your income to change the balance in your favour. A sample budget planner is provided in Appendix 2. Fill this in to see where your money is going and provide an indication of how and where you can cut down on your expenditure. If you feel that you really cannot cut down on your expenditure, think about how you can increase your income. Do this as soon as possible, because once you get into debt you could find that this debt can quickly get out of control.

Part Two of this book provides in-depth information about how you can increase your income: consult these pages and make sure that you exhaust all sources of income. Only try reputable sources, and stay away from any loans with extortionate interest rates attached (see below). To summarise, the following sources of additional income may be available to you as a student:

- student loans;
- government grants or bursaries;
- parental contribution/extra money from parents or relatives;
- grants or bursaries from educational trusts and charities;
- university grants, bursaries or scholarships;
- NHS bursaries;
- social work bursaries;
- allowances for disabilities;
- grants for teacher training;
- private sponsorship;
- wages from paid employment;
- Access to Learning Funds (England);
- Hardship Funds (Scotland);
- Financial Contingency Funds (Wales);
- Support Funds (Northern Ireland).

In addition, you may be entitled to a tax rebate if you have paid too much income tax or tax on your savings. Similarly, you may be entitled to a rebate on your National Insurance Contributions if you think you have overpaid.

Managing your money

You will need to open a bank account to manage your money. Banks work hard to attract student customers and will offer a number of incentives that may be attractive to you. However, in addition to these, you will need to think about the following issues, which will help you to reduce costs.

Current account

- What is the interest rate? (This will be minimal on a current account.)
- Is a free overdraft facility offered with the account?
- What are the charges on the account should you go overdrawn accidentally?
- Do you receive a cheque book, cheque card and switch/debit card?
- Will you be charged to use the cash machines of other banks?
- Does the account let you use telephone and online banking?
- Is Saturday or late-night opening available?
- How often will you receive statements? What are the bank charges if you need extra statements?

Savings account

- What are the interest rates, and do these differ depending on the amount you have in your account and how much money you withdraw?
- Does the account let you use telephone and online banking? Can you transfer your money easily to your current account?
- How do you access your money? Is this by card that can be used in cash machines or do you have to go into a branch with a book? If you have to visit the bank, is there a branch close to your university and in your home town? Can you access your account 24 hours a day?
- Do you have to give notice when you want to withdraw money?
- Is there a limit to how much you can withdraw? Are there financial penalties if you withdraw more than this amount?

Most banks have resident student advisers. Visit the bank to arrange an appointment and the adviser will guide you through the application process. You will need to take at least two forms of identification containing your name and address. Make sure that you remain on good terms with your bank manager or student adviser. At the first sign of trouble arrange an appointment to discuss the problems. They will recognise that you are taking a responsible attitude and will want to sort out problems before they escalate.

Credit cards

You need to think carefully about whether you need a credit card. To make the most of a credit card you need to pay off your balance each month so that you can avoid paying interest. However, many students find that this is difficult to do and that the interest gradually adds up, making the balance harder to pay off. Some students find that they end up in serious debt because they have taken out a credit card. The best advice is that you only use credit cards as a last resort. The same rule applies for store cards.

Bank loans

In general, bank loans are also not a good idea when you are a student. They will have a much higher annual percentage rate (APR) than your student loan and you may struggle to pay off the loan for years to come. Before taking out a loan you should talk to your bank manager or student adviser to find out whether you can raise the limit on your interest-free overdraft.

However, some students find that they have to take out a loan because they have got themselves into so much debt. If you have an unauthorised overdraft, it may be better to turn this into a loan because the interest charged may be less than the interest payments and financial penalties on an unauthorised overdraft. If you do decide to take out a bank loan you should be aware of the following points:

- Sometimes banks will add on optional extras without making this clear when you sign the form. Make sure that extras such as payment protection insurance have not been added without your agreement.
- Watch out for other charges such as arrangement fees.
- Make sure you know exactly how long the loan will last; the longer the duration of the loan, the more interest you will pay.
- Make sure that you only take out as much money as you need to cover your debts.
- Keep up your repayments. The financial penalties will be severe if you don't, and the bank could take legal action to recover any monies owed.

If you feel that you must take out a loan, seek advice from your students' union first, as they may be able to tell you about additional sources of income. If you still want to go ahead with a bank loan, hunt around for the best deal. You do not have to take out a loan with your existing bank, so shop around for the lowest APR.

Summary

The cost of going to university has been highlighted throughout this book. This final chapter has pulled together all the strands and presented a series of bullet points on how you can reduce these costs. Advice has also been offered on knowing how to budget, managing your money and being careful with loans and credit cards.

Studying for three or four years at university can be very expensive, especially when tuition fees and accommodation costs are taken into account. However, with careful planning and budgeting, and with better knowledge about the grants, loans and bursaries that are available, you can significantly reduce the costs of university. This book has provided a complete guide to paying for university for both students and parents. I hope that you have found it useful and that it will help to reduce the costs of going to university for you or your children. I wish you every success with your studies and hope that your financial management runs smoothly.

Further information

Student budget sheets and a student money manual can be downloaded from the student section of the Credit Action website: www.creditaction. org.uk/student.html.

If you find that you are experiencing financial problems and you want to talk to somebody, you can try the following organisations:

Consumer Credit Counselling Service (CCCS) (www.cccs.co.uk)
Tel: (0800) 138 1111
e-mail: contactus@cccs.co.uk

Student Debt Advice Helpline (part of the CCCS – see above)
Tel: (0800) 328 1813

National Debtline (www.nationaldebtline.co.uk)
Tel: (0808) 808 4000

Use the contact form on the website if you wish to e-mail an adviser.

Useful websites

www.support4learning.org.uk

The support 4 learning website contains a regularly updated summary of student bank account offers and a large amount of useful information about student finance.

Appendix 1: Case studies

Case study 1: Sally

Sally is 18 years old and is in the first year of a three-year, full-time degree course in social sciences at Kingston University. Sally began her course after having left care and was therefore able to receive the following money to help her to pay for her studies:

- £1,000 bursary from Kingston University;
- £1,000 care leaver's bursary from Kingston University;
- £5,215 student loan for maintenance from the Student Loans Company (the full loan of £6,475 for a university in London, minus £1,260, which is taken off when a student receives a full maintenance grant);
- £3,145 student loan for tuition fees from the Student Loans Company;
- £2,835 maintenance grant from the government.

This meant that Sally received a total of £13,195 for her first year of study. She has paid her £3,145 tuition fees straight away and has set aside a total of £4,060 for accommodation costs (£101.50 per week for a 40-week contract). This leaves Sally with a total of £5,990 for the year. Sally says:

> I have almost £150 a week to spend for the 40 weeks of study in my first year. To me this seems like a lot of money because I've not had much money before. But I'm determined to keep control of my spending. To start with it was a bit tempting to go out and buy lots of stuff, but I know I've got to be careful if I want the money to last. I've got an en-suite room with a shower, toilet and sink... It's really, really nice and all the heating and electricity is included in the cost, so I don't have to budget for that... I've got some books from a second-year student who was selling them, so they were cheap, and I can get other

cheap stationery locally… I haven't got a computer, but there are plenty for us to use here. I've never had a problem getting one so I don't think I will buy one at the moment, although I might decide to later. At the moment it's all so exciting and new. I'm loving it!

Case study 2: Robbie

Robbie is 17 and from a low-income family. At the moment he is studying for his A-levels at a sixth-form college in Dorset. In the first year of his A-levels he received £30 a week Education Maintenance Allowance (EMA), which is paid to 16–19 year olds from low-income families to encourage them to stay in full-time education. However, this year his payments have been delayed due to problems experienced by the company administering the scheme. Robbie's college has been able to help him financially by providing meal vouchers until he receives his payment.

Robbie is hoping to go to university this year (2009/10 entry). He is expected to get good A-level results and has found out that some universities offer a larger bursary to students from low-income households who obtain good results in their A-levels. Robbie says:

> I'm hoping to study on some sort of media course… No, I'm not really bothered exactly what course, there are so many I like the look of… I'm not bothered about which university, as long as it's one in a good place. It's going to cost me loads to go to university but I've found that some pay a lot more in bursaries than others… Well, my brother told me 'cos he went to Cardiff last year… I looked at places that offered more… As long as it's some sort of media course. There's some that do some study abroad as well, you know, like South America, so I might look at that. But all this thing with the EMA, you know, it's made me think money is the most important thing to think about. So I'm not sure about going abroad yet, 'cos I don't how I will pay for that.

As Robbie is from a low-income household he should qualify for a maximum university bursary and the maximum maintenance grant. He should also be able to obtain a student loan for tuition fees and another for maintenance. As he rightly points out, some universities also offer bursaries purely on academic merit. This has been a controversial issue

for some people who believe that bursaries should not be a means to attract talented students, but should rather help under-represented groups to enter higher education.

However, Robbie, as a white, working-class male from a low-income household would certainly be classed as coming from an 'under-represented' group, and should be able to take advantage of extra funds that might be available to him. For example, he could choose to study at the University of Birmingham, which in 2009/10 is offering an £840 bursary for students from low-income households and an additional scholarship of £1,260 per year for students achieving high A-level grades from low-income families. Bournemouth University is offering a £1,000 bursary for students from low-income households and academic achievement scholarships of £1,000 for the first year for students demonstrating an outstanding academic profile on entry.

Case study 3: Martina

Martina is a mature student who is studying on a diploma course at an adult residential college in Yorkshire. She is in receipt of an adult education bursary and additional money for her two children while she is studying on the course. Also, accommodation and meals for Martina and her children are free while she is studying. The children go to a local school and a free bus is arranged for them to travel to school from the college each day.

Martina said that the experience is 'amazing'. The standard of accommodation is 'excellent' and, although the food is a 'little stodgy', she feels that she can't complain because it is all free. There is a bar at the college and the students' union arranges various types of entertainment throughout the year. Everybody else on the course is 'mature and unconfident' but the tutors are excellent and are helping them 'to grow in confidence'.

Martina hopes to go to university when she has finished the diploma. The college has links with the local university and places are set aside for adult students who have successfully completed the diploma course. Bursaries are available for students from the local area and there is additional financial support for mature students. Martina is a 'little worried about making ends meet' but knows that university is something that she really 'wants to do'. She is determined not to let lack of money stop her,

as returning to education has been 'the best decision' she has ever made.

Case study 4: Uma

Uma studied for a Master's degree at Kent University. She had to pay for the course herself and took out a bank loan of £7,000 to cover tuition fees and living expenses for the year. However, she soon found that this loan wasn't enough and she had to take a further £4,000 loan from her bank. The bank manager didn't seem to have a problem with loaning this amount of money. Uma feels it was because she was a mature student, already had a first-class honours degree, and intended to get a well-paid job when she had finished her course. Uma says:

It may seem rash borrowing that amount of money. But I really wanted to do the course and I couldn't get a scholarship so I had to pay for it myself. I felt it would be worth it because if I was careful I could pay back the loan within a couple of years. Obviously I was taking a gamble on getting a job, but I managed to get one straight after university... It was with a market research organisation and my wage was nearly £25,000 so I did manage to pay off... well I think it took three years... anyway I did manage to pay it off fairly soon so I know I did the right thing. It makes you wonder now though whether banks would still lend that much to students... I was a mature student though and I can be quite persuasive when I want to be.

There are a variety of grants, scholarships and teaching assistance posts available for students with good honours degrees who wish to study on a postgraduate course. However, as Uma found, these can be hard to obtain, so many postgraduate students decide to fund their own studies. If you wish to study at postgraduate level, more information about all aspects of funding for postgraduate study can be obtained from www.prospects.ac.uk and www.postgrad.hobsons.com.

Appendix 2: Budget planner

A comprehensive budget planner has been reproduced below. You can use this form (or develop your own) to plan your budget in the first few weeks of your university course. It will help to show how you are managing financially and point to areas of large expenditure on which you can cut down if necessary. It will also help to indicate the best sources of income for you, personally, while you are studying.

Course costs	Amount of expenditure
Tuition fees	
PC	
Laptop	
Disks	
Memory	
Books	
Pens	
Notepads	
A4 paper (draft)	
A4 paper (good)	
Photocopying	
Laser printing	
Sub-total	

Living costs	Amount of expenditure
Rent	
Gas	
Electricity	
Water rates/meter	

Living costs	Amount of expenditure
Transport (local)	
Travel (home and abroad)	
Telephone (landline)	
Telephone (mobile)	
Laundry	
Leisure	
Entertainment	
Sports	
Hobbies	
Food	
Drink	
Clothes	
Household goods	
Insurance	
TV licence	
Credit commitments	
Miscellaneous expenditure	
Sub-total	
Total expenditure (course costs plus living costs)	

Sources of income	Amount of income
Student loan	
Parental/household contribution	
University bursary	
Sponsorship	
Income from employment	
Income from self-employment	
Income from savings	
Benefits	
Other loans	
Other grants	
Miscellaneous income	
Total income	
Total profit/loss **(expenditure and income: larger figure minus smaller figure)**	

Appendix 3:
Graduate employment opportunities and wages

As we have seen previously, new funding arrangements for undergraduate students mean that you can take out a student loan to help you to pay for your university education, which you do not need to start to pay back until the April after your studies when you are earning over £15,000. So, as a graduate, how much could you be earning, for what type of job?

This appendix provides a selection of the type of jobs you could get and the wages that you could expect as a graduate (2009 figures). More information about graduate job opportunities can be obtained from your university careers office, from national newspapers (such as the *Guardian* and *The Times*) or from the following websites:

- www.prospects.ac.uk;
- www.thegraduate.co.uk;
- www.just4graduates.net;
- www.milkround.com;
- http://graduate.monster.co.uk;
- www.ukgraduatecareers.net;
- www.get.hobsons.co.uk.

Examples of graduate jobs

Business and finance	
Job title:	Graduate business account manager
Salary:	£18,000–£20,000 per annum
Sector:	Telecommunications
Location:	Nationwide

Job title:	Graduate trainee recruitment consultant
Salary:	£20,000 per annum + London allowance
Sector:	Finance
Location:	London

Job title:	Graduate trainee credit risk analyst
Salary:	£10,000–£21,000 per annum
Sector:	Banking
Location:	Yorkshire

Information technology	
Job title:	IT professional
Salary:	From £24,500 per annum + benefits
Sector:	Civil service
Location:	Nationwide

Job title:	Graduate data analyst
Salary:	Up to £28,000
Sector:	International business (marketing)
Location:	Worldwide

Job title:	Graduate software engineer
Salary:	£23,000–£24,000 + benefits, per annum
Sector:	International business (software development)
Location:	Worldwide

Administration and management	
Job title:	Graduate trainee manager
Salary:	£20,000–£25,000 + benefits, per annum
Sector:	Financial (accountancy firm)
Location:	Nationwide
Job title:	Graduate operations manager
Salary:	£20,000–£25,000 per annum
Sector:	Postal service
Location:	Nationwide
Job title:	Personal secretary
Salary:	£17,000 per annum + London weighting
Sector:	Financial
Location:	London
Sales and retail	
Job title:	Graduate sales account manager
Salary:	£19,000–£20,000 per annum
Sector:	Retail
Location:	Midlands
Job title:	Graduate medical sales representative
Salary:	£18,500 per annum + commission
Sector:	Pharmaceutical sales
Location:	Nationwide
Job title:	Graduate trainee business development manager
Salary:	£19,000–£20,000 per annum
Sector:	Business consultancy
Location:	West Midlands

Health and medical	
Job title.	Trainee clinical scientist
Salary:	£25,000 per annum
Sector:	NHS
Location:	Nationwide

Job title:	Graduate safety consultant
Salary:	£18,000–£22,000 per annum
Sector:	Safety and environmental engineering consultancy
Location:	Somerset

Job title:	Care manager
Salary.	£18,000–£21,000 per annum
Sector.	Private health
Location:	Warwickshire

Non-profit and charities	
Job title:	Marketing manager
Salary:	£18,000–£20,000 per annum
Sector:	National charity
Location:	London

Job title:	Finance manager
Salary:	£22,000–£25,000 per annum
Sector:	National charity
Location:	London

Job title:	Fund-raiser
Salary:	£18,000 per annum + commission
Sector:	Local charity
Location:	Nottinghamshire

Media	
Job title:	Production assistant
Salary:	£18,000–£24,000
Sector:	TV company
Location:	London

Job title:	Graduate media sales executive
Salary:	£16,000 per annum + commission
Sector:	Publishing
Location:	Southern England

Job title:	Designer
Salary:	£25,000 per annum
Sector:	Retail (publishing)
Location:	London

Building, planning and engineering	
Job title:	Graduate engineer
Salary:	£23,000–£25,000 per annum
Sector:	Construction
Location:	Norwich

Job title:	Graduate project coordinator
Salary:	£20,000 per annum
Sector:	Construction
Location:	Northumbria

Job title:	Product design engineer
Salary:	£32,000–£35,000 per annum
Sector:	Car manufacturing
Location:	Berkshire

Useful websites

Government funding

www.studentfinanceengland.co.uk

This website will direct you to all the information that you require about financial support in England.

www.studentfinancewales.co.uk

If you are a Welsh student, more information about student finance can be obtained from this website.

www.saas.gov.uk

If you are a Scottish student, more information about student finance, including application forms and procedures, can be obtained from this site.

www.studentfinanceni.co.uk

You can find out all the information you need about funding for students from Northern Ireland on this website.

Charities and funding organisations

www.uniaid.org.uk

Uniaid is a charity that offers advice and support for students who may experience financial difficulty at university. On its website you can find useful interactive tools to help you to work out your finances, along with a useful student calculator.

www.acu.ac.uk

The Association of Commonwealth Universities offers a variety of scholar-ships, fellowships and bursaries for students who wish to study in another commonwealth country.

www.iefa.org

This is the International Education Financial Aid website. You can find information about international grants, bursaries and sponsorship oppor-tunities on this site.

Student services and discount schemes

www.nussl.co.uk

This is the website of NUS Services, which provides goods and marketing services for students' unions. On the website you can find information about student discount cards and links to all students' unions in the country.

www.isiccard.com

You can purchase an International Student Identity Card (ISIC) from this site. You can receive discounts on entertainment, books, food and drink, cultural events and travel worldwide if you purchase one of these cards.

Advice and information for students

www.ucas.com

UCAS is the organisation responsible for managing applications to higher education courses in the United Kingdom. On this website you can find all the information you need about applying for higher education and there is a useful student budget calculator available.

www.ukcosa.org.uk

This is the website for the UK Council for International Student Affairs. If you are an international student, visit this site for comprehensive information about sources of funding for international students and for information about how to pay for university. There is also a section for UK students who intend to study abroad.

www.teachertrainingwales.org

This is a useful site for anyone who is thinking about teacher training in Wales and includes useful links to Welsh university sites and relevant funding sites.

www.socialworkcareers.co.uk

More information about becoming a social worker and obtaining funding for social work courses can be obtained from this website.

www.connexions-direct.com

Information about company sponsorship and various career opportunities can be obtained from this website, along with general advice and guidance for school leavers.

www.scholarship-search.org.uk

This website provides a comprehensive guide to student finance and has been developed by Hot Courses in association with UCAS. There is a useful budget planner and funding database available on this site.

www.support4learning.org.uk

The support 4 learning website contains a regularly updated summary of student bank account offers and a large amount of useful information about student finance.

www.hotcourses.com

This website provides comprehensive and up-to-date information about all universities in the United Kingdom, containing useful reviews to help you with your course and university choice.

www.push.co.uk

You can look at each university profile on this website. Universities are rated in the following categories: academic, booze index, sports, activities, housing, welfare, reputation and living costs. You can also find out about leisure and entertainment, along with up-to-date prices of alcoholic drinks at each university.

Careers and work experience

www.nases.org.uk

The National Association of Student Employment Services (NASES) is the national representative body for practitioners from all styles of student employment services. This site contains an alphabetical list of student employment services in colleges and universities, along with information leaflets covering issues such as applying for jobs, income tax and national insurance.

www.prospects.ac.uk

Prospects is an organisation that provides advice and guidance to university students and graduates about careers, work experience and study abroad.

www.targetjobs.co.uk

This website has a useful database that you can search for all kinds of jobs, including short-term jobs for work experience. Your can search the database by sector, keyword and region.

www.itraineeship.com

This website seeks to match graduates with international employers. It provides detailed listings of a variety of international employers, work and placement opportunities, including short and long-term contracts before, during and after your course.

www.topinternships.com

This website provides information on internships and placements for UK undergraduates. You can search the database by sector, discipline, date, location and keyword. You will need to register to view the results of your search.

Books and copyright

www.cla.co.uk

This is the website of the Copyright Licensing Agency (CLA). On this site you can find useful information about copyright issues and CLA licences.

www.uni-trader.co.uk

You can buy a wide variety of items and textbooks from this site. It is a useful site to access because you can search for items at specific universities and arrange to meet the person selling the item so as to cut down on postage costs.

www.tso.co.uk/bookshop

You can buy a number of specialist books about study abroad from this website. You can also obtain books about further and higher education and books about graduate careers. In some cases, publications are available in both printed and electronic format.

Useful organisations

Government funding for students

Adult education bursaries

A booklet called *Adult Education Bursaries: A guide for applicants for courses at the long-term residential colleges* is available from the address below:

Awards Officer
Adult Education Bursaries
c/o Ruskin College
Walton Street
Oxford OX1 2HE
Tel: (01865) 556 360
e-mail: awards@ruskin.ac.uk

The Student Awards Agency for Scotland (SAAS)

More information about all aspects of student financial support in Scotland can be obtained from the SAAS:

The Student Awards Agency for Scotland
3 Redheughs Rigg
South Gyle
Edinburgh EH12 9HH
Tel: (0845) 111 1711
Fax: (0131) 244 5887
e-mail: use contact form on website
www.saas.gov.uk

Education and Library Boards

ELBs provide information about all aspects of study for students from Northern Ireland.

If you live in Belfast, contact:

Student Awards Section
Belfast Education and Library Board
40 Academy Street
Belfast BT1 2NQ
Tel: (028) 90 564000
e-mail: student.awards@belb.co.uk

If you live in Antrim, Ballymena, Ballymoeny, Carrickfergus, Coleraine, Larne, Magherafelt, Moyle or Newtownabbey, contact:

Student Awards
North Eastern Education and Library Board
182 Galgorm Road
County Hall
Ballymena BT42 1HN
Tel: (028) 2565 5025
e-mail: student.awards@neelb.org.uk

If you live in Ards, Castlereagh, Down, Lisburn or North Down, contact:

Student Awards Section
South Eastern Education and Library Board
Grahamsbridge Road
Dundonald
Belfast BT16 2HS
Tel: (028) 9056 6200
e-mail: info@seelb.org.uk

If you live in Armagh, Banbridge, Cookstown, Craigavon, Dungannon or Newry & Mourne, contact:

Student Awards Section
Southern Education and Library Board
3 Charlemont Place
The Mall
Armagh BT61 9AX
Tel: (028) 37 512432
e-mail: student.support@selb.org

If you live in Fermanagh, Limavady, Londonderry, Omagh or Strabane, contact:

Student Awards Section
Western Education and Library Board
1 Hospital Road
Omagh
Co Tyrone BT79 0AW
Tel: (028) 82 411411 / 411499
e-mail: student.awards@welbni.org

Student Loans Company Limited

The Student Loans Company (SLC) administers government-funded loans and grants to students throughout the United Kingdom.

Student Loans Company Limited
100 Bothwell Street
Glasgow G2 7JD
Tel: (0141) 306 2000
Fax: (0141) 306 2005
www.slc.co.uk

Funding for specialist courses

Dance and drama

Advice about careers and funding in dance and drama, and tips for passing auditions, can be obtained from the following organisations:

Council for Dance Education and Training (CDET)
Old Brewer's Yard
17–19 Neal Street
London WC2H 9UY
Tel: (020) 7240 5703
Fax: (020) 7240 2547
e-mail: info@cdet.org.uk
www.cdet.org.uk

National Council for Drama Training
249 Tooley Street
London SE1 2JX
Tel: (020) 7407 3686
e-mail: info@ncdt.co.uk
www.ncdt.co.uk

Social work

Welsh students should contact the Care Council for Wales:

Student Funding Team
7th Floor
South Gate House
Wood Street
Cardiff CF10 1EW
Tel: (0845) 070 0249
e-mail: studentfunding@ccwales.org.uk
www.ccwales.org.uk

Scottish students should contact the Scottish Social Services Council:

Scottish Social Services Council
Compass House
11 Riverside Drive
Dundee DD1 4NY
Tel: (0845) 60 30 891
e-mail: enquiries@sssc.uk.com
www.sssc.uk.com

Students in Northern Ireland should contact the Northern Ireland Social Care Council (NISCC):

Northern Ireland Social Care Council (NISCC)
7th Floor
Millennium House
19–25 Great Victoria Street
Belfast BT2 7AQ
Tel: (028) 9041 7600
Fax: (028) 9041 7601
e-mail: info@nisocialcarecouncil.org.uk
www.niscc.info

Further information about bursaries and working in social work in England can be obtained from:

NHS Student Bursaries
Hesketh House
200–220 Broadway
Fleetwood
Lancashire FY7 8SS
Tel: (0845) 358 6655
Fax: (01253) 774490
e-mail: bursary@nhspa.gov.uk
www.nhsstudentgrants.co.uk

Fine and performing arts

Further details about funds for fine and performing arts can be obtained from:

The Leverhulme Trust
1 Pemberton Row
London EC4A 3BG
Tel: (020) 7822 5220
e-mail: enquiries@leverhulme.ac.uk
www.leverhulme.ac.uk

Healthcare

For enquiries concerning NHS financial support in England contact:

Student Grants Unit
Hesketh House
200–220 Broadway
Fleetwood
Lancashire FY7 8SS
Tel: (0845) 358 6655
Fax: (01253) 774490
e-mail: bursary@nhspa.gov.uk
www.nhsstudentgrants.co.uk

For enquiries concerning NHS financial support in Wales contact:

The NHS Wales Student Awards Unit
3rd floor
14 Cathedral Road
Cardiff CF11 9LJ
Tel: (029) 2019 6167 (bursary enquiries)
Tel: (029) 2019 6168 (childcare enquiries)
e-mail: use contact form on website
www.nliah.com

For enquiries concerning NHS financial support in Scotland contact:

The Student Awards Agency for Scotland
3 Redheughs Rigg
South Gyle
Edinburgh EH12 9HH
Tel: (0845) 111 1711
Fax: (0131) 244 5887
e-mail: use the contact form on the website
www.saas.gov.uk

For enquiries concerning NHS financial support in Northern Ireland contact:

Central Services Agency
Bursary Administration Unit
Nursing Board NI
2 Franklin Street
Belfast BT2 8DQ
Tel: (028) 9055 3661
e-mail: use the contact form on the website
www.centralservicesagency.com

Information for students

National Union of Students (NUS)

The NUS is a voluntary membership organisation that represents the interests of students across the United Kingdom. You can obtain a wide range of information about all aspects of university life from the NUS.

NUS HQ
Centro 3
19 Mandela Street
London NW1 0DU
Tel: (020) 7380 6649
Fax: (0871) 221 8222
e-mail: nusuk@nus.org.uk
www.nus.org.uk

Skill: the National Bureau for Students with Disabilities

Skill is a national charity that promotes opportunities for young people and adults with any kind of impairment in post-16 education, training and employment.

Skill: the National Bureau for Students with Disabilities
Chapter House
18–20 Crucifix Lane
London SE1 3JW
Tel: (0800) 328 5050
Textphone: (0800) 068 2422
e-mail: info@skill.org.uk
www.skill.org.uk

Charities and funding organisations

UNIAID

Uniaid is a charity that offers advice and support for students who may experience financial difficulty at university. Accommodation bursaries are available through UNIAID.

UNIAID Foundation
CAN Mezzanine
Downstream Building
1 London Bridge
London SE1 9BG
Tel: (020) 7785 3885
e-mail: info@uniaid.org.uk
www.uniaid.org.uk

Educational Grants Advisory Service

The Educational Grants Advisory Service is an independent advice agency for people who want to obtain funding for post-16 education.

Educational Grants Advisory Service (EGAS)
501–505 Kingsland Road
Dalston
London E8 4AU
Student advice line: (020) 7254 6251
www.family-action.org.uk

The Helena Kennedy Foundation

More information about funds available from this charity can be obtained from the following address and website:

Helena Kennedy Foundation
The Mansion
Bletchley Park
Bletchley
Milton Keynes MK3 6EB
Tel: (01908) 363452
e-mail: admin@hkf.org.uk
www.hkf.org.uk

The Leverhulme Trade Charities Trust

Information about grants, awards and bursaries available from the Leverhulme Trade Charities Trust can be obtained from their office and websites:

The Leverhulme Trust
1 Pemberton Row
London EC4A 3BG
Tel: (020) 7822 5227
Fax: (020) 7882 5084
e-mail: enquiries@leverhulme.org.uk
www.leverhulme-trade.org.uk
www.leverhulme.ac.uk

The Gilchrist Education Trust

More information about grants for individual students can be obtained from the following address:

The Gilchrist Education Trust
13 Brookfield Avenue
Larkfield
Aylesford ME20 6RU
e-mail: gilchrist.et@blueyonder.co.uk
www.gilchristgrants.org.uk

Index

access agreements 114
Access to Learning Fund 84, 86, 171, 185
accommodation
  accommodation officers 18
  booking fee 25
  catered 17, 75–76
  contracts/agreements 24–24, 27, 220
    individual agreement 27, 49–50
    joint agreement 27, 49
  costs 1, 17–35, 72, 73, 74, 75–76, 288–90, 301
  deposits 25, 27
  en-suite 17
  full-board 29
  halls of residence 17, 24, 29, 33, 195
  house in multiple occupation 221
  instalment plans 24, 25, 75–76
  inventory 27, 220–21
  licence 25
  living at home 17, 28, 195, 196
  lodgings 17, 30
  private rented 17, 24, 30, 31
  rent 27, 29, 72
  reservation fee 25
  retainers 25
  room cancellations 25
  self-catered 17, 26, 30
  semi-catered 29–30
  student owner-occupiers 34

accommodation debts see debts
Adult Dependant's Grant see grants
Adult Education Allowance Scheme
    (Scotland) 165, 167, 185
adult education bursaries see bursaries
adult residential colleges 173–74
art shops 39
Assembly Learning Grant see grants
Association of Commonwealth
    Universities 152, 313
Association of Investment Companies
    208–09
Association of Residential Letting
    Agents 219

bank accounts 12, 25, 128, 246–47, 296–97, 300
bank transfer 11, 24
benefits 170–71, 175
bike storage 26
books 1, 36–42, 72, 74, 292–93, 301, 316
bookshops 40
British Council 59, 151
budget planning 2, 294–96, 305–06
bursaries
  adult education bursaries 164–67, 172, 185, 303, 317
  care leaver's bursary 301
  NHS bursary 134, 146–47, 155–56, 185, 322–23

Research Council bursary 134
social work bursary 149–50,
    157–58, 185
sports bursary 258
Students' Outside Scotland Bursary
    100, 185
university bursaries 1, 13, 16, 25,
    72, 114–131, 145, 161, 185,
    194, 301, 302–03
Welsh Bursary Scheme 93
Young Students' Bursary 100, 185

Capital Gains Tax 214, 225, 226, 234
capped tuition fees 7–8
car-parking 26
charitable funding 2, 269–75, 312,
    324–25
Chartered Institute of Taxation 238
child benefit 199
Child Tax Credit 163, 169–70, 175
Childcare Grant see grants
Copyright Licensing Agency, the 38,
    42, 316
Council of Mortgage Lenders, the 237
council tax 33–34, 226, 245
    benefit 171
    exemption 33, 34
    single person discount 34
course materials 1, 36–42, 74,
    292–93
credit cards 298

dance and drama courses 148–49,
    319–20
debts
    accommodation debts 11
    tuition fee debts 11
    university debts 11–12
degree ceremony 11
Department for Innovation,
    Universities and Skills 102
Diploma in Higher Education 84, 93,
    101, 110
Disabled Student's Allowances 93,
    102, 132–38, 185

General Disabled Students'
    Allowance 133
non-medical helper's allowance
    133
postgraduate allowance 133
specialist equipment allowance
    132–33
travel costs 133
DIUS see Department for Innovation,
    Universities and Skills
downsizing 2
DSAs see Disabled Student's
    Allowances

Education and Library Boards 111,
    112–13, 132, 133, 134, 145,
    310–19
Education Maintenance Allowance
    302
Educational Grants Advisory Service
    274, 324
ELB see Education and Library Boards
ELQs see equivalent and lower
    qualifications
EMA see Education Maintenance
    Allowance
e-mail 60, 61, 62, 65–66
employment
    graduate employment opportunities
        307–11
    overseas 57
    part-time 2, 72, 74–75, 249–57
    salary levels 243–44, 252,
        308–11
    self-employment 2, 276–87
    vacation 2, 249–57
    working conditions 253
    working hours 251
entertainment 1, 43–52, 72, 74, 293
entertainment card 44
entertainment committee 43, 44
entrepreneurship 2, 276–87
equity release 2, 231–33
equivalent and lower qualifications
    9–10, 110

ERASMUS *see* European Region
   Action Scheme for the Mobility
   of University Students
EU students 15, 115, 166
European Region Action Scheme for
   the Mobility of University
   Students 55–56
exchange students 34, 58, 59, 151

field trips 1, 53–55
financial advisers
   independent financial advisers 175
   student financial advisers 12
finance officer 12
financial barriers 2, 3
Financial Contingency Fund 92, 95, 185
financial penalties 11–12, 25
Financial Services Authority 199,
   204–05, 208, 213, 232, 294
Financial Services Compensation
   Scheme 185, 213
fine and performing arts courses
   150–51, 158, 321
foundation degrees 84, 93, 101, 110
Freshers' Fair 43, 45, 48, 51
FSA *see* Financial Services Authority

gap year 2, 108, 241–48
Gilchrist Education Trust, the 272–73,
   275, 325
Graduate Endowment 103
grants
   Adult Dependant's Grant 83, 92,
      108, 164, 171, 185
   Assembly Learning Grant 89, 185
   Childcare Fund (Scotland) 164, 185
   Childcare Grant 83, 92, 108,
      160–63, 170, 171, 185
   Childcare Grant for Lone Parents
      (Scotland) 163–64, 185
   Dependants' Grant (Scotland) 164,
      185
   Lone Parents' Grant (Scotland)
      163, 185

maintenance grant 74, 81–82, 107,
   146, 171, 180, 185, 301
Parents' Learning Allowance 83,
   92, 108, 163, 171, 185
Special Support Grant 83, 89–90,
   108, 132, 170, 171, 185
travel grants 93, 185
Tuition Fee Grant (Wales) 13, 90,
   185

hardship funds 181, 185
healthcare courses 134, 146–47,
   155–56, 185, 322–23
Helena Kennedy Foundation, the
   270–71, 274, 325
Higher Education Funding Council for
   Wales 145
Higher National Certificate 10, 84,
   93, 101, 110
Higher National Diploma 10, 84, 93,
   101, 110
HNC *see* Higher National Certificate
HND *see* Higher National Diploma
Home Office Identity and Passport
   Service 56

income tax 226, 244–45, 253–56
information technology 1, 60–70, 73,
   74, 195
   computer shops 61, 62
   educational discounts 61, 62
   file recovery service 61
   firewall 64
   IT services departments 61, 65
   laptops 60, 63, 69, 115
   network connection services 61
   PCs 50, 60, 62, 63, 64, 68–69
   reducing IT costs 267
   remote access service 61, 65
   safe computer configuration 64
   sanitised equipment 61, 62
   second-hand equipment 62–63
   software 60, 62, 63, 68
   viruses 62, 64

inheritance tax 2, 191–93, 214, 226,
    229, 234
  annual exemption 191–92
  maintenance gifts 192
  potentially exempt transfers 192
  regular gifts out of income 192–93
  small gifts 191
insurance
  accommodation 26
  computing equipment 63, 69–70
  documents 26
  household insurance 26, 194
  mobile phones 66
  personal belongings 26
  sports 46
  travel 55–56
International Education Financial Aid
    152, 313
international exchange programmes
    152
International Student Identity Card 57,
    313
International Youth travel Card 57
internet access 26, 63–65, 68
Investment Management Association
    207, 209, 211
ISIC see International Student Identity
    Card

Law Society, the 198, 284
leisure 1, 43–52, 72, 74, 294
Leverhulme Trade Charities Trust, the
    271–72, 274–75, 325
Leverhulme Trust, the 158, 321
library 36–37
  borrowing 37
  card 37, 41, 62
  fines 11
  inter-library loan service 36
  ratio of books 36
  resources 37
  short-term loans 37
  tour 37
loans
  bank loans 33, 298–99, 304

extra attendance loans 107
maintenance loans 10, 74, 82–83,
    301
overseas loans 56
parental loans 2, 193
student loans 1, 10–11, 13, 25, 27,
    72, 90–91, 99, 105–07, 132,
    171, 180, 185
tuition fee loans 10, 13, 14, 74,
    82–83, 91, 301
low-income households 1, 13, 81–82,
    114–15, 302

mature students 2, 9, 30, 160–75
meals 17, 26, 29–30
mobile phones 60, 66, 68
mortgages 33, 217, 210, 227, 235
  interest-only mortgages 233
  lifetime mortgages 233
  remortgaging 233–34

National Approved Letting Scheme 219
National Association of Estate Agents
    231, 236
National Association of Student
    Employment Services 250, 257,
    315
National Insurance Contributions 83,
    91, 245, 256, 283
National Union of Students 27, 249,
    273, 323
  NUS card 41, 43, 293
  NUS Extra 45
  NUS Services 41, 43, 44, 51, 313
NICs see National Insurance
    Contributions
non-traditional students 2
NUS see National Union of Students

OFFA see Office for Fair Access
Office for Fair Access 129, 130–31
Ombudsman for Estate Agents 231,
    236
Open University 102, 134
overseas students 11, 24, 30, 152

parental contribution 1, 189–91
parental gifts 2, 191–93
Parents' Learning Allowance *see* grants
part-time fee grant 14, 84, 93–94, 109
part-time tuition fees 14, 84
passports 56
PGCE *see* Postgraduate Certificate in Education
PGDE *see* Postgraduate Diploma in Community Education
photocopying 38, 60, 66–67, 68, 72
plagiarism 63
Postgraduate Certificate in Education 84, 93, 102, 110
Postgraduate Diploma in Community Education 102, 145, 146
printing 60, 61, 66–68, 72
prospectus 18

reading lists 39–40
rent-a-room relief 226

SAAS *see* Student Awards Agency for Scotland
Safe Home Income Plans 232
savings plans 199–207, 208–15
   Child Trust Funds 199, 200–01
      savings CTF 200
      stakeholder CTF 200–01
      stock-market-linked CTF 201
   children's bonds 199, 202–03
      baby bonds 202–03
      National Savings Children's Bonus Bonds 203, 206, 209
      university bonds 203
   children's savings accounts 199, 201–02
   deposit guarantee scheme 204, 205
   individual savings accounts 211–12, 214, 247
   National Savings and Investments 209–10, 214
      Fixed Interest Savings Certificates 210

Index-linked Savings Certificates 210
   Premium Bonds 210
scholarships 1, 114–15
self-employment *see* employment
Skill: the National Bureau for Students with Disabilities 137, 324–24
SLC *see* Student Loans Company
social work courses 149–50, 159, 320–21
societies 47–48
Society of Trust and Estate Practitioners 197–98, 217
Society of Will Writers and Estate Planning Practitioners 237
Special Support Grant *see* grants
sponsorship 2, 258–68
   armed services sponsorship 263–66
      army sponsorship 266
      Defence Technical Undergraduate Scheme 263–64
      Royal Air Force sponsorship 264–65
      Royal Navy sponsorship 265
   company sponsorship 261–63
   sports sponsorship 258, 261
sports 1, 43–52, 72, 74, 294
   aerobics 46
   badminton 46
   clubs 47, 48
   football 46, 47
   free facilities 47
   gym 46
   scholarships 47
   sports card 46, 115
   swimming 46
   tennis 46
   yoga 46
stamp duty land tax 225, 234
stationery 36–42, 72, 292–93
statutory funding 1, 193–94, 312
Student Awards Agency for Scotland 10, 14, 97–104, 132, 133, 134, 138, 145, 167, 317

Student Finance England 85, 87, 128, 138
Student Finance Northern Ireland 111, 113, 128, 138
Student Finance Wales 94, 96, 128, 138
Student Loans Company 11, 16, 102, 163, 164, 319
Students' Outside Scotland Bursary see bursaries
students' union 33, 41, 43–45, 51, 57
study abroad 55–59, 77
support funds (Northern Ireland) 108–09, 185

TDA see Training and Development Agency for Schools
teacher training
  bursaries 146
  funding 139–46
  golden hellos 146
  initial teacher training 139, 146
  qualified teacher status 139
  school centred initial teacher training 139, 146
  Teaching Information Line 153
  Welsh medium incentive supplement 146
tenancy agreement see accommodation
tenancy deposit scheme 27, 222
top-up fees 7, 8
trade union funding 167–68
  General Federation of trade Unions 168, 174
  GMB 168, 174–75
  Union Learning Fund 167

Unison 168, 175
Unite 168, 175
Training and Development Agency for Schools 146, 158
travel expenses 72, 74, 101, 109, 291–92
traveller's cheques 11
tuition fee debts see debts
Tuition Fee Grant (Wales) see grants
tuition fees 1, 7–15, 17, 55, 73, 74, 75–76, 97–99, 165
TV licences 27, 49–50, 65

UCAS 51, 77, 248, 262, 313
UK Council for International Student Affairs 77, 314
UNIAID 35, 312, 324
university applications 8
university bursaries see bursaries
university debts see debts
utilities 17, 26, 27, 30–33, 74, 290
  electricity 30, 31, 32
  gas 30–31
  water 30, 31, 32–33

vacations 24, 25–26, 29, 195
Valuation Office Agency 34
variable fees 7, 9, 114
visas 56–57
VOA see Valuation Office Agency

Welsh Assembly Government 15, 92
Welsh Bursary Scheme see bursaries
Working Tax Credit 108, 160, 169–70, 175

Young Students' Bursary see bursaries

Index of advertisers

Balfour Beatty 259–60   www.bbcl.co.uk
Brunel University 183–84   www.brunel.ac.uk
Department for Employment & Learning,
    Northern Ireland 106   www.studentfinanceni.co.uk
Hillcroft 161–62   www.hillcroft.ac.uk
Institution of Civil Engineers 140–41   ice.org.uk/questundergrad
Institute of Engineering &
    Technology 142–44   www.theiet.org/undergradawards
Student Awards Agency for Scotland 98   www.saas.gov.uk
University of Edinburgh 116–19   www.scholarships.ed.ac.uk/bursaries
University of Sheffield 177–79   www.sheffield.ac.uk/bursaries
University of York 126–27   www.york.ac.uk/admissions
Welsh Assembly Government 88   www.studentfinancewales.co.uk

The sharpest minds
need the finest advice

visit
www.koganpage.com
today